Writing on the Job

Quick, Practical Solutions To All Your Business Writing Problems

by

Cosmo F. Ferrara, Ed.D.

PRENTICE HALL
Englewood Cliffs, New Jersey 07632

Prentice-Hall International, Inc., *London*
Prentice-Hall of Australia Pty., Ltd., *Sydney*
Prentice-Hall Canada, Inc., *Toronto*
Prentice-Hall Hispanoamericana, S.A., *Mexico*
Prentice-Hall of India Private Ltd., *New Delhi*
Prentice-Hall of Japan, Inc., *Tokyo*
Prentice-Hall of Southeast Asia Pte., Ltd., *Singapore*
Editora Prentice-Hall do Brasil, Ltda., *Rio de Janeiro*

© 1995 by
PRENTICE-HALL, INC.
Englewood Cliffs, N.J.

Library of Congress Cataloging-in-Publication Data

Ferrara, Cosmo F.
   Writing on the job : quick, practical solutions to all your
business writing problems / by Cosmo F. Ferrara.
        p.   cm.
   Includes index.
   ISBN 0-13-068727-8. — ISBN 0-13-068735-9 (pbk.)
   1. Business writing—United States.   2. Business communication–
–United States.   I. Title.
HF5718.3.F48   1995
808'.06665—dc20   94-28367
                                                               CIP

ISBN 0-13-068727-8
ISBN 0-13-068735-9 (pbk.)

PRENTICE HALL
Career and Personal Development
Englewood Cliffs, NJ 07632
Simon & Schuster, A Paramount Communications Company

PRINTED IN THE UNITED STATES OF AMERICA

I dedicate this book with gratitude to the many people who have taught me the importance of effective communication. I include my grammar school teachers, who laid the foundation with countless drills and exercises; my high school teachers, who required—and read—a composition a week; my college profs, who considered expression an element of content. I also owe a debt to the men and women I've worked with in corporate settings who place a premium on clear, readable business prose.

To the User of This Book

When writing for business, you—like most writers—may come face to face with a problem. At one time it may be a problem of content, such as how to respond to a customer's letter of complaint. At another time the problem may center around word choice, such as *affect* or *effect*. One day the problem may center around the conventional requirements of a business letter. On another day, you may be struggling to write crisper, clearer sentences.

In each instance you want a quick solution to the problem. You're not looking for a lecture on the writing process or for Composition 101. You just want quick guidance to get you through the crisis of the moment. You want to go to one source for a solution to this writing problem, just as you go to a phone book for a telephone number.

If you've found yourself in this type of situation, then *Writing on the Job: Quick, Practical Solutions to All Your Business Writing Problems* is for you. You can go to it when your supervisor says things like, "Draw up job descriptions for each of the administrative positions in the office." You've never written a job description before. How do you do it? Well, just turn to *Writing on the Job* and you'll find your problem in the Table of Contents: "Problem No. 9: How Do I Develop a Job Description That Works?"

Or your boss writes *"Dull!"* across the first page of your report. How do you turn "dull" into "lively"? Check Problem No. 19, "How Can I Put More Snap into My Writing?" There you'll find sound, practical advice.

You'll find in this book help with most types of business documents—all sorts of letters, memos, resumes, proposals, requests, instructions. You'll find useful tips on collecting information, organizing material, and getting started, even when faced with a "block." You'll learn from real-world samples how to achieve flow and write clearly, forcefully, and persuasively. There are tips for dealing with the most common troublespots of grammar, language, spelling, and punctuation. And because we are such a visually oriented society, you'll find easily workable suggestions for sprucing up the look of your documents and using visual cues that make key points jump off the page.

MODELS AND CHECKLISTS GUIDE THE WAY

In fact, you'll get more than advice in *Writing on the Job*. You'll get *models* of sales letters, memos, and resumes; of coherent and persuasive correspondence; of documents with an inviting physical appearance. You'll be aided by models illustrating every solution to every writing problem treated in the book.

In addition, each "solution" concludes with a *checklist*, a bullet-point list of tips for writing a letter of recommendation, achieving a friendly but businesslike tone, or putting emphasis on the key elements in your sentences. For some problems, the checklist alone may be sufficient to set you on course.

REAL-WORLD PROBLEMS AND PRACTICAL SOLUTIONS

The problems treated in this book are those I have come across in more than a dozen years of editing business documents and conducting seminars for executives, managers, secretaries, and other office workers. Skim through the Table of Contents and note how many of the problems listed you have wrestled with at one time or another.

The solutions offered to these problems are practical and do-able. They've worked with hundreds of my colleagues and seminar participants. They can work for you, too.

HOW TO USE THIS BOOK

The problems have been grouped into three categories:

❏ *Part One: All You Need to Know About Business Documents* gives you useful tips on the content requirements of the most common types of business writing. You'll learn where to place the key information, how to highlight and downplay, when to ask for the order or lower the boom.

❏ *Part Two: Collecting Information, Organizing, Getting Started, and Writing Clearly and Forcefully* offers proven methods of overcoming the blank page and "writer's block," of organizing disparate pieces of information into a unified plan. This section shows you how to measure the readability of your writing and express your ideas to suit your audience and purpose. You'll learn how to add punch, persuasiveness, tact, directness, and imagination.

❏ *Part Three: Revising for Correctness, Precision, and Visual Appeal* offers you a systematic way of revising content and expression. You'll learn answers to the most common questions about word choice, punctuation, and grammar. This section offers tips for giving your documents an appealing look that wins points with the reader. The material goes beyond margins and line length to show how you can use subheads, underlining, and bullets to convey messages more effectively.

Why Writing on the Job Works

You can improve your writing on the job by using this book because

❏ *It is easy to use.* Its Table of Contents enables you to find just what you need immediately, as the contents are expressed in terms of your writing problems, not academic constructs.

❏ *It gives models, analyses, and guidelines.* These enable you to see what your document might look like and help you adapt your material to the model.

❏ *It does not require a major commitment.* You can use it when you need help, without having to read the whole book.

❏ *It gets the job done quickly.* Because it treats each problem in a few pages, you won't waste time with this book; rather, it will save you time.

❏ *It is comprehensive.* That is, it treats all the major problem areas in writing for business today.

WHO CAN BENEFIT FROM THIS BOOK?

Writing on the Job is intended for anyone who writes for business, whether CEO or worker bee. The book can help writers with all kinds of documents—from single-page memos to lengthy reports and manuals. It is neither a primer nor a compendium of all that has ever been said about writing. Instead, it is a handy, useful guide for the busy woman or man who uses writing as a tool for doing business. I can't promise you a Pulitzer Prize, but I can say that this book will enable you to write clear, effective business prose.

Cosmo F. Ferrara, Ed. D.
Hillsdale, New Jersey 1993

Table of Contents

Problem No. 7
HOW CAN I DEMYSTIFY MY MEMOS?—*60*

PART TWO

COLLECTING INFORMATION, ORGANIZING, GETTING STARTED, AND WRITING CLEARLY AND FORCEFULLY—*137*

Problem 14

WHERE CAN I FIND AND HOW DO I COLLECT THE INFORMATION I NEED?—*139*

Problem No. 17

HOW CAN I MAKE THE MOST OF MY GOOD IDEAS?—*165*

Problem No. 18

HOW CAN I WRITE CLEAR, EMPHATIC SENTENCES?—*180*

Problem No. 19

HOW CAN I PUT SNAP INTO MY WRITING?—*193*

Problem No. 20

HOW CAN I MAKE MY WRITING PERSUASIVE?—*203*

PART THREE

REVISING FOR CORRECTNESS, PRECISION, AND VISUAL APPEAL—233

Problem No. 23

HOW EXACTLY DO I REVISE?—235

Problem No. 24

HOW CAN I SPOT AND CORRECT ERRORS IN MY SENTENCES?—243

Part 1

ALL YOU NEED TO KNOW ABOUT BUSINESS DOCUMENTS

Problem No. *1*

WHAT MAKES A SALES LETTER SELL?

Your organization wants to generate some business and thinks an announcement of a new service or product can do that. But the company's marketing department limits its activities to companywide announcements. So the task of writing the letter has fallen to you.

Or you are the owner of a small business and think a sales letter can help broaden your customer base. Since you do the marketing, as well as the selling, servicing, book-keeping, and sweeping up for your small company, that means you write the sales letter.

How do people in these and other situations write sales letters, without specific training or background in marketing?

Well, it's not an impossible task. In fact, such people—people like you—are often better prepared than the marketing department to write such a letter. As the creator of the product or service, or as proprietor of a small business, you know it better than anyone else. You know what a service or product can do for your customers. You know what need prompted the creation of the product or service. And you know what is competing with it out there in the marketplace.

In other words, the creator has the advantage of product (service) knowledge and customer knowledge. This information is the essence of every sales letter. What a nonmarketer may lack, however, is the expertise in selecting the information for the letter and putting it down in the best form and the best order. That's what you'll learn in this chapter.

3

What a Well-Written Sales Letter Can Do For You

In the best case, a sales letter will prompt the reader to pick up the phone and place an order for your product or service. It is more likely, however, that a successful sales letter will do something less than make a sale. Be delighted, for example, if your sales letter prompts a call for more information. In fact, consider your letter successful if the reader reads it and makes a mental note about your company and your offering. What you may be trying to do with a sales letter is raise your audience's awareness, to prepare readers for a follow-up letter or phone call. If your initial sales letter works, your follow-up will have greater impact.

Poor Sales Letters Ignore the Reader; Successful Letters Focus on Them

You probably receive many sales letters. Many come to your home, making up the bulk of what we appropriately call "junk mail." You probably receive sales letters at the office, too, selling everything from seminars to books to computers. What makes you stop and read some letters and just toss others away almost immediately?

You probably begin tossing the letter if it:

- ❐ Is too long
- ❐ Looks too difficult to read at the moment
- ❐ Does not grab your attention immediately
- ❐ Offers nothing you need

Too often, writers of sales letters get wrapped up in themselves and what they're selling and forget about the buyers—the readers. Letters that make no effort to appeal to readers are destined for the recyclable bin.

Read the following sales letter. How would you respond to it? What in the letter accounts for your response?

Dear Resident:

I have 30 years of experience in accounting and in the preparation of individual and business tax returns and offer year-round tax planning as well. I am an Enrolled Agent of the Internal Revenue Service and work with several hundred clients. I hold a BBA in Accounting and a Masters Degree in Taxation from Sobright University. I offer very competitively priced services for income tax preparation and other year-round advisory service.

I am also a Certified Financial Planner through the College of Financial Planning and offer financial planning services to my clients during the year including some very extraordinary investments of my own creation. The emphasis is on increasing profits and reducing taxes. I am licensed by the S.E.C. and manage an investment portfolio of $6 million. My investment reviews always look at tax-cutting measures.

I am also a Real Estate Broker and Insurance Agent and use my expertise in real estate and tax matters to develop tax avoidance and wealth accumulation transactions including tax-free exchanges.

I offer a free consultation for analysis of income tax returns and a discussion of preparation costs. In addition, I review individuals' financial situations to assess objectives, goals, and current portfolios.

Sincerely,

A. J. Wright, CPA

A CASE OF EGOCENTRISM

If you did not run to your phone book looking for A. J. Wright's number, you're not alone. For though Wright's credentials seem sound, the letter does not do a good job of selling them.

For one thing, the letter is so "I-conscious." Notice that every paragraph begins with *I*. As a result, the letter focuses on the writer and pays little attention to the readers and their needs. One of the most important principles of writing sales letters is: *Express your offerings in terms of the reader's needs.* For instance, Wright should have spelled out how his experience and his being an Enrolled Agent with the IRS can benefit the client. He might have said: *As an Enrolled Agent of the IRS, I can keep you abreast of the most recent changes in tax law and use that information to your advantage.*

The writer leaves too much for readers to interpret for themselves. A good sales letter spells out how the product or service can help the customer.

Another problem with the letter is that *it is difficult to read*. The sentences are long and often contain three or more different ideas. Readers cannot focus on one idea at a time. Paragraph 3 contains some very marketable services, but they are lumped together in one sentence and will escape all but the most diligent readers.

Third, the letter just ends. It makes no *call for action* and offers no enticement for picking up the phone and calling.

FIVE STEPS TO AN EFFECTIVE SALES LETTER

1. *Freeze Readers with a Strong Beginning*

People recognize a sales letter when they see one. So you have little time to draw them into yours. If your first paragraph doesn't click with them, chances are they will not go any further. Therefore, consider your first 15 words the most important. Make them:

Emphasize the *you* not the *I*
            or
Lure the reader with an imaginative lead.

EMPHASIZE THE *YOU* NOT THE *I*

As you saw in the analysis of A. J. Wright's letter, singing your own praises is no way to get a reader onto your bandwagon. The surest way to generate interest is to focus on your readers' concerns.

By nature we are all most interested in ourselves, our families, our jobs. Play to this self-interest. Give center stage to reader problems, activities, needs, and benefits, so you keep them reading long enough to absorb your message. Rephrase your *you* statements as *I* statements. For example:

not:	Our system has the following features ...
but:	You benefit from the following features in our system.
not:	*We* are pleased to announce ...
but:	*You* will be pleased to hear ...

not:	*We* use this approach because …
but:	*You* can save money with this approach because…

In writing a sales letter, keep the self-centered attitude of the consumer in mind. It might be summed up in this way:

Don't tell me about your grass seed;
tell me about my lawn.

You should be very prominent in any sales letter. To persuade people you must focus on their interests. Stress what gives them results, saves them money, is easy to use, and brings them love and success.

Here's an example of how A. J. Wright could have made his credentials more of a selling point by shifting from *I* to *you*, from a writer-centered perspective to a reader-centered perspective:

I, or Writer-Centered Perspective:

I have 30 years experience in accounting and in the preparation of individual and business tax returns and offer year-round tax planning as well. I am an Enrolled Agent of the Internal Revenue Service and work with several hundred clients. I hold a BBA in Accounting and a Masters Degree in Taxation from Sobright University. I offer very competitively priced services for income tax preparation and other year-round advisory service.

You, or Reader-Centered Perspective:

Are you struggling with your income tax return? Would you like some help that can prevent your being in the same predicament next year? You might find my 30 years experience just what you need to get your taxes in order. With a BBA in Accounting and a Masters Degree in Taxation from Sobright University, I have helped hundreds of clients just like you. And you may be pleasantly surprised to find how reasonable my fees are for tax preparation and year-round advisory services.

In writing your sales letter, then, think about the service or product you have to offer. Think about why you offered it in the first place. Most products or service grow out of some need. Determine what that need is and make it a major theme of the beginning of your sales letter.

Lure the Reader with an Imaginative Lead

You can also generate reader interest with an imaginative lead. This is a sentence or two that draws reader interest because it is clever, startling, or fanciful in some way. This approach may require more creativity and may be more risky than a more conventional opening. But remember that a sales letter is not your everyday business document. If it's going to sell, it must be "salesy."

Consider these leads:

- Travelers reported 2,399,457 baggage complaints in a single year.

- Are your profits going up in smoke? Cigarette smoke, that is. In offices where smoking is permitted ...

- In the widget industry, when the going gets tough, the wise get CLUTCH.

- Plan-a-head. That's good advice when expecting a hundred or so picnickers. Let Portable Heads provide the relief your visitors will need.

A. J Wright may have used one of the following imaginative leads to draw interest in his services:

- Are you swamped right now by W-2s, canceled checks, and regulations you can't understand?

- Why is it that every time they *simplify* our income tax returns, most of us get more lost than ever?

- Next year'll be different! Is that what you're saying now as you struggle with your income tax return? Is that what you said last year?

You may have noticed that some of these imaginative leads also focus on the reader's needs, using the word *you* and mentioning the reader's concerns. An imaginative lead matched with a reader-centered focus creates a powerful tandem to draw readers into a sales letter.

2. Make Your Pitch Sound, Sharp, and Swift

Once you've drawn the readers into your sales letter, you must provide the substance to keep them reading. Offer them concrete information about your company, product, or service. As in the beginning, present this information from a reader-centered perspective.

SOUND. Be selective in the information you present. The sales letter should not be a dissertation. Rather it should highlight points that would be of interest to these readers—uses, benefits, savings, quality, and other items that will make readers take notice and consider the offer.

A. J. Wright's letter lacks soundness. For example, he spends many of his words naming degrees and certifications and schools. While these may suggest credibility, they don't offer the specifics people need. For instance, what are the particulars of his *other year-round advisory service?* Why not give some examples of *financial planning services* and the *very extraordinary investments of my own creation?*

SHARP. Keep your paragraphs and sentences short, so readers can concentrate on one idea at a time. Wright's letter crams too much into a single sentence. The opening sentence presents two separate ideas—two services—that would be more emphatic if treated separately. As they are lumped together, readers may lose sight of one or the other. In the last paragraph, he reduces the effectiveness of his offer of a *free consultation* by throwing into the same sentence the idea of preparation costs.

In addition, use plain, conversational language, including contractions (*you're, that's, haven't*). Remember, you're trying to sell, not impress.

And use action verbs with punch. For instance,

instead of:	"… to develop tax avoidance and wealth accumulations transactions"
write:	"…to avoid taxes and build wealth"

SWIFT. Make your letter easy to read so it can be read quickly. Highlight key points with bullets, underlining, and subheads. Had he used some visual cues, A. J. Wright's strengths might have jumped off the page and pulled the reader in. For example:

If you'd like help planning your finances, consider the fact that I

❑ emphasize increasing profits and reducing taxes

❏ am licensed by the S.E.C.

❏ manage an investment portfolio of $6 million

❏ have created extraordinary investments of my own

The information in these bullets is essentially the same information as in Wright's second paragraph, but the reader can grasp it more quickly in bullet form.

3. Close with Impact

If readers stay with you to the close of your letter, they are interested in what you're selling. So don't hose down their interest with some empty ending like *if you have any questions...* The closing is almost as important as your beginning. Leave the reader with a particular feeling, thought, urge, or responsibility.

For instance, a good ending to a sales letter may refocus on the reader's key need and how the product (service) meets that need. (*So if you're spending too much time doing your taxes and earning too small a return from your investments, shouldn't you be talking to a professional?*) Or the ending may project readers to a point at which they could be enjoying life more with the product or service. (*Next year at this time your return could have been completed and you may have already received a refund.*) Or the ending may excite the sense of urgency by reminding readers how their situations can worsen if they do nothing. (*Why leave to chance the quality of your family's future and your retirement?*)

With each approach, be sure to *ask for the order*. That is, tell the readers to take action. Specify what it is you want them to do—*subscribe today*, *call for your free consultation*, *complete the enclosed form and send it in today*.

A. J. Wright's letter ends weakly. It does not rehighlight any particular need. In fact, it confuses readers by introducing a totally new subject in the last sentence: *In addition, I review financial situations to assess objectives, goals, and current portfolios.* This ending also fails because it does not in any way make a call for action.

THE POWER OF A P. S.

You may notice that many sales letters end with a P. S. The P. S. often repeats the call for action—in a more dramatic way. Sometimes the P. S. will extend a special offer: *If you call by March 1, you will receive two sets for the price of one.* Or the P. S. might heighten the sense of urgency: *Act now! This offer ends on March 31 and will not be repeated.*

Studies have shown that when people receive a sales letter, they read the opening paragraph first, then jump to the P. S.—which explains why so many sales letters carry a P. S. In addition, the P. S. stands out from the text of the letter, as a set of bullet points would, and is likely to draw attention.

4. Give It Visual Appeal

Just as a sales rep making a call in person wants to look presentable to create a favorable impression, the sales letter should also have visual appeal. The letter need not be on expensive stock or have fancy graphics. Try, though, to space the text well on the page, so reading the letter does not seem like a monumental task. Keep the letter short—one side of a page, if possible. Keep working at your letter to prune away all but the most useful information. Use a good-size typeface and a fresh typewriter ribbon or printer cartridge, if you do your own production. These are "musts" for visual appearance and ease of reading. And be sure to highlight the phone number or address readers are to use in responding to your letter.

Looking at A. J. Wright's letter, we see it is one solid block of print. In our visually oriented society, readers shy away from documents that look challenging. Had Wright used one or two subheads to break up the text, it would look less daunting.

5. Anticipate Reader Objections

Before considering your sales letter finished, read it from your readers' perspective. You know the kinds of reasons they give for not buying. Undercut the resistance by raising those objections against your own letter and then answering them.

For example, if you assume readers will object to the cost of a new piece of equipment, point out that the piece will pay for itself in so many months. If you know readers may be leaning toward larger companies for these services, don't skirt the issue of size. Confront it with a statement such as: *Unlike some of the behemoths in this industry, we offer you personal service and a customized solution.*

— MODEL SALES LETTERS —

<u>SELLING A SERVICE</u>

Dear Neighbor:

opening:
focus on
reader

Are you struggling with your income tax return? Would you like to prevent your being in the same predicament next year? If so, you might find my 30 years experience just what you need *to get your taxes and finances in order.*

short
paragraphs

With a BBA in Accounting and a Masters Degree in Taxation from Sobright University, I have helped hundreds of clients just like you. And you may be pleasantly surprised to find how reasonable my fees are.

offerings
in terms
of you

If you'd like help *planning your finances*, I can help you there, as I am also a Certified Financial Planner through the College of Financial Planning. As you think about where you'd like to be heading financially, consider the fact that I:

highlight
with
bullets

❏ emphasize increasing profits and reducing taxes
❏ am licensed by the S.E.C.
❏ manage an investment portfolio of $6 million
❏ have created extraordinary investments of my own

persuasive words:
health,
wealth

You may be thinking about real estate, certainly one viable approach to financial health. As a Real Estate Broker with tax expertise, I can help you *accumulate wealth and avoid major tax assessments.* I can also show you the advantages of tax-free exchanges.

short sentences
emphasize
each idea

In fact, the best way to ensure financial security is to review your situation overall. Together we can assess your goals, objectives, and current portfolio. Then we can map out a strategy that best matches your means and goals.

subhead
anticipate
reader objection

Free Consultation

If you've never worked with a financial planner or tax professional before, or have been burned doing so, let me calm your fears. You can come in for a free consultation, and I will analyze your tax return with you. I'll tell you what my fee for completing your return will be. *No hidden surprises!*

close;
call for
action

Why be stuck in the mire of regulations and forms any longer? Why leave to chance the quality of your family's future and your retirement? Put your finances on firm footing. Call me today TOLL FREE at 1-800-123-4567.

Sincerely,

A. J. Wright, CPA

urgency

P. S. To have your tax return completed for this year, call me by March 1.

SELLING A PRODUCT

Dear Widget Manufacturer:

opening: focus on readers

Training your sales reps costs you time and money. And that cost repeats itself every time you introduce a new product. The longer the learning curve, the higher the cost.

To help speed that education process and reduce training costs, our company has developed the SALES AND TRAINING TEACHER. The TEACHER:

highlight with bullets

❏ is a state-of-the-art knowledge-based computer program
❏ disseminates information quickly
❏ facilitates training

focus on you

From a central location *you can put on-line* information about new products and how to sell them. Your sales reps can tie into the system from their remote locations and retrieve that information at any hour of the day.

support

The training departments of many major widget manufacturers with needs like yours have already accepted SALES AND TRAINING TEACHER enthusiastically. They find it to be a quick and inexpensive way of keeping their reps informed and up to date.

short paragraphs and sentences

For more information on the benefits of the TEACHER, please review the enclosed brochure. See if you don't agree with many widget companies that this user-friendly technology offers you immediate marketing and sales advantages. And *savings.*

subhead persuasive words

Free Demonstration

After reading more about the TEACHER, you will `probably want to *see for yourself* just how beneficial it can be for you. We would be happy to demonstrate its capabilities for you—at no cost to you, of course. The demonstration will enable you to see how *easy* TEACHER is to use, and how it will *save you time and money.*

anticipate

The demonstration takes only a few minutes. To schedule a demonstration in your office, please call me **TOLL FREE** at 1-800-123-4567. I look forward to putting you together with the TEACHER.

call for action

Very truly yours,

M. E. Owens

highlight

P. S. If you wish, we can program your information into the TEACHER and demonstrate exactly how you can use it with your people.

— Sales Letter Checklist —

GENERATE READER INTEREST WITH A STRONG BEGINNING

- ❏ *Put the focus on the reader, not the writer.*
- ❏ *Lure the reader with an imaginative lead.*

MAKE YOUR PITCH SOUND, SHARP, AND SWIFT

- ❏ *Be selective in what you say.*
- ❏ *Highlight key points.*
- ❏ *Make the letter easy to read.*
- ❏ *Use conversational language.*
- ❏ *Use persuasive words.*

CLOSE WITH IMPACT

- ❏ *Reemphasize key needs/benefits.*
- ❏ *Call for action.*
- ❏ *Use a P. S.*

MAKE THE LETTER VISUALLY APPEALING

- ❏ *Keep it short.*
- ❏ *Be neat.*
- ❏ *Use white space well.*

ANTICIPATE READER OBJECTIONS

- ❏ *Read from the reader's perspective.*
- ❏ *Raise issues and deal with them.*

How Do I Write Claim and Adjustment Letters That Get Results?

You continue to receive a bill that you know has been paid. Your phone calls have not stopped this annoying stream of bills. You must resort to writing.

Or you have received a shipment that does not match the order you placed. Some items are missing and the quantities are not what you ordered. The invoice, however, reflects your original order exactly.

Or a customer has notified you that work your company performed for him is unsatisfactory. You look into the matter and find that his claim is legitimate, but not to the extent he does.

The writing you do in the first two instances falls under the heading of claim letters, when you are the "victim." When you are being asked to rectify what a customer sees as an inequity, your response is an adjustment letter. This chapter gives you tips for writing both.

MAKE A CLAIM, DON'T PLACE BLAME

Errors do occur from time to time in business-to-business transactions, as well as in transactions we conduct as individuals. The best way to approach these situations is calmly. And impersonally. You will save yourself much aggravation if you assume that someone made an error, rather than assume someone is trying to cheat you. In addition, instead of seeking an apology or admission of error, just go for retribution.

In writing a claim letter:

❐ Explain the problem.

❐ Give all the details the company needs to understand the problem.

❐ Suggest what you want them to do to rectify the problem.

Be businesslike and reasonable, but firm.

— MODEL CLAIM LETTERS —

STOP BILLING ME—BILL PAID

> Gotcha Collection Agency
> 123 Sleuth Street
> Anywhere, USA 01234

Subject:
> Rubber Glove Medical Labs
> Account Number 12333444
> Patient: Frances Lee
> Service: Analysis of Throat Culture
> Date: January 15, 1999
> Balance: $200.00

Dear Mr. Gotcha:

You continue to send me letters regarding this bill, though the bill has been paid. Please adjust your records and stop sending me these letters.

I have called your office and notified "Patti March" that my insurance company—Coverall Insurance—has paid this bill in full. I faxed Coverall's verification of that payment to Ms. March on April 6. I am enclosing with this letter another copy of that statement. Please use it to correct the records at either Gotcha or Rubber Glove, whichever are incorrect and responsible for these letters to me.

Aside from the annoyance of receiving these letters, and having to take time to answer them, I fear my credit rating can be adversely affected. For this reason, I appreciate your rectifying this matter and clearing my account as soon as possible. Thank you.

Sincerely,

Frances Lee

The letter makes it easy for the recipient to deal with the claim. It provides all the information regarding the issue, and it presents that information in an easy-to-read format—the list. With this information, the reader can quickly locate his paperwork on this account, or go into his computerized database, to begin to work on your claim.

You can put this information in the text of the letter, but if you do, be sure to have it stand out so the reader can grasp it easily. If your claim involves more than two or three details, use a bullet-point list, rather than force the reader to wade through a paragraph searching for invoice number, dates, amounts, merchandise ordered, and so on.

Address the letter to an individual whenever possible. Doing so gives you a better chance of someone's taking responsibility for resolving the case, particularly if it is somewhat involved and may require some digging.

Note that the letter states the problem and the desired solution in the first paragraph. The background to the problem and the inconvenience it has caused can come later. Up front, identify the problem and tell what you want done about it. At this point you can speak in general terms, giving the reader the "big picture."

Then give the other information. In the case of the example, the writer explains why he feels the bill has been paid and how he has tried before to prove that to the agency. He then states in more detail what he expects the agency to do to correct the problem. Do not assume that by stating a problem the reader will know what you expect to happen. As you "ask for the order" in a sales letter, you state what you expect in a claim letter.

The sample letter then spells out the hardships this problem has caused—the annoyance, loss of time, and potential impact on the credit rating. This kind of information varies in importance from letter to letter, but it may help to move an otherwise disinterested individual on the other end to try to resolve the issue.

The letter closes by repeating the writer's expectation—that the problem will be resolved. Leave no ambiguity as to what you want done.

Error Made

Weatherspoon Office Supply
888 Route 24
Anywhere, USA 09876

Subject: Invoice #64578   *highlight for quick search*

Dear Ms. Rasper:

purpose   The purpose of this letter is to call to your attention   *problem*
errors made in a shipment of office supplies to our office,
and to ask you either to send the materials we ordered or
to make the required adjustments to the invoice.   *solution*

background   On September 3, 1999, we placed an order with your company for a variety of office supplies. We received delivery on September 16, but the shipment had some significant discrepancies from the order. Your invoice, however, reflects our original order exactly. Specifically,

list of needed details

- ❐ we *ordered 16 cartons* of Hammermill Bond 8 1/2 × 11 long grain white paper but we *received only 12 cartons.*
- ❐ we *ordered 100* Sony 2HD high-density 3.5-inch diskettes; we received 100, but your invoice shows 1000.
- ❐ we ordered *4 cartons* of fax paper, but we did not receive any. This item, however, appears on your invoice as "delivered."

effects of problem   Rather than complicate the matter, we are withholding   *suggested*
payment on the entire invoice. Please let us know if you   *solution*
will ship the material not delivered, and adjust the invoice   *repeated*
accordingly. Thank you.

Sincerely,

Marcia Wilson

THE ADJUSTMENT LETTER: YOUR RESPONSE TO A CLAIM

In responding to a claim letter, you have three options: you can say yes, you can say no, or you can compromise. Your answer depends on the legitimacy of the claim, your company's adjustment guidelines, and its relationship with the customer. Regardless of the response you make, you want to keep the customer happy and doing business with you. Be polite and be positive.

Let's look at some examples.

— MODEL ADJUSTMENT LETTERS —

THE YES LETTER

Dear Mr. Smith:

We checked our bookkeeping as you suggested in your letter of June 6, and you are right. We did charge you twice for our spring maintenance, done on April 29. We have corrected that error, as you will see on the enclosed invoice.

We apologize for the error and any inconvenience it may have caused you. We value your business and look forward to serving you again soon.

Sincerely,

Herman Reusch
A-1 Air Conditioning

This letter is short and to the point. The first paragraph refers to the previous correspondence, quickly acknowledges the error, and gives the writer's response to it. The letter apologizes for the error, and shows thoughtful understanding of the customer. But the letter quickly moves off the negative to the positive, to doing business again with this customer.

THE NO LETTER

Dear Ms. Washington:

acknowledgment

Thank you for your letter of August 6 requesting reimbursement for the cost of repairs to your 1979 Zephy. Unhappily, I must tell you we cannot agree to your request.

facts
first

personal
tone

The warranty on your vehicle expired some years ago. The fact that you have had it serviced regularly since you bought it is one reason you have been able to get so many years of untroubled use from it. But, Ms. Washington, even the most well-maintained machines wear down with age and use. And unless certain parts are replaced, they will eventually fail to operate effectively. That, we believe, is the case with your car.

positive

We are pleased that you have enjoyed your Zephy these many years, and we look forward to serving you again in the future.

Sincerely,

Whitney Green
Customer Service Representative
Zephy Motors

The first paragraph refers to the previous correspondence, summarizing the claim made by the customer. The writer gives her decision to the claim letter in this paragraph. Get by the unpleasant task as quickly as possible. Delaying your answer, by giving the explanation first, may seem as if you are uncertain of your decision or are toying with the customer. Give the decision; then in the next paragraph give the rationale for your decision.

Consider facts first, as facts are more difficult to refute than opinions or "judgments." In the sample, the fact is that the warranty is expired. That fact supporting the decision is really all the writer must say, but to stop there might seem cold. And in this letter, the writer does not want to alienate the customer, or she may lose her forever. So the writer supplements the facts behind the response with an explanation. In this case, the writer compliments the customer for keeping the car serviced and gently explains the reality of life with mechanical things. Note how the writer softens this information by using the customer's name in the text of the letter: *But, Ms. Washington, even the most well-maintained machines wear down with age and use.*

The letter ends on a positive note, reminding the customer that she has received her money's worth for the vehicle.

The Compromise Letter

There may be times when the customer has a legitimate complaint about your service or product, but he asks for more than he is entitled to. In such cases you try to offer what you think is a fair settlement. At times you may even feel the customer's claim is weak, but because he has been a long-time customer, you do not want to give an outright NO. In these instances you may want write a compromise letter. As in the other letters, keeping the customer is a prime concern.

Dear Mr. Williams:

acknowledgment

Thank you for your letter of September 16. We are sorry for what seems to be a misunderstanding and would like to propose a reasonable solution. While we cannot waive the cost of the chimney cover,

decision

as you request, we will split the cost of that cover with you. The enclosed invoice reflects that change.

rationale

We arrived at this decision after speaking with you and our serviceman, Jeff Thatcher. You and Jeff agree that he told you about the cement cracking at the top of your chimney and that he could install an aluminum cover that would prevent such cracking in the future. You both agree that Jeff told you there would be an additional charge for installing this cover. While Jeff maintains he told you

soften with personal tone

what the cost of the cover would be, you feel he did not. As we have no way of replaying that conversation, Mr. Williams, we feel it would be fair for you to pay us half the cost of the cover and installation.

goodwill close

We hope you see this solution as our way of letting you know how much we value your business. We do look forward to serving you again.

Sincerely,

Doris Van Dyke
Chim Chimney Sweeps

The opening paragraph refers to the customer's claim letter and gives the writer's decision on the claim. The writer tactfully calls the situation a "misunderstanding." This kind of word tries to placate the customer and yet save face for the company. The writer also uses the word "reasonable" in referring to the solution, hoping to put the reader in a mind-set to go along with the compromise.

The details of this kind of situation could get involved. The writer here, however, summarizes briefly the events that led to the stand-off. The paragraph closes with a restatement of the compromise, strengthening its merits by describing it as "fair."

The close implies that the writer is doing more than is legally called for by offering this compromise solution and is doing so to show goodwill. So the letter ends on a positive note.

— Claim/Adjustment Letter Checklist —

IN YOUR CLAIM LETTER, SEEK RETRIBUTION, NOT APOLOGIES.

EXPLAIN THE PROBLEM, GIVE THE DETAILS NEEDED TO INVESTIGATE IT, AND SUGGEST A SOLUTION.

STATE THE GIST OF YOUR CLAIM AND EXPECTED SOLUTION UP FRONT.

IN THE ADJUSTMENT LETTER, BE CONCERNED ABOUT MAINTAINING GOODWILL WITH THE CUSTOMER.

GIVE YOUR DECISION IN THE FIRST PARAGRAPH AND THE RATIONALE IN THE SECOND.

USE WORDS WITH PERSONAL, FRIENDLY CONNOTATIONS TO MAINTAIN A CONGENIAL RELATIONSHIP WITH THE CUSTOMER.

CLOSE ON A POSITIVE NOTE.

What Kind of Collection Letters Induce Payment?

You've been given the unenviable but vital task of writing to customers who are late in paying for services rendered or products delivered.

Or your company has instituted a policy that each account representative or project manager will contact his or her own customers delinquent in their payment.

Or as the owner of a small business, you realize that writing collection letters is another of the many skills you have to learn as an entrepreneur.

How do you approach the task of writing letters that will induce people to pay their bills?

How to Get Paid *and* Keep the Customer Happy

Your primary objective in writing a collection letter is to get past-due bills paid. But you also have a secondary objective—to keep the customer. In coaxing payment out of the customer, you do not want to offend or in any way turn the customer off to your company.

So the tone you use in asking for payment has to be friendly, at least at first. What you say has to serve both your objectives. In a way your task is similar to that of the dentist who tries to pull a tooth without causing any pain.

But where the dentist *extracts,* what you want to do is move the customer to pay up willingly. You want to make her feel it is in her best interests to pay the bill, to keep her good reputation, or to keep a good relationship with trusted suppliers such as you.

Model Letters That Build Your Case with
A Series of Graduated Demands

You don't threaten a lawsuit if a customer is 30 days late with a payment. You build up to that gradually, hoping you never have to use that "litigation" channel.

Start with the Overdue Notice

Your first notice is not a letter at all. It may be a short message that goes on a copy of the original invoice with a rubber stamp or stickers. This process simplifies the task yet makes the message stand out, so this invoice receives special attention.

The message may be as simple as:

2nd notice. 30 days past due.
Please send payment. Thank you.

This message is impersonal and objective, and it is not likely to give offense. People will see it for the "form" message that it is. They will not take it "personally," because they assume—rightly—that this message goes out almost automatically. There is no one at your company saying, "That no good XYZ hasn't paid its bill."

The downside, however, is that some customers may not take this message seriously, and might not be moved by it to pay the bill. But most people do react positively. So rather than run the risk of offending the majority, start the collection process with this low-profile, impersonal "reminder."

Your First Real Letter: "Perhaps It's an Oversight"

The first letter conveys your assumption that nonpayment is not intentional. It is an oversight. Perhaps the check is already in the mail. This kid-glove approach strives to be inoffensive and keep the customer relationship, while, of course, coaxing payment.

> If you have already paid this bill, please disregard this notice. But our records show that the attached invoice is now more than 30 days past due. We look forward to continuing our relationship with you. Please use the enclosed envelop to send your payment.

The letter implies that the bill may have been paid, showing your confidence in the customer. By saying that "our records show" the bill is past due, you place the focus not on the customer but on the impersonal records. Personalities are not a factor here. But by including the number of days past due, you indicate that there is legitimate cause for the reminder.

The letter briefly mentions your desire to continue doing business with the customer. It lets the customer know that this one overdue bill is not causing you to write her off your customer list. That statement is a conciliatory note to your customers. To those who rely heavily on your servicing them, however, that statement may seem a veiled threat, but a very mild one. The letter closes with a firm, but not hostile, "please—send your payment."

The Second Letter: Turn It Up a Notch

The bill is now perhaps 45 days past due, so you have to draw on heavier persuasive weapons to induce payment. You are still trying to *induce* payment, not coerce it, because you do not want to jeopardize your relationship just yet.

In the second letter, you become more personal. This is no longer *your* accounts receivable system addressing *her* accounts payable system. This letter brings the people into play and considers how they are thinking and why they are acting the way they are.

Making the letter more personal, try to develop some pleasant, clever way of ingratiating yourself with the customer to get her to make payment. One way of doing this is to suggest that you think she is holding up payment *deliberately* because she is not satisfied with the services or products you delivered. for example:

> Have we done something wrong? Is that why we haven't received payment from you? If you were not satisfied with the service we provided you [the equipment we installed, the product we delivered], please call to let us know how we can rectify the problem.
>
> If the delay in payment is simply an oversight, we can understand that too. But this bill is now 45 days overdue, and we're sure you can understand our position. So please call us or make payment on this bill soon.
>
> Thank you.

This letter tries to tell the customer that you are being reasonable and hope the customer will be, too. As in all collection letters, this one indicates the number of days that payment is overdue.

Here's another way you might approach this second letter.

> Though every business is unique, your business is just like ours in one important way—we both need money to keep operating. And we both expect to be paid for the services or goods we provide.
>
> Our records show, however, that you haven't paid us for the services [goods] we provided you. In fact, the bill is now 45 days past due.
>
> As a business operator, you can understand the position we are in. You can fully realize that a business can't "carry" its customers. So we would appreciate your showing that understanding and paying this bill promptly.
>
> Thank you.

This letter is a little stronger than the other sample. It does not suggest that payment is being withheld because of the customer's dissatisfaction with you. (You may, however, add that element to this letter if you think that may be the case or may help your cause.) This letter appeals to the integrity of the customer as a business operator. The letter puts the two companies in a fraternity and plays on the reader's sense of "business partnerships."

The Third Letter: Put the Pressure On

At this point you have to be ready to quit the sniper fire and confront the delinquent customer with all but your heaviest artillery. You are still concerned with keeping her as a customer, but payment is a much greater concern. If she persists in not paying you, then she is not the kind of customer you want to do more business with. But the condition at her company causing the delay in payment may be temporary, so it's worth one more effort to induce payment.

You may incorporate some of the ideas of the previous letters, such as her dissatisfaction being the reason for nonpayment. And you may want to suggest she pay you in installments or contact you about working out a solution. Half a loaf is, indeed, better than none. But this letter is conciliatory only to a point. The letter exerts pressure on the customer to pay up. It lets the customer know that you are running out of patience. But it cannot be too heavy-handed either. You are still trying to induce payment, not coerce it.

Question: What's the worst thing that a business can lose?

Question: What's the worst thing a business can gain?

Answer to both questions: Reputation.

A business whose good reputation is tarnished will have a hard time making it shine again.

Companies that don't pay their bills risk putting themselves in this position. Unfortunately, it seems you are running that risk.

Your payment of our invoice is now more than 90 days overdue. We want to continue doing business with you. But if we can't expect to be paid for the services we perform (products we deliver, etc.), it would be pointless to do so.

If you haven't paid this bill because you're disappointed in the service (products) we delivered, let me know and I'll rectify the situation.

If there's been an oversight in your accounts payable department, we can understand that. But let us know that's the problem.

And if for some reason you're strapped at the moment and cannot pay this entire bill right now, call me and we'll work out a payment schedule you can live with.

As you can see, we are doing what we can to keep our reputation as a reasonable, responsible business partner. So please, you do the same. Don't ignore us. Contact me by phone, letter, or with your check.

Thank you.

This letter tries to work a different psychological element from the previous letter. The second letter tries to appeal to the reasonableness, integrity, and camaraderie of the customer. In this one you appeal to baser motives—pride and self-preservation. By calling the customer's reputation into question, and by implying the devastation a bad reputation can cause to her company, you work the opposite end of the hierarchy of motivating factors.

The letter softens the strike by offering the customer a face-saving "out," as well as options for payment. But the letter closes firmly, referring again to the idea of reputation and asking for a response.

The Fourth Letter: The Last Straw

You don't have many options left, and you want to tell the customer that. In this letter you tell the customer that if payment does not arrive in so many days, you will turn the matter over to the lawyers or to your collection agency. Your letter should indicate how the legal process can be annoying as well as costly to the customer and that payment now is a neater alternative. But stress that this is the last request you will make for payment.

We're just about out of words and suggestions to get your bill cleared up. It's now 120 days overdue.

We've said we'd rectify a problem if that's the reason you haven't paid us. We've suggested a payment schedule to pay the bill in installments.

But you've not responded. And you leave us no choice but to turn to litigation.

So before putting both of us through this costly and messy process, please send us payment. Or call me to discuss how you'd like to pay the bill.

If we do not hear from you within ten days of the date on this letter, we will turn this matter over to our lawyers. What'll it be?

The letter makes the same offers as the earlier ones did about helping the customer save face and pay the bill in installments, but it makes less of an effort to promote those approaches. This letter is to be perceived as a threat—one that can be averted—but still a threat.

EASY WAYS TO PERSONALIZE YOUR FORM LETTERS

Though collection letters are usually form letters, try to make them look personal. Have each freshly printed; they should not look like copies. And address the letter to an individual at the customer's company, not to a department. Word processing equipment makes this kind of personalization relatively easy. And personalization may get more attention and a faster response.

— Collection Letter Checklist —

WRITE THE LETTER WITH THE PRIMARY OBJECTIVE OF GETTING PAYMENT FOR THE BILL.

REMEMBER THAT YOUR SECONDARY OBJECTIVE IS ALMOST AS IMPORTANT—TO KEEP A GOOD RELATIONSHIP WITH THE CUSTOMER.

USE PERSUASION TO INDUCE PAYMENT RATHER THAN FORCE TO COERCE IT.

PLAN A SERIES OF NOTICES AND COLLECTION LETTERS, BUILDING UP FROM FRIENDLY AND CONCILIATORY TO VERY FIRM.

OFFER THE CUSTOMER FACE-SAVING OUTS AND OPTIONS FOR PAYMENT.

INCLUDE THE NUMBER OF DAYS PAST DUE IN EACH LETTER.

PERSONALIZE FORM LETTERS WITH THE NAME AND ADDRESS OF THE CUSTOMER.

How Should I Respond to a Complaint?

A customer has just sent you a letter complaining about a product or service someone in your department has delivered to her. The customer has asked you to look into the situation and respond in writing. What do you write, especially if you can't give the customer what she expects?

Or you work as a Customer Service Representative for a large manufacturer. Your entire day is spent talking with customers on the phone or writing letters to them. For every compliment you receive, there are nine problems and complaints. How do you deal with these, and deal with them quickly, so you don't fall behind in this never-ending litany of woes?

THREE KEYS TO SUCCESSFUL RESPONSES TO COMPLAINTS

When writing to customers, you must be concerned primarily with three key issues. First, you must try to satisfy or at least *placate the customer*, so he or she continues to remain your customer. But you cannot give away the store in doing so. There are times—many times—when customers make unreasonable requests and you cannot agree to them. Therefore, it is necessary to be correct in your first response. Giving the wrong answer—whether yes or no—could cause you additional problems with either the customer, your boss, or both. So be sure to consider all aspects of the situation and review documents such as warranties, promotional literature, and policies, paying particular attention to dates that may qualify or disqualify a customer for a refund or free repair.

Second, *be tactful* in your response. Even though tact is the last thing you'd want to use on some customers, tact is essential in meeting your first objective—keeping the customer. Bear in mind that words you put on paper cannot be taken back. Being tactful, however, does not mean slobbering all over the paper or apologizing profusely. As you will see a little later in this chapter, a few words of apology and a factual explanation of your position often work best in saying NO.

And, third, you want to be *quick*, to make sure the customer receives a response in a reasonably short time. In addition, if you write these letters frequently, you can't spend a half-day writing each one, or you'll never be able to dig out from the pile of letters waiting to be answered. Knowing what to say and how to say it can help you cut down the time you spend writing such letters.

HOW TO SHAPE A RESPONSE WITH IMPACT

Generally, in responding to a customer, consider the letter as having three parts: introduction, body, and closing. Let's take a look at what goes into each part.

Introduction: Don't Duck the Issues

The introduction should be short—just a few sentences—but should deal with a number key issues.

Reference to the Complaint

At the beginning of the letter indicate your purpose—to respond to the customer's complaint. You can say this in a number of ways, but try to be specific. That is, *state the nature of the problem so the customer feels she is not receiving a form letter*. The more specific you are, the more the customer feels she is getting personal attention. For example:

Generic: We're sorry about the problem you have had with your Kramer appliance.

Specific: We're sorry about the problem you have had with the ON\OFF switch on your Kramer Koffee-maker.

Apology

Another key element in your introduction is the apology. No matter what kind of problem the customer is having, apologize for it. You may combine the apology with your reference to the problem, as in the preceding example. Or you may devote a separate sentence to it.

But don't overdo the apology. Some writers feel the need to go on for two or three sentences apologizing and "regretting" and saying how important customer satisfaction is to the company. Customers really don't want that. They want a resolution to the problem. So make your apology and move on. An elaborate apology may give the impression you are waffling on the question rather than being straightforward. For example:

Waffling: It was regrettable to learn that your correspondence was prompted by a problem with your new Ticking Watch. Please accept our sincere apology for any inconvenience you may have experienced as a result. Let us assure you that your satisfaction with Ticking products is our primary objective.

Straightforward: We apologize for any inconvenience the faulty face on your new Ticking Watch may have caused you.

In the "waffling" apology, the writer is redundant, as "it was regrettable" and "please accept our apology" say the same thing. With too long an apology, readers may feel "the lady doth protest too much," and doubt your sincerity.

REFERRALS FROM EXECUTIVES

In many instances, customers take their complaints to a top-level executive, often the president of the company. Frequently these letters are referred to Customer Service. Explain this referral in the introduction.

Bear in mind, though, that customers can be very sensitive about referrals, particularly when the item in question has a high sticker price. The language you use in handling these referrals, therefore, can further alienate or win back the customer. Some wording makes these customers feel as if their letter to the president has been *dismissed out of hand*. Other language treats the same referral as an action step by the president on the customer's behalf. The writer can give the impression he has been *directed by the executive* to handle the matter. Note the difference in connotation and the impact on the customer:

Dismissed:	Thank you for your letter to our president, Miss Frances DeMiglio. *She has asked me to respond on her behalf.*
Directed:	Thank you for your letter to our president, Miss Frances DeMiglio. After reviewing your letter, she *directed me to expedite the handling of your request.*
	or
Directed:	Thank you for your letter to our president, Miss Frances DeMiglio. After reviewing your letter, she *directed me to resolve the issue.*

Customers don't like to feel their letters are just being shuffled from one desk to another. Phrases such as "asked me to respond" convey such inaction. On the other hand, phrases like "directed me to resolve the issue" and "to expedite the handling of your request" convey a proactive stance by the executive. That's what the customer wants.

Body: State Your Decision Clearly

The body of the letter varies with the nature of the complaint and your decision. Generally, though, it includes your decision and an explanation of it or details that follow from it.

SAY YES OR NO

The range of assistance that customers seek is unimaginably broad. Those requests may range from asking for a list of dealers in the area to demanding a replacement for an item bought ten years ago. Whatever the request, your response can be either YES or NO. If your answer is YES, tell the customer:

- ❑ What the company will do to deal with the request
- ❑ How this action will unfold
- ❑ When it will be completed

For example:

We have tested the widget you sent to us and have found it to be defective. Because your widget is still under warranty, we will be sending you a new widget. You should receive it through the mail within five weeks. If you do not receive it by then, call 1-800-123-1234. Refer to claim number 98765 when inquiring about the replacement.

Note the kinds of details included. The writer has obviously *anticipated* the customer's questions and planned for the most likely eventualities. By giving a timeframe in which the problem will be solved, the writer wards off a premature follow-up by the customer. By giving the phone number and claim number, the writer helps the customer further, facilitating a follow-up if necessary. Providing this information takes the writer out of the loop, eliminating his having to handle another call or letter.

If your answer is NO, there are two approaches you can take, the inductive and deductive.

INDUCTIVE. In this approach, you give the rationale behind your decision first, and then the decision. For example:

rationale   The problem with the Ticking Watch you sent us does not appear to have resulted from a flaw in the design, in the parts, or in the manufacture of the item. A number of aspects point to the watch's having been soaked in water. For instance, the wrinkled band, the discoloration of the face, and the moisture on the underside of the crystal all suggest this watch is not running because it has been wet. This watch is not waterproof, as is clearly stated on the back of the watch and in the instruction sheet that comes with each Ticking Watch #123.

decision   Therefore, we must inform you that we cannot replace this watch or offer any compensation for it.

Writers who prefer the inductive approach feel a NO answer at the beginning might be perceived as a frontal assault. These writers prefer to give the rationale and evidence for the decision first, building the case that leads naturally to the conclusion.

DEDUCTIVE. This is the opposite approach, giving the answer at the beginning of the letter, then following up with the reasoning. The thinking here is that customers are anxious for your answer and don't want a lengthy discussion, which might be seen as a "tease." In some instances, customers might interpret the explanation incorrectly, expect a YES, and then be crushed when the answer is NO. To prevent that possibility, you can use the approach that is standard for most business letters—give the main point up front and then explain it with the detail. For example:

decision   We are sorry to inform you that ABC Bikes cannot grant the financial assistance you seek for repainting your 1999 Whirlwind.

rationale   The clause you quote from in your warranty contract covers repainting as a result of conditions caused by manufacturing defect. Your dealer informs us, however, that the paint condition on your bicycle was not caused by a manufacturing defect. Rather, the nicks and scratches on it could have been caused only by an accident or mistreatment of the bicycle. They did not result from conditions caused by a manufacturing defect.

You may choose either the inductive or deductive approach, depending on which works best for each letter's circumstances. If you use the inductive approach, be wary of sending the wrong signal to the customer, which might aggravate his disappointment with your negative response. If you use the deductive approach, soften the blow with a mild apology, such as "we are sorry to inform you."

WHAT TO SAY WHEN YOU HAVE TO PASS THE BUCK

In many instances, the action you take on a letter will be to refer it to someone else for action or a decision. As with the executive referral to you, be careful in the words you choose to explain your action. Use language that implies you are expediting the matter, not just shuffling paper, or passing the buck.

Paper Shuffling:	To ensure that this matter receives the attention it deserves, we are forwarding your letter to our District Manager for Service.

What does "receives the attention it deserves" mean? Are you implying it might deserve much attention, some, very little? And what is the connotation of "forwarding your letter"? Do people see this as an active step toward a solution or a side-step out of the matter? Note how some changes in word selection can convey a different attitude, thereby generating a different, more favorable response from the customer.

Taking Action:	To have this matter addressed immediately, we have contacted our District Manager for Service to look into your complaint.
	or
Taking Action:	The District Manager for Service, the individual responsible for resolving this type of problem, has been asked to look into your complaint.

Closing: A Positive Look to the Future

In closing, try not to rehash what's already been said, particularly in a NO response. Try to use the closing to *stabilize your company's relationship* with the customer for the future. Try to win back or maintain customer loyalty. Here are examples of ways to do that:

Close in a YES Letter:	We hope this solution meets with your satisfaction. Please feel free to contact us at any time, as we appreciate your patronage of GBT Products.

Close in NO Letter:	Though this may not be the response you had hoped for, we thank you for allowing us to explain the basis on which we've made this decision. We hope you will continue to support GBT Products.

BREAK BARRIERS WITH PERSON-TO-PERSON LANGUAGE

A letter to a customer should carry a businesslike tone yet establish a cordial, person-to-person relationship with the reader. Too often, however, writers slip into archaic, impersonal language that simply puts barriers between them and their readers. Note the difference between the archaic, impersonal language in the sentence below and the fresh, conversational language in the sentence that follows.

Archaic, Impersonal:	This office is in receipt of your correspondence of March 2.

Has "the office" actually received anything? And why not call the letter a "letter" instead of "correspondence"?

Fresh, Conversational:	We have received your letter dated March 2.

Business writing can get very stiff and impersonal when the writers use archaic clichés such as "in receipt of." Avoid these archaic clichés. They not only sound stiff and impersonal to the reader, but they can also lead you to writing an entire letter of warmed-over phrases that are not your own. Other clichés of this type to avoid are

Per your request ...

Please be advised that...

Herewith are forwarded...

In regard to the above-referenced claim...

Regarding yours of June 6...

Pursuant to our conversation...

Per the agreement...

Instead of using these clichés as a crutch, choose words and expressions of your own, which can create a more personal link with your reader.

Personal letters have more impact than impersonal letters. You can personalize by using more pronouns—*I, we, you, she, he, they*. Note the difference between the sentences below.

Impersonal:	As previously discussed, the following information is supplied per your request for an explanation of the warranty provisions.
Personal:	As *you* requested, *we* are sending *you* the following explanation of *your* warranty provisions.

Pronouns bring people into the picture and the reader can visualize people doing things.

— MODEL RESPONSES TO CUSTOMER COMPLAINTS —

<u>YES RESPONSE</u>

July 9, 199_

Mr. Jack Armstron
123 Seventh Avenue
Some City, State 12345

Dear Mr. Armstron:

referral
"directs"

    Thank you for your letter to Ms. Willa Paget describing the problem you've been having with you new Paget lawn mower. After reviewing your letter, Ms. Paget directed me to expedite the handling of your request.

short apology;
decision first

    First, please let me apologize for the difficulty you have had in getting your Paget serviced. We have taken a number of steps, however, that should resolve the problem.   *specifies problem*

details
actions

    We have contacted your dealer, M. Landow, and discussed the issue with him. He assures us that he will work on your mower himself to ensure its being put in running order quickly. Please bring your mower to the dealer, leaving it in Mr. Landow's hands. You   *personal pronouns* may want to bring this letter with you to remind Mr. Landow of my conversation with him.

closing

Thank you for your patience. We trust the repair will lead to many years of dependable service from your Paget lawn mower.

look to future

Sincerely,

Arlene J. Thomson
Customer Service Representative
Paget Lawnmower Company

NO RESPONSE

April 4, 199_

Ms. Amy Lew
999 Holstein Way
City, State 12345

Dear Ms. Lew:

apology; specifies problem

We are sorry that the Vango painting supplies you purchased from Masterpiece Art Supply did not meet with the success you had hoped for.

inductive approach

Though the photographs on the cartons do show children busily at work on interesting paintings in a classroom setting, Vango does not make any claim on the carton or elsewhere that the supplies on their own will get students to work diligently. We feel you may have expected too much from these materials.

explains rationale

decision

Therefore, we do not feel a refund is warranted in this case.

closing

We hope you understand our reasoning in making this decision and look to will try Vango materials again.

look to future

Sincerely,

Chris Estaban
Customer Service Representative
Vango Art Materials

— Complaint Response Checklist —

Try to Satisfy or Placate the Customer.

Be Tactful and Quick in Your Response.

In the Introduction, Refer Specifically to the Customer's Complaint.

Make Your Apology Brief.

In Handling Referrals from Executives, Suggest a Proactive Stance by the Executive.

In a *YES* Response, Give Details of How You Will Accede to the Customer's Request.

In a *NO* Response, Use the Inductive Approach (Explanation then the Decision) or the Deductive Approach (Decision then the Explanation).

When You Forward the Customer's Letter, Don't Make It Seem Like Mere Paper Shuffling.

Anticipate the Customer's Questions and Objections to Your Response.

In Closing, Try to Stabilize Your Company's Relationship with the Customer.

Avoid Clichés and Archaic, Impersonal Language.

Use Fresh, Conversational Language.

Personalize the Letter with Pronouns.

How Do I Write Letters of Reference and Recommendation That Do Their Jobs?

You have been asked by a summer intern for a letter of reference that she can use in applying to other companies for employment.

Or you receive an inquiry from a peer in another company about an individual who has worked for you and is a candidate for a position there.

In each case you have to write a letter about a person. How do you do it?

THE SLIGHT BUT REAL DIFFERENCE BETWEEN
REFERENCES AND RECOMMENDATIONS

In a letter of reference you verify facts about the individual. In a letter of recommendation, you verify facts *and* endorse the person for a position.

Both letters are short and to the point. Both require a blend of the general and the particular. That is, you make a general statement about the individual or the job the person has done for you, and you support that general statement with specifics.

— MODEL LETTER OF REFERENCE —

Dear Ms. Fraser:

This letter is a response to your request for verification of Frances Demig's work history at Stil Manufacturing Company.

Ms. Demig served as my secretary for four years, from 1989 to 1993. She ably performed a diverse range of secretarial duties. Among those duties were handling all incoming and outgoing correspondence and interacting with customers, employees and executives of the company on my behalf. She maintained schedules for the sixteen people in the department, monitored invoices, and assisted me in preparation of the annual budget.

Ms. Demig has always been a willing worker, one who does not watch the clock, who accepts a challenge, and is willing to pitch in to get a job done, regardless of the kind or amount of work involved.

Sincerely,

Roberta Goodheart
Distribution Department Manager, Stil Manufacturing

REFERENCES: CONCENTRATE ON SKILLS, PERFORMANCE, AND ATTITUDE

The reference letter begins, as most business letters do, with a statement of purpose. That is, the writer indicates the letter is in response to a request for this information.

The second paragraph begins with two general statements about the person's work history. The writer gives the individual's job title, duration of service, and an *overview* of her responsibilities: "She ably performed a diverse range of secretarial duties." Then the writer gives some specifics of those responsibilities. Even when the job title is a universal one and people have an idea of what it entails, give some specifics of what it entails in this particular case. Don't assume that "a secretary is a secretary is a secretary."

The last paragraph focuses on the character or work habits of the individual. Potential employers want to know something about the character of the person they are considering. Here again, the writer leads with a general statement (*a willing worker*) and supports that with a few specifics.

While this letter speaks highly of the individual, it falls short of a recommendation. There may be a number of reasons for that restraint. First, the request may not have asked for a recommendation. Second, the writer may not be familiar with the position the candidate is applying for, and so is not in a position to make a recommendation. Or the writer may simply feel more comfortable stating the facts about the person's work history without venturing a prediction about how she might perform in the future.

Sometimes you may be asked to write a letter of reference for an individual who may want to copy it and include it in applications for different positions. In such instances, you would be unable to make a recommendation. You'd write the same letter but address it: *To Whom It May Concern.*

RECOMMENDATIONS: PERSUADE THE READER

The letter of recommendation verifies information as the letter of reference does, but it goes even further. It tries—mildly—to persuade the reader that the individual in question is highly qualified and suited for the position. To persuade, choose details carefully to support the general impressions you present of the person. Specific details "show" rather than "tell," and they raise your credibility level. Use words in stating your impressions that are likely to strike an emotional chord within the business heart of the person you are writing to. Here's an example.

— MODEL LETTER OF RECOMMENDATION —

Dear Mr. O'Rourke:

Amy Estaban worked as an intern at Insightful Consulting last summer, and I am happy to comment on her experience here, as you asked.

Ms. Estaban proved to be a quick learner and hard worker. She began by doing research for a number of projects. Soon she was interpreting data and providing summaries for project leaders. In every case we found her work to be thorough, precise, organized, and well written.

During the four months she was with us, Ms. Estaban worked closely with about ten people on our professional and support staffs. Everyone agrees she is pleasant, cooperative, and a true team player.

Based on this experience, and the intelligence, diligence, and people skills she displayed, I would highly recommend Amy Estaban for the position of associate consultant.

Sincerely,

Johanna L. Kohlmann
Partner, Insightful Consulting

The letter states the purpose in the first paragraph, identifying the individual in question. In telling what the individual did, the second paragraph begins with a general statement and then provides specifics. The third paragraph focuses on the "character" element and gives enough detail to be helpful and credible. The statement of recommendation in the last paragraph is direct and unambiguous. It uses terms that summarize or supplement what has been said previously.

In addition, the letter uses words connoting the kinds of effort and attitude business executives like to hear about employees: *quick learner, hard worker, thorough, precise, team player, diligence.* And, of course, the letter backs up these words with specifics of what the individual did—*doing research, interpreting data, providing summaries.*

IF YOU CAN'T SAY SOMETHING NICE ...

Both sample letters are highly complimentary toward the candidates. You may face situations, however, when you do not feel comfortable making a recommendation or even writing a letter of reference. In such instances, you are better off not writing it. Should you write something negative, or even state a fact that can be interpreted as negative, that letter may come back to haunt you. Especially in today's litigious climate, you will be better off begging out of a request for a letter of reference than running the risk of a messy legal entanglement.

— Reference/Recommendation Checklist —

KNOW THE DIFFERENCE BETWEEN A LETTER OF REFERENCE AND A LETTER OF RECOMMENDATION.

IN BOTH LETTERS, MAKE GENERAL STATEMENTS AND SUPPORT THEM WITH SPECIFICS.

ADDRESS THE INDIVIDUAL'S SKILLS, PERFORMANCE, AND ATTITUDE.

IN THE LETTER OF RECOMMENDATION, TRY MILDLY TO PERSUADE, USING CONNOTATIVE WORDS, SPECIFIC DETAILS, AND A STATEMENT CLEARLY ENDORSING THE CANDIDATE.

How Do I Set Up
a Business Letter
That Looks Impressive?

With *downsizing, you no longer have the luxury of a secretary. So you type your own correspondence. You want to know the proper way of laying out a business letter. There seems to be no consistency in the company letters you have seen, and you don't know which to model your letters on.*

Or you are the owner of a small business. Though you have part-time help to do the typing, you want to make sure the typist follows all the conventions for letter writing. In addition, you're concerned about where to place things in a letter, the tone to strive for, and the language to use.

For these and other situations, this chapter shows you the conventions followed most frequently in business letters. You'll also find some tips for the content and expression in a business letter.

ELEVEN ESSENTIALS OF BUSINESS LETTER

Although business writing is becoming less formal all the time, a number of conventions are still observed. But even among these there are some options and variations that you should be aware of. As you read, refer to the model on page 48. The numbers preceeding each entry correspond to the number in the left-hand margin of the sample.

1—LETTERHEAD OR WRITER'S ADDRESS. When you are writing for a company, the company's letterhead gives the formal name of the company, its mailing address, and its phone numbers. If you are writing as an individual and do not have letterhead, type your street and city address, but not your name, as the first element in your letter.

On some letterhead, the company name begins at the left margin, as in the example. That should be the left margin for the entire page. On other letterhead, the company name is centered. You must then create your own left margin. For more details on margins, see "Margins" later in this chapter.

2—DATE. On company stationery, type the date between four and eight lines below the company address, depending on the length of the letter. For a long letter, use the minimum spacing; for a short letter, the maximum. If you are not using letterhead and type in your address, type the date on a separate line just below the address.

123 State Street
Happy Valley, ST 12345
July 5, 1999

3—INSIDE ADDRESS. Type the name, title, and company name and address of your reader. Put the zip code on the same line as the city and state, with two spaces but no punctuation between the state and zip code. Be detailed and specific here about titles and department names. Should the individual leave the department, your letter can still be received by someone in the department who can handle it properly. Skip as many lines between the inside address and date as between the letterhead and the date (between four and eight).

1

Ace
Construction Company   234 Shilho Road
                         Utopia, MO 12345

4 lines

2   November 1, 199_

4 lines

3
Ms. Diana Smith
Vice President, Corporate Development
City General Hospital
One Stac Plaza
Downtown, MO 13579

2 lines

4   Subject: Proposed Agreement for West Wing Renovation

2 lines

5   Dear Ms. Smith:

2 lines

I have enclosed for your review the drafts of the proposed agreement by which Ace
Construction Company will renovate the West Wing at City General Hospital. Please
review this agreement in preparation for our final discussion of it with our respective
attorneys on December 1, 199_.

6   If you need any portions of the agreement clarified, please do not hesitate to call me at
(123) 456-7890.

I look forward to seeing you again on December 1 and working with you on this renovation.

2 lines

7   Sincerely,

4 lines

8   Joseph Ace
President

9   ab

10   Enclosure

11   c: W. McCormack, Esq.

4—Subject. As in the memo, you can help your reader into the letter by indicating its subject. Type the word *Subject* and follow it with a colon (:) and a short description of the subject of the letter. Rather than using an abbreviated or generic subject head, such as *Agreement*, be as detailed and specific as you can in one line. An informative subject head often has more "drawing power" in getting a reader to read the letter immediately. And a specific subject head makes it easy to file the letter and retrieve it *from the files* when needed later. Skip two lines between the inside address and the subject line. (Some writers prefer to place the subject two lines *below* the greeting.)

5—Greeting. Always try to address a business letter to an individual. If you cannot locate the addressee's name, use the person's title. If you don't know how a woman prefers to be addressed, use *Ms.* Some people use only the first name in addressing letters to business associates with whom they feel a close or friendly relationship. When you use the full name, follow it with a colon. When you use first name only, follow it with a comma. Skip two lines between the subject line and the greeting.

6—Text. Present the details of the letter, giving careful attention to your introduction and closing as well as to the message in between. In the introduction, *state the purpose of the letter.* In the closing, repeat a key point or convey a particular attitude toward the reader. Skip two lines between the greeting and the beginning of the letter. Single space the letter unless it is very short. Skip a line between paragraphs.

7—Complimentary Close. In a formal letter, typical closes are *Respectfully yours, Yours truly.* Note that only the first letter in two-word closings is capitalized. In a less formal—increasingly more common—business letter, you might use a less formal closing, such as *Sincerely, Sincerely yours, Best wishes, Cordially,* or *Thanks.* Skip two lines between the last line of the text and the complimentary close.

8—Name of Writer. Type the name of the writer of the letter, as he or she wants to be addressed in business. Leave enough room between the complimentary close and the name for the individual's normal signature, generally four lines. This spacing may vary with the length of the letter and the height of the writer's signature. Put the person's title on the next line. Some writers and companies will type in the company name before the writer's name, when the person is writing as spokesperson for the company. In these instances, the complimentary close and signature portion might look like this:

Sincerely yours,

Ace Construction Company

Joseph Ace, President

In all other cases, if the company name appears on the letterhead, it is unnecessary to repeat it. However, if you are employed by a large company, with many divisions, you may wish to add that after your signature to facilitate correspondence or add information. If so, the signature portion and complimentary close might look like this:

Sincerely yours,

Joseph Ace, President
Ace Construction Company

9—Typist's Initials. As a point of reference, it is conventional to indicate who prepared the letter. At one time, the writer's initials, in caps, would precede the typist's initials. But the writer's initials seem superfluous, since the writer's entire name and signature are on the letter.

10—Enclosure Reminder. The word *enclosure* reminds the reader to look in the envelop for the enclosed materials. Were you to attach something to your letter with a clip, indicate that in this spot in the letter, replacing *enclosure* with the word *attachment.*

11—**Copy To.** The notation *c:* identifies for the reader others who are receiving a copy of this document. Traditionally, the letters *cc* were used in this notation, signifying *carbon copy.* But since few people use carbon paper anymore, the single *c* for *copy* is sufficient.

Choose a Format and Follow It

There is some choice in the format of the business letter. Your company, however, may have made its choice for you. Basically the choices are the following:

Full Blocked

In this style, every line begins *at the left margin.* That includes the date and complimentary close. If you are not using company stationery, type your return address at the left. In the full-blocked style, you do not indent the beginning of a paragraph. The model above is in full-blocked style. This style obviously is the most efficient from a typing standpoint. There is no tabbing to be done and little room for error in terms of placing elements on the line.

Modified Blocked

Every line begins at the left margin *except* the date, complimentary close, name and title of writer. These begin at the center of the line. Some writers using this format also indent the subject line, so it will stand out.

Indented

Every line begins at the left margin *except* the first line of each paragraph, which is indented five spaces.

Once you have chosen or been assigned a letter style, be consistent in following it.

— MODEL FORMATS —

<u>FULL BLOCKED</u>

Ace
Construction Company   234 Shilho Road
                                    Utopia, MO 12345

4 lines

November 1, 199_

4 lines

Ms. Diana Smith
Vice President, Corporate Development
City General Hospital
One Stac Plaza
Downtown, MO 13579

2 lines

<u>Subject: Proposed Agreement for West Wing Renovation</u>

2 lines

Dear Ms. Smith:

2 lines

I have enclosed for your review the drafts of the proposed agreement by which Ace Construction Company will renovate the West Wing at City General Hospital. Please review this agreement in preparation for our final discussion of it with our respective attorneys on December 1, 199_.

If you need any portions of the agreement clarified, please do not hesitate to call me at (123) 456-7890.

I look forward to seeing you again on December 1 and working with you on this renovation.

2 lines

Sincerely,

4 lines

Joseph Ace
President

ab

Enclosure

c: W. McCormack, Esq.

<u>MODIFIED BLOCKED</u>

Ace
Construction Company 234 Shilho Road
Utopia, MO 12345

November 1, 199_

Ms. Diana Smith
Vice President, Corporate Development
City General Hospital
One Stac Plaza
Downtown, MO 13579

<u>Subject: Proposed Agreement for West Wing Renovation</u>

Dear Ms. Smith:

I have enclosed for your review the drafts of the proposed agreement by which Ace Construction Company will renovate the West Wing at City General Hospital. Please review this agreement in preparation for our final discussion of it with our respective attorneys on December 1, 199_.

If you need any portions of the agreement clarified, please do not hesitate to call me at (123) 456-7890.

I look forward to seeing you again on December 1 and working with you on this renovation.

Sincerely,

Joseph Ace
President

ab
Enclosure

<u>INDENTED</u>

Ace
Construction Company   **234 Shilho Road**
Utopia, MO 12345

November 1, 199_

Ms. Diana Smith
Vice President, Corporate Development
City General Hospital
One Stac Plaza
Downtown, MO 13579

<u>Subject: Proposed Agreement for West Wing Renovation</u>

Dear Ms. Smith:

I have enclosed for your review the drafts of the proposed agreement by which Ace Construction Company will renovate the West Wing at City General Hospital. Please review this agreement in preparation for our final discussion of it with our respective attorneys on December 1, 199_.

If you need any portions of the agreement clarified, please do not hesitate to call me at (123) 456-7890.

I look forward to seeing you again on December 1 and working with you on this renovation.

Sincerely,

Joseph Ace
President

THE KEYS TO A SUCCESSFUL BUSINESS LETTER: CONTENT AND ORGANIZATION

More important than any of the conventions of the business letter are the content and organization—what you say and how you present it.

Generally, begin a letter with a sentence or short paragraph stating why you are writing. For example:

> This letter summarizes the points we discussed at our meeting yesterday. Please review them and let me know of any errors or omissions.

Then give the details, explanations, and descriptions required. Try to keep these brief, giving the reader what she wants to know and needs to know for you to accomplish your purpose.

Close with a reminder or statement of what you'd like the reader to do with the information, or with a date by which you would like a response. You may conclude with an expression of feeling. For example:

> If I do not hear from you by Friday of this week, I will assume you agree with my summary of our meeting.

DON'T OVERLOOK THE SMALLER CONVENTIONS

To convey a professional image with your business letters, be alert to the following points, for conventional as well as practical reasons.

ENVELOPE

In addressing the envelope, use full names and specific titles and department identification. It is possible that when your letter arrives, a trainee may be working in the mailroom. He may not know there are two Ms. Smiths in the company and delivers your letter to the wrong person, delaying action on it.

In addressing the standard business letter envelope (No. 10), which measures 9-1/2 × 4-1/8 inches, start the address on line 14 from the top and four inches from the left edge of the envelop. Special notations such as *confidential* or *attention* are typed three lines below the return address. Special mailing notations *(air mail, special delivery)* are typed below the stamp.

Ace Construction Company
234 Shilho Road
Utopia, MO 12345

Confidential

Ms. Diana Smith
Vice President, Corporate Development
City General Hospital
One Stac Plaza
Downtown, MO 13579

ABBREVIATIONS

In the address, use the two-letter abbreviation for the state. But write out words such as *street* and *avenue*. In writing the titles of individuals in the address and greeting, use these abbreviations: *Mr., Mrs., Ms., Dr.* But spell out titles such as *Senator, Reverend, Captain, Professor.* Do not abbreviate the month in the date.

NUMBERS

"Building" numbers generally are given in figures rather than words:

123 Madison Avenue

Spell out building numbers when they are less than ten. For instance,

One Gateway
Six WorldWide Plaza

When numbered streets are under ten, spell them out. When they are over ten, use the figures:

West Fifth Avenue
East 77 Street

When figures are used in the street address, it is not necessary to use the letter suffix:

77 Street not 77*th* Street
32 Avenue not 32*nd* Avenue

ATTENTION LINE

You may see an attention line following the inside address in a letter. For example:

Dajon Associates
123 Kermack Road
Emerson, WI 65432

Attention: Personnel Director

The attention line is useful when you do not know the name of the addressee. For the greeting in such a letter, use a title such as *Dear Personnel Director* or *Dear Sir or Madam*. Do not use *Dear Sir* on the assumption that the person in this position is male.

TONE

Your choice of words can convey an attitude in a letter, just as the sound of your voice can convey an attitude in speech. Generally, you want your letters to be professional yet carry a friendly, personal tone. You can create such a tone by using conversational language. For example, use *try* instead of *endeavor*, and *fix* instead of *rectify*. Personal pronouns also help to convey a personal tone and imply a person-to-person communication. Note the difference in tone:

Impersonal: Enclosed herewith are the specifications as requested.

Personal: *I* have enclosed the specifications *you* requested.

Contractions *(can't, it's, won't)* also give a personal, informal tone to writing. Although once forbidden in business correspondence, contractions are finding their way into more and more letters, as some of the constraints of formality are being disassembled. Consider your audience, however, before deciding to use contractions. If you think your reader will object to contractions, don't use them.

BLIND COPIES

Sometimes you may want to send a copy of the letter to someone without the addressee's knowing it. Such a copy is called a blind copy. The notation for a blind copy is *bc:*, which is to be placed in the same position you'd place *c:* or just below it, if you use both notations. Naturally, you'd have to type the blind copy notation on all copies but the one sent to the addressee.

MULTI-PAGE LETTERS

Use letterhead for the first page only. Use blank sheets of the same stock as the letterhead for subsequent pages. On these pages, use a heading giving the name of the addressee, page number, and date. You may put that heading across the top of the page or at the top left. For example:

Ms. Diane Smith   2   November 1, 199_

or

Ms. Diane Smith
Page 2
November 1, 199_

Begin each type of heading at the seventh line from the top of the page. Then skip three lines before continuing with the text of the letter.

PAGE BREAK

In making a page break, try to have more than one line in the paragraph at the bottom of the first page and more than one at the top of the succeeding page. You may end a page in the middle of a paragraph, but not in the middle of a word.

POSTSCRIPT

A postscript is an effective way of calling attention to an important point. Type the postscript as a single-spaced paragraph, beginning at the left margin.

(Indent the postscript if all of the paragraphs are indented.) Place the notation *P. S.* two lines below the last notation. Skip two spaces following the second period and begin the text of the postscript.

MARGINS

If your letterhead begins at the left side of the page, the beginning of the company name is your left margin for the entire letter. Have every line in your letter, beginning with the date, align with the first letter in the company name. If you must set your own left-hand margin, set it at 1 to 1-1/2 inches for most letters. You may use more ample margins for a very short letter. Set a right-hand margin of one inch.

— BUSINESS LETTER CHECKLIST —

INCLUDE DATE, INSIDE ADDRESS, GREETING, TEXT, COMPLIMENTARY CLOSE, NAME AND TITLE OF WRITER, TYPIST'S INITIALS, AND NOTATIONS FOR COPIES TO, ENCLOSURES, OR ATTACHMENTS.

FOLLOW THE STANDARD PUNCTUATION AND SPACING BETWEEN LINES.

OBSERVE THE RULES FOR ABBREVIATING TITLES AND NAMES OF STATES.

GENERALLY, SPELL OUT ALL NUMBERS UNDER TEN AND USE FIGURES FOR THOSE OVER TEN.

SET A LEFT-HAND MARGIN OF 1 TO 1-1/2 INCHES, OR USE THE FIRST LETTER IN THE LETTERHEAD AS THE LEFT-HAND MARGIN.

SET A RIGHT-HAND MARGIN OF 1 INCH.

FOR MULTIPAGE LETTERS, USE LETTERHEAD FOR THE FIRST PAGE ONLY, AND USE A HEADING ON EACH SUBSEQUENT PAGE.

CREATE A PROFESSIONAL BUT PERSONAL TONE THROUGH YOUR CHOICE OF LANGUAGE AND USE OF PERSONAL PRONOUNS AND CONTRACTIONS.

USE A "SUBJECT" LINE TO IDENTIFY THE SPECIFIC ASPECT TREATED IN THE LETTER.

BE CONSISTENT IN YOUR USE OF THE LETTER FORMAT YOU CHOOSE.

HOW CAN I DEMYSTIFY
MY MEMOS?

You're straight out of school, where the only writing you did was for tests and term papers. Your boss has just asked you to write a memo. You've heard of memos, but what exactly is a business memo? What's the best way to write one?

Or you've been writing and reading memos for a number of years now. Some seem to generate positive response, while others generate indifference or confusion. You've decided it's time to find out what makes memos work so yours can be more effective. This chapter shows you how to clear up muddled memos and make them effective vehicles of communication.

THE WHAT AND WHY OF MEMOS

A business memo is a short, written document that conveys requests, directives, advice, or information from one member of an organization to another. Despite the widespread use of telephone mail and electronic mail, the memo still prevails as the cornerstone of official interoffice communication because it offers a tangible, durable record of a message being sent.

With the rapid movement of personnel from job to job and from company to company, hard-copy records enable those left behind to carry on without major disruptions to the organization. Memos often provide such records.

Memos are written on a range of subjects, from the office picnic to a company restructuring. Memos should be clear and brief. And because it is an interoffice communication, the memo is generally informal in style.

HOW *NOT* TO WRITE A MEMO

If you were a manager and received the following memo, would you read it? Why? How would you respond to it? Would you know exactly what it is asking you to do?

To: All Managers
From: Mr. Bigg
Date: 9/9/9_
Subject: Professional Appearance

I had a client visit me at the office yesterday, and as we were walking out, we passed a number of staff, both professional and support. While everyone was polite, the client made some remarks about the way some people were dressed. As I walked back to my office alone, I was thinking about the client's remarks and the potential effect of them on our business relationship. I then took a closer look at the same people we had passed. Feeling now that this was becoming an issue, I proceeded to walk around the entire floor (some of you may have noticed me) to make an overall assessment of our appearance. On a scale of 1 to 10, I'd have to rate us about a 6, which is not acceptable.

So I went back to my office to think about the problem. Last night before going home I stopped off at the library and picked up a copy of *Dress for Success*, by John T. Molloy. It includes some good material on business dress. I'd like to share some of it with you.

One suggestion he makes, which I will ask all managers to apply, is to hold a staff meeting and discuss appropriate attire. Molloy goes on to say that a poor first impression loses more sales than anything else. He also says that you have a better chance of making the sale if you are dressed conservatively. Conservative need not be corny, however. So be informed about fashion issues so you're not considered way out of touch with today's world.

You can get your people to improve their appearance by setting a good example and dressing professionally yourself. Be clear about how you want employees to dress for work. Compliment employees who look great; express dismay when they don't. When you have to criticize a person's appearance, don't mix that in with other work issues.

I realize that telling people how to dress is no easy task, but no one said managing people is easy.

What Gets a Memo Read?

Managers in Mr. Bigg's office might read his memo, but only because his authority commands their doing so. On its own, the memo has little going for it.

For one thing, the memo is long and rambling, taxing the reader's patience to find out where it is going. The excess verbiage not only bores the reader but also buries the memo's key points and purpose. Some managers may feel the purpose is merely to convey information, because of Mr. Bigg's statement: "I'd like to share some of it with you." Actually, the purpose is to get managers to do something. But the directive is not emphasized. It is given almost as an aside: "One suggestion he makes, *which I will ask all managers to apply,* is to hold a staff meeting…." Only the most alert managers would see that statement as a directive.

Similarly, Mr. Bigg is vague about the dress standards he wants set. What does he mean by "conservative"? Or by "corny"? Or by being "informed about fashion issues"?

In addition, what Mr. Bigg wants from his managers is no easy task. Yet he gives no real help as to how they can accomplish it.

Furthermore, does Mr. Bigg expect any reporting from his managers? Does he want to know of their progress? By a certain date? Mr. Bigg gives no indication of when he wants this task accomplished or how he wants managers to report to him. Such open-ended directives can easily be ignored.

Mr. Bigg no doubt spent much time writing this memo. And his managers spent time reading it and trying to interpret it. Chances are, though, their time was wasted, because the memo as constructed probably will not achieve what the writer wants. He has not made that clear.

SIX PRINCIPLES OF GOOD MEMO WRITING

1. Specify the Subject

Most companies use a preprinted form to standardize and simplify memo writing. Use the "subject" line on these forms to bring the reader close to the subject quickly. Instead of a generic subject head like "Professional Appearance," as in Mr. Bigg's memo, use a more specific title like "Improving the Professional Appearance of the Staff." This kind of heading tells more about the subject—that something is going to be done about *improving* personal appearance. Readers react more strongly when they infer from the subject heading that something is being asked of them.

Another reason for using a specific subject head has to do with *future use of the memo*. A typical project in most offices may produce as many as twenty or thirty memos. A generic head on those memos does not help someone researching the project some time later. For example, if all thirty memos carry a generic subject head like "Loss Protection Plan," the researcher will have to read the contents of each memo to find the one he wants. To eliminate all that reading and simplify the search, use a more specific subject head like "Implementing the Loss Protection Plan." Or use the generic head with various subheads, such as

Loss Protection Plan—Equipment Needs

Loss Protection Plan—Cost-Benefit Analysis

Loss Protection Plan—Implementation: Phase I

A specific subject head indicates more precisely what the memo covers. Such specificity helps the reader get into the memo. It also helps in filing the memo and searching the file later.

2. State Your Purpose Clearly

Most memos are written for one of three reasons:

To give readers information

To get readers to make a decision

To move readers to act

When you know beforehand the purpose you are working toward, you will cut out extraneous matter and highlight the critical—ideally, in the first sentence or paragraph. In the example, Mr. Bigg's purpose is to get managers to act, to take steps to improve appearance. But he does not state his purpose until the third paragraph. Some readers may not get that far with some memos. And by stating the purpose almost parenthetically as he does (*which I will ask all of our managers to apply*) he does not call attention to it.

Stating the purpose up front is like running a meeting from an agenda—you have an outside discipline focusing you on the essentials. You are less likely to ramble. And by stating the purpose up front, you make it obvious to your readers what you are about.

If you find yourself having trouble stating the purpose of your memo, use this basic trigger: "The purpose of this memo is to…". That statement can get you started in the right direction, and it cannot be ignored or misunderstood by your readers.

One exception to this principle of stating the purpose up front occurs when persuasion is involved. In such instances, you may want to coax the reader into the memo before stating your purpose. To see how that's done, read the material on "The Sales Letter," page 12.

3. Limit the Content

Restrict the content of the memo to:

❒ What the reader *needs* to know

❒ What the reader *wants* to know

In the example, the only background needed is that Mr. Bigg is displeased with staff dress. The managers do not need to know all the details of his sojourn around the office and of his trip to the library. What they *do* need to know, however, and what they *want* to know, is what they should do about the problem. The worst thing a memo can do is imply that something is expected of the reader but not be clear on what that something is.

By being conscious about limiting the content, you're more likely to include the important information. Having done that, you'll see no need to add extraneous matter. Therefore, learn to review your memos and cut out all that is not helpful to the reader.

4. Save the Details for the Attachments

When readers need more than a few details to follow a directive, put those details in attachments. You saw in the example what happened when Mr. Bigg did not do that. He tried to summarize the book he read, doing little justice to the book and giving little real help to his readers. But by putting the specific guidelines and suggestions in attachments, you can give the level of assistance readers need to do what's asked and still keep the memo itself short and focused.

5. Put the Most Important Information First

If you put unimportant information up front, hoping to "build up" as you go, you may lose your readers. They may never get to the important stuff. Mr. Bigg, for example, may be justified in thinking his managers need an explanation for his call for this action, but that explanation is less important than the directive. That explanation may be included, but more succinctly, and later in the memo.

6. Highlight with Visual Cues

Effective memos make it easy for readers to grasp key thoughts. Highlight important information by using:

- ❏ A specific subject title
- ❏ Meaningful headings and subheads

❏ Underlining and boldfacing

❏ Bulleting

❏ Numbering and lettering

Mr. Bigg's memo is one solid block of print. Readers are forced to read every sentence of every line to grasp the message. That may be asking too much of busy people. By using visual cues, you can draw attention to key elements. Such highlighting may be enough to pique the reader's interest, and it will certainly emphasize key points.

SOME POINTERS ABOUT FORM

Use first and last names on the "To" and "From" lines in the logistics portion of the memo. Memos often become part of a project's permanent file and remain with it long after individuals connected with it have moved on. Full names make tracing either party more realistic.

The memo does not need a greeting, as a letter does. Some people, however, like to use a greeting when writing to someone they know. They feel a simple "Jack" or "Hi, Joan," softens the formality of the printed communication. A closing is not required either, but *the writer's signature or initials are.* They verify that the person whose name appears on the "From" line did indeed write the memo.

Include your telephone extension number next to your name in the logistics portion of the memo. You may get a quicker response if you make it easier for readers to contact you. Don't give the reader a reason not to respond, and do all you can to encourage a quick response.

Try to limit memos to one page. A one-page, double-spaced memo is visually inviting, and is more likely to be read than a longer, cramped memo. If you must use single spacing to keep the memo to one page, do so. Whenever your memo is single-spaced, be sure to skip a line between paragraphs.

Whether you indent the first line of each paragraph or use the block form is a personal or company choice. If you use the block form (no indenting), however, skip a line between paragraphs.

MODEL MEMO

To:	All Managers	Date:	9/9/9_
From:	Mr. Bigg	Ext.	1234
Subject:	Improving the Professional Appearance of the Staff		

specific subject head

The professional appearance of some of our staff is not what it should be. I'd like you to hold a group meeting with the people reporting to you to raise the level of appearance to a professional standard.

purpose

subhead

The Standard to Maintain

One of the attachments to this memo gives *seven guidelines* for professional dress I'd like you to convey to your people. These guidelines were drawn from *Dress for Success*, a book by John T. Molloy, which many individuals and companies are now using as their standard.

highlight

details in attachment

I have also attached some *detailed suggestions* that can help you explain the issues and make this a positive experience for all. I suggest you read these before calling your meeting.

space between paragraphs

subhead

What Prompted This?

A client walking through our office made a disparaging remark about staff appearance. I'm taking that as a signal to address the situation before it becomes a problem.

less important

due date

Please let me know by 10/9/9_ how you have handled the matter and what the results were.

highlight

initials of writer

ajb

— Memo Checklist —

DECIDE ON YOUR PURPOSE:

- ❏ *To inform*
- ❏ *To call for a decision*
- ❏ *To move to action*

SPECIFY YOUR SUBJECT ON THE SUBJECT LINE.

STATE YOUR PURPOSE IN THE FIRST SENTENCE OR PARAGRAPH.

SELECT YOUR CONTENT TO ACHIEVE YOUR PURPOSE.

LIMIT THE CONTENT TO WHAT THE READER NEEDS AND WANTS TO KNOW.

PUT THE MOST IMPORTANT INFORMATION FIRST.

HIGHLIGHT THE MOST IMPORTANT INFORMATION WITH VISUAL CUES.

USE ATTACHMENTS FOR LENGTHY DETAILS.

FOLLOW THE CONVENTIONS OF YOUR COMPANY'S MEMO FORM.

How Do I Make Requests That Elicit Responses?

You are responsible for engaging speakers for the monthly meetings of your professional association. You want to get some ideas from members—all as busy as you—on topics they are interested in and suggestions for speakers they'd like to hear.

Or you run a small business and want to update your mailing list. How do you get customers to take time to verify or change a mailing label?

Or you are conducting a survey for your company or association, or for a graduate school project, and need information from many companies. How do you get them to share proprietary information with you?

In each of these instances you are writing a letter of request.

THREE KEYS TO ACHIEVING COMPLIANCE

Nowhere is it more important to consider the reader than in letters of request. Their sole purpose is to move busy people to drop what they are doing to do something for you, with little or no benefit to themselves. Therefore you must be your most persuasive, and persuasion, we know, begins with understanding the reader.

To persuade your readers to put aside their own priorities to meet yours, follow these three principles:

❏ Keep the letter short and to the point.

❏ Make your request reasonable and easy to comply with.

❏ Offer *some* benefit to the reader.

To keep the letter brief and increase your response rate, *know exactly what you want*. If you are precise in your request, readers can quickly ascertain if they have the information and can get it to you. Letters of request that are vague are often ignored. They do not give the reader enough to work with, or do not channel her thinking. For example:

> Please provide me with some information about productivity in your department.

This kind of request is so broad it is daunting. The department manager does not know where to begin. Unless the request comes from a supervisor (which puts it in another category), the manager will more than likely ignore the request. A more targeted request, however, might have a better chance with the same manager. For example:

> Please send me annual output-to-staff ratios for your department for the last three years.

A specific request is easier for someone to deal with than a general, open-ended one that requires more time and thought.

Once you decide exactly what you want, *be sure what you want is reasonable* and that the reader can easily get her hands on it. In the precise example just given, the writer is familiar with the ways her readers measure productivity. So she phrases the request in those terms. Do not expect people to reconfigure their data to come up with the kind of information you want.

Another aspect of the reasonableness of a request concerns *proprietary and sensitive information*. Just how much of their operation can you expect people to divulge? And can you expect them to reveal sensitive information, such as the number of sexual harassment cases filed against the company, or the number of employees suffering from addiction? There are no hard rules here other than using judgment in making requests.

Give clear directions for responding. Don't assume they know you want a written response or you want figures as well as commentary.

And work hard to *make it easy for readers to respond*. If people have to write their own letters, they are less likely to respond than if you provide a form on which they can respond. You might provide a response card. For a lengthy response, provide a questionnaire calling for checkmarks or short answers. For a short response, you might simply create a tear-off section at the bottom of your letter. When readers have to get back to you by mail, a self-addressed, stamped envelope raises the level of response.

Think of *benefits you can offer* the reader for complying with your request. In some instances you might be able to offer something tangible in return, such as a copy of the report you are building with the information you collect. With many requests, however, you must play on the goodwill or professionalism of people to respond. Think of an intangible benefit they receive, even if it is only your suggesting that "I owe you one."

— MODEL REQUESTS —

"IT ONLY TAKES A MINUTE" LETTER

Dear SHEP Member,

*benefit
to the
reader*

    As a frequent attendee at SHEP meetings, you know the impact the fea-
tured speaker has on the entire evening. Good speakers and timely topics
generate a lot of discussion that often carries over long after dinner.

*specific
request*

    That's why, as this year's chairperson for dinner speakers, I'm polling the
membership for ideas. Please take a minute to give me some TOPICS or
SPEAKERS you think would invigorate our meetings.

directions

    To simplify this process, call me at (222) 555-9999, or use the lower por-
tion of this letter and return it to me as soon as you can. Thanks.

Sincerely,

Marsha Nichols

---

easy

TOPICS   SPEAKERS

response

————————————————   ————————————————

form

————————————————   ————————————————

————————————————   ————————————————

————————————————   ————————————————

Member: _____

    This letter begins not with the request but with an appeal to the reader's
self-interest. This kind of beginning may draw the reader into the letter, whereas an outright request might turn her off. This beginning offers the intangible
benefit the reader will ultimately receive by complying with the request.

In making the request, the letter specifies the information sought: topics and speakers. Being precise about the information sought and providing two easy means for response raise the chances of getting a sizable number of returns.

APPEAL TO PRIDE LETTER

Mr. and Mrs. Bill Marakovits
288 Hobart Court
Niceton, USA 15790

Dear Mr. and Mrs. Marakovits,

purpose of the letter

You have been welcome guests at PONTE'S RESTAURANT for some years. And we'd like to keep our "regulars" informed of our innovations, special events, and discount offerings. To do that, we have to make sure we have your current mailing address.

simple directions

So please take a moment to make any necessary changes in the name and address on this letter. If there are no changes, write OK next to the address.

benefit

Please return the letter in the enclosed envelope. *Or, bring the letter to the restaurant and enjoy a bottle of wine—on the house.*

Thank you. We look forward to seeing you soon.

Buon Gusto,
Carlo Ponte

This letter opens with an attempt to draw the readers in by appealing to their sense of pride at being considered a "regular." The task requested is simple and can be done right on the letter itself. Returning the information is made simple, too, with the enclosed envelope. The offer of a free bottle of wine is a tangible benefit that might increase response.

THE PERSUASIVE LETTER

Dear Ms. Ring:

*pique
curiosity*

     Voicemail systems are becoming as common as the telephone, because they seem to offer great savings. But those savings have never been documented.

request

*directions;
easy response*

     That's why I am conducting a study on the uses and effectiveness of voicemail systems *in companies of fewer than 500 people.* I am asking you to participate in the study by completing the short questionnaire that is enclosed and returning it to me in the envelop provided.

*tangible
benefit*

     For participating in the study you will receive a copy of the report it generates—free of charge. The report will include the results collected from many companies like yours. I'm sure it will offer you some useful insights into how you might improve the use and cost-effectiveness of your system.

*address
concern*

     All the information you provide will be kept proprietary. The report will name participating companies but all responses will be reported only in aggregate. None of your responses will be identified as yours.

*intangible
benefit;
appeal to
professionism*

     This study is long overdo for this population and can provide significant benefits. The success of the study, however, depends on the professionalism of people like you to participate. So please review the enclosed questionnaire and complete and return it as soon as possible. If you have any questions, call me at (222) 555-1333.

Sincerely,

Cecile Beamer
Research Associate
Pinchot Consulting

    The request in this letter carries a number of burdens. It asks readers to complete a questionnaire, which is much more time consuming than listing a few names or topics and correcting an address label. In addition, the questionnaire is asking for information about the company's operation. Many companies are reluctant to reveal to the world—including their competitors—how they operate. Thus the letter works hard to convince the reader to comply.

First, the writer tries to pique the curiosity of the reader with a question the reader herself may have—whether the voicemail system actually saves money. Second, the letter highlights the exclusivity of the study—to companies under five hundred employees. That exclusivity may make the study more appealing to the reader. Third, the writer offers a copy of the report. Last, the letter appeals to the professionalism of the reader, indicating how useful the study will be and how vital the reader is to its success.

More than the other letters, therefore, this one works harder at persuasion, at convincing the reader to persuade.

The letter also anticipates a concern many of its readers might have—the privacy issue. A full paragraph of the letter is devoted to assuring the reader that no one will gain any knowledge about her operation. Thus the writer fully realizes who the reader is and how she might react to the request. By anticipating the objection, the writer may help readers over that hurdle.

— Request Letter Checklist —

UNDERSTAND WHO THE READERS ARE AND ANTICIPATE THEIR REACTIONS.

KEEP THE LETTER SHORT AND TO THE POINT.

BE PRECISE ABOUT WHAT YOU WANT.

BE REASONABLE IN YOUR REQUEST.

GIVE CLEAR DIRECTIONS FOR RESPONDING.

MAKE IT EASY FOR READERS TO RESPOND.

OFFER SOME BENEFIT TO THE READER.

HOW DO I DEVELOP A JOB DESCRIPTION?

Your company is growing and its personnel matters can no longer be maintained in the corner of your mind. It's time to formalize who does what in the company. It's time to write some job descriptions.

Or you want the Human Resources Department to advertise an open position. HR asks you for a job description on which to base the ad.

Or the people in your department are overworked and you want to request assistance. You want to use the opportunity to create a new position. Before you can sell management on the need, you have to draw up a list of responsibilities and qualifications— a job description.

GET RIGHT TO THE POINT:
KEEP IT SHORT, STRAIGHTFORWARD, AND INFORMATIVE

The purpose of a job description is to inform, not to persuade or inspire or entertain. Its primary purpose is to inform applicants what will be expected of them if they are chosen for the position. Therefore, write the job description to inform. Make it short, one or two pages. Be direct and straightforward, keeping sentences free of qualifiers. And in addition to making the description easy to read, lay the information out in an attractive format that highlights different aspects of the job and requirements.

WHAT GOES INTO THE JOB DESCRIPTION?

Although the job description is short, it must contain quite a bit of information. It must give the range of duties and responsibilities so people can determine if they are interested in applying for the job and qualified to do it. The job description must also provide management with enough information on which to rate the job appropriately.

If you think in terms of *categories of information*, you are more likely to write a job description that gives people who read it a clear and accurate representation of the job. For example, you may have noted in the model job description that, as you read down the page, you gained more and more detail of the job. First, you are given just a title, then an overview, then some dimensions of the job, and then finally a list of specific duties. So through these categories of information the job description moves from a higher level to a lower level of detail. Let's look at those categories of information.

TITLE, LOCATION, REPORTS TO

Give the title of the job, the department in which it resides, and the position to which it reports. In some organizations *Job Title* may be written as *Job Classification* or *Position Title*. Use the term your company uses. If you have a choice, why not use *Job Title?* That seems to be the simplest yet clearest term.

— MODEL JOB DESCRIPTION —

JOB TITLE: Manager of Payroll
DEPARTMENT: Finance
REPORTS TO: Director of General Accounting

OVERVIEW:

Responsible for the processing, accounting, and financial control of all company payrolls. Implements accounting and operating policies and procedures related to payroll.

DIMENSIONS:

Administrative: Directs the activities of three Section Managers and approximately 25 professional and clerical employees engaged in payroll functions.

Financial: Directs the payment of more than 4,000 employees.

Other: Files reports to and interfaces with various external parties including the IRS and unions.

MAJOR DUTIES:

❑ Directs the processing of payrolls to ensure timely and accurate payment to employees in accordance with corporate policy, union contracts, and IRS and state regulations.

❑ Manages the data entry of weekly and biweekly payroll timesheets.

❑ Directs the payment of employee payroll deductions to governmental and third-party agencies. Manages the preparation of reports mandated by the government, including tax returns and W-2s.

❑ Interfaces with Human Resources on matters such as promotions and increases in pay.

❑ Interacts with all levels of management to facilitate the development and flow of information, as well as the resolution of problems related to payroll issues.

MINIMUM QUALIFICATIONS:

Education: Bachelor's degree in accounting, business administration, finance, or a related field

Experience: Six years in payroll or related areas; three years at a supervisory level

Other: Knowledge of automated payroll systems and accounting

In some instances you may have to include other information in addition to that shown in the model. For example, some companies use codes to identify level, such as G-7 and IN-3. In multidivisional companies, you may want to include the division. In companies spread out in various locations, identify the location of the particular opening. In other words, give potential applicants all the information they need when deciding whether or not to apply. And give management the information it needs to understand exactly where a position fits in the overall company structure.

Position this information at the top of the page and use some combination of typefaces, underlining, boldface, upper- and lowercases to make the most important information stand out. The model uses all caps for the classifications and puts the job title in boldface.

Overview: The Scope of Responsibilities and Duties

Under this head you give a general understanding of the job. Go beyond the job title to give a big picture statement, identifying the job's responsibilities at the broadest level. For example:

- ❐ Responsible for providing technical support to users throughout the company
- ❐ Responsible for all internal and external publications
- ❐ Responsible for analysis of financial records and reports where no clear precedent exists

In the Overview you also identify the job's principal range of duties, again in general terms. For example:

- ❐ Makes all technical decisions to ensure operation of the network
- ❐ Writes, edits, and produces all publications
- ❐ Initiates the adjustment of records and inclusion of detailed information

You may see this information under headings such as *Job Definition, General Description,* and *Purpose and Authority of the Position.*

In the Overview, and throughout the job description, do not use a subject in setting down responsibilities or duties. For example, you write: *"Responsible for"* not *"The Manager of Payroll is responsible for."* Because readers know the title of the job being described, repeating it would be superfluous.

Dimensions: Type, Degree, and Level of Responsibilities

The information under this heading expands on the broadbrush statement in the Overview. Here you might provide the *types of responsibilities* involved, such as administrative and financial; the *degree of responsibility,* such as the number of people to supervise or serve; and the *levels of interfacing* the job entails.

By presenting this information separately, you make it easy for readers to note the range of activity and responsibility involved.

In introducing various dimensions of the job, give this information in the form of actions, not *"territories,"* so you can further the reader's understanding of what the person actually *does.* Use action verbs like *directs, files, evaluates, manages,* instead of *"is responsible for."*

Dimensions is an effective heading for this information because the term suggests an image of range and space. You may, however, want to use another term such as *Degree of Responsibility, Scope of Activities, Areas of Responsibility,* or *Interfaces.*

Major Responsibilities

In this section you move still lower in detail, specifying the most important functions of the job. To decide what's most important, consider:

❑ What others in the department and outside the department look to this job for, such as reports, direction, advice

❑ Things that would not get done if this person did not do them

❑ Things that, if done poorly, would come back to this person for redressing

Here especially, begin each item with an action verb. Where you think readers may not fully understand the action, give a short example, as in the model: "Interfaces with Human Resources on matters such as promotions and increases in pay."

You may see this information under other headings, such as *Typical Duties* or *Specific Duties and Responsibilities.*

How many duties do you include? Enough to give a clear picture of what the person does on a day-to-day basis. And don't forget an important duty that might be done once a year, such as "prepares the annual budget."

The example lists only five duties for the sake of convenience. The job description for the position of Manager of Payroll would probably show more. But do not provide every duty the person could conceivably be asked to perform. Remember, you want to keep the description to two pages maximum.

Qualifications

The information in this section lets people know who should and should not apply for the position. By breaking the qualifications into categories as in the model, you highlight each set of requirements. Remember that this is a job description not an advertisement, so it seems appropriate to set *minimum* requirements.

— Job Description Checklist —

MAKE IT SHORT, STRAIGHTFORWARD, AND INFORMATIVE.

LIST TITLE, LOCATION, REPORTS TO, AND OTHER GENERIC INFORMATION AT THE TOP.

PROVIDE AN *OVERVIEW,* STATING BRIEFLY THE SCOPE OF RESPONSIBILITIES AND DUTIES.

UNDER *DIMENSIONS,* GIVE THE TYPES AND DEGREES OF RESPONSIBILITIES OR LEVELS OF INTERFACES THE JOB ENTAILS.

UNDER *MAJOR DUTIES,* SPECIFY THE MOST IMPORTANT FUNCTIONS OF THE JOB.

UNDER *QUALIFICATIONS,* SET DOWN MINIMUM EDUCATIONAL, EXPERIENCE, AND SKILL REQUIREMENTS FOR THE JOB.

USE VISUAL CUES AND SPACING TO HIGHLIGHT INFORMATION AND CREATE AN ATTRACTIVE, EASY-TO-READ DESCRIPTION.

How Can I Write Instructions People Can Easily Follow?

*Y*ou are in charge of security for your building and must issue a set of instructions covering the admittance of visitors.

Or you are the recording secretary for a task force on vendor relations and you must put into writing the new procedures you have developed.

Or because people are misusing a new piece of equipment, you must replace the instructions in the user's manual with a set of your own.

Or you have developed a marketing kit for a new product and must prepare a set of instructions so sales reps will use it advantageously.

Or with a change in health insurance coverage, you must provide a new set of instructions for choosing doctors and filing claims.

In each of these instances, you want to tell through some written document how people are to do things. Some of these writing tasks require technical knowledge and others do not. But they all require a directness and clarity of expression if people are to follow the instructions. How do you write such documents? This chapter will show you.

EFFECTIVE INSTRUCTIONS REQUIRE PRECISION

To write instructions that employees, or customers, can follow unaided, it is not enough for you to know how to complete the process, run the machine, or file the claim. For, like tying shoelaces, some procedures come so naturally to us after a while, we are no longer aware of all the steps involved. To write effective instructions, put yourself in the place of the typical users of your instructions, the people who know little, or perhaps even nothing at all, about the procedure or piece of equipment you might be instructing them to follow or use. Writing for these users, you will be more likely to provide all the steps, as well as the required detail and explanation needed to understand the steps.

Be Specific: Identify the Procedure Clearly

Label the process or procedure for which you are writing instructions and be as specific as possible. *Admittance to Our Building,* for instance, would be too general for the instructions in the model on page 84. That heading might indicate admittance of employees and not draw much attention. Because the heading specifies *Admitting Visitors,* those employees who have visitors to the office will take note of the announcement.

Highlight the Action Steps

Through instructions you are telling people how to do something. Therefore, the actions are most important. *Keep these action steps short,* so readers do not have to struggle to comprehend them and will take note of each.

Begin each step with a verb, the primary action in the step, such as *notify, provide, plan, come.* Beginning with the verb, you get to the heart of the matter and write a more direct action step.

You may have to *supplement the action of the step with additional information.* Rather than including too much information in the action step, supplement it with another sentence giving other pertinent information. In the example that follows on page 84, the main action in step 1 is to *notify the receptionist.* But the time of that notification is also important. So, the writer includes that additional information, putting it in another sentence.

<u>MODEL NONTECHNICAL INSTRUCTION</u>

Procedures for Admitting Visitors to Our Building

Effective February 1, 199_, when bringing an outside vendor, consultant, or other visitor to the office, follow these steps:

1.   **Notify the lobby receptionist that you are expecting a visitor.** Do this on the day before or the day of the visit, *no later than one hour before* the visitor is expected to arrive.

2.   **Provide the visitor's full name and the expected time of arrival.** The receptionist will prepare a name tag for him or her in advance.

3.   **Provide the receptionist with the telephone extension number at which you can be reached when your visitor arrives.**

4.   **Be at that extension about the time of the expected visit,** so you can receive the receptionist's call and not keep your visitor waiting. If your plans change regarding the time of the visit or your location, keep the receptionist informed.

5.   **Greet your visitor at the reception desk and lead him or her personally to your office or conference room.** NO VISITORS, REGARDLESS OF THEIR FAMILIARITY WITH OUR BUILDING, WILL BE ALLOWED BEYOND THE LOBBY UNESCORTED.

Inform Your Visitors of the Procedures

So your visitors know what to expect, tell them that, upon entering the main lobby, they should approach the reception desk and sign in with the receptionist. They must then sign the visitors' log book and wear a name tag authorizing their presence in the building.

By following these steps, you will be keeping the building safe and providing an efficient, professional welcome to your visitors.

You may also want to *supplement the action step with rationale.* Sometimes knowing why an action is required makes it easier for people to remember to do it. The supplemental information for step 2, for example, explains why the advance notification is required, and may make the step more palatable.

When the steps in the procedure must be done in a specific order, number them. Readers can then more easily complete the procedure.

Don't Overlook Related Activities

Some procedures require users to know or do other things that do not fall within the sequence of actions described. Again, rather than cluttering the action steps, give this information elsewhere, either before or after the action steps.

In the example, the writer put the information about informing the visitor *after* the action steps because they make more sense if the reader has first read the action steps. Sometimes, though, you may want to put this kind of information *before* the action steps. For example, if the instructions deal with sensitive machinery, you may want to give a warning about handling the pieces *before* giving the steps. Giving them after may be too late.

Put additional information under a separate heading. Try to make this subhead as specific as possible to draw reader attention to it.

MOTIVATION: THE MOST CRITICAL ELEMENT IN INSTRUCTION

Even though you have the authority to insist that people follow your instructions, try to move them to do so willingly, even eagerly. When people want to do something, or at least see the reason for doing it, they are more faithful to the letter and spirit of the law.

As in all persuasion, try to find benefits to the readers as the source for motivation. The last paragraph in the model gives reasons for the instructions, that offer benefits to each individual, as well as to the company.

Writing Style: Plain and Simple but Not Clipped

Use a plain, simple style in writing instructions. But do not strip the writing to make it "telegraphic." Instructions should be less wordy and conversational than other business prose but not so clipped that they seem cryptic or lacking in critical detail. You are writing instructions, not code. For example:

Clipped:	Notify receptionist of visitor.
Plain:	Notify the lobby receptionist that you are expecting a visitor.
Clipped:	Leave extension number.
Plain:	Provide the receptionist with the telephone extension number you can be reached at when your visitor arrives.

Use the *imperative* style, by which you speak directly to the reader and begin sentences with the verb.

| *Expository:* | You must notify the lobby receptionist… |
| *Imperative:* | Notify the lobby receptionist… |

As you can see, the imperative style is more direct and focuses attention on the action. This style also shortens the wording of the step.

In situations that call for you to refer to the user, use the second person pronouns *you* and *your*, rather than the third person, such as *he/she, one,* or *the employee.* For example:

| *Not:* | If *the employee's* plans change regarding the time of the visit or *his/her* location, keep the receptionist informed. |
| *But:* | If *your* plans change regarding the time of the visit or *your* location, *keep* the receptionist informed. |

ADDITIONAL TIPS FOR WRITING TECHNICAL INSTRUCTIONS

The guidelines given for writing nontechnical instructions also apply when writing technical instructions. But, depending on the procedures being described and the audience, you may want to consider doing some additional things.

Whittle the Job Down to Manageable Size

In giving instructions for an involved technical procedure, break it down into stages. What would otherwise seem like an overwhelming challenge seems more manageable when broken into stages. For instance, in Hewlett-Packard's *LaserJet IIIP Printer Getting Started Guide,* instructions are broken down into twenty-four short stages, from "Prepare a Location for the Printer" to "Verify Communication Between the Computer and Printer." Each stage is given on a separate page, with its own set of action steps. A drawing illustrating the action accompanies some steps; see Figure 1.

Note the two *caution boxes* shown before the steps, to prevent the user's mishandling the cartridge. Note, too, the additional information given with step 1 (*It is in a separate box*) and step 2 (*Save the bag for possible storage.*)

Instructions in stage W in the same guide are more technical and complicated, but the presentation removes much of the difficulty from them (see Figure 2). The writer employs a number of techniques to simplify the material for the user. In these instructions the writer

- ❏ Identifies in boldface at the top the primary action in the step.
- ❏ Spells out the purpose of the step.
- ❏ Gives an overview of what the step accomplishes. (By making users aware of what they are doing and why, you make it easier for them to perform the tasks.)
- ❏ Specifies the actions to take, how to take them, and what the result of each will be.
- ❏ Uses a three-column format to make this information easy to read.
- ❏ Numbers the actions in sequence.
- ❏ Uses subsets (7b and 7c) when variables are involved.

In writing instructions, then, from the most technical to the nontechnical, keep the needs of the readers in mind. Provide all information that will help them accomplish the task, but no more. And present that information with whatever visual cues are necessary to enable readers to follow the instructions unaided.

Unpack the Toner Cartridge

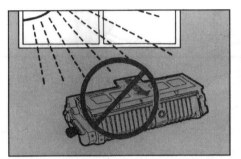

CAUTION: Do not expose the cartridge to direct sunlight. Do not expose it to room light for more than a few minutes.

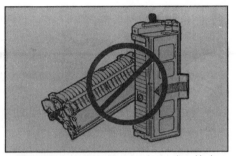

CAUTION: Do not stand cartridge on end or turn it upside down after it has been unpacked.

Locate the toner (EP-L) cartridge. It is in a separate box.

Remove the cartridge from its bag. Save the bag for possible storage.

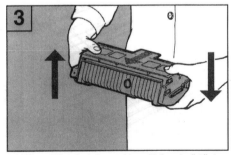

Rock the cartridge slowly from end to end 5 times to distribute the toner.

Reprinted with permission of Hewlett-Packard Company.

Edit Your AUTOEXEC.BAT File

This section applies only to DOS users who do not have another method to edit their AUTOEXEC.BAT file. If you do not work in a DOS environment, skip to section X.

For DOS users, the AUTOEXEC.BAT file is used to set up the communication link between the computer and printer. When you enter the printer configuration (for example, LPT1, COM1) into this file, the computer knows what port to send data to.

The following procedure:

- Verifies you have an AUTOEXEC.BAT file.

- Prepares the computer to accept printer configuration commands.

- Inputs the MODE statement(s) in your AUTOEXEC.BAT file.

If you have DOS 4.0 or above, substitute the P with a B in the parallel MODE statement. (MODE LPT1:,,B)

Step	WHAT to do:	HOW to do it:	Computer Displays:
1	Select your root directory	Type: `CD\` `ENTER`	`A:\>` or `B:\>` or `C:\>`
2	Make a backup copy of your AUTOEXEC.BAT file	Type: `COPY AUTOEXEC.BAT AUTOEXEC.LJ` `ENTER`	`1 file(s) copied`
3	Review your AUTOEXEC.BAT file	Type: `TYPE AUTOEXEC.BAT` `ENTER`	Your AUTOEXEC.BAT file. (If you don't have one, skip to Step 5.)
4	Look for a MODE statement in the file. If the correct statement is there, continue with section **X**. (If there is an incorrect MODE statement, you cannot use this procedure to edit your AUTOEXEC.BAT file.)		
5	Look for the `MODE.COM` in your root directory. If you can't find it, check in subdirectories on your computer, or on your original DOS disks.	Type: `DIR *.COM` `ENTER`	A list of files with the .COM extension.
6	If `MODE.COM` appears in the directory listing, skip to Step 9a		
7a	If `MODE.COM` does not appear in the root directory listing, copy it from your DOS disks to your root directory	IF YOU HAVE A HARD DRIVE: Insert the "startup" DOS disk in drive A and type: `COPY A:MODE.COM` `ENTER`	`1 file(s) copied`
7b		IF YOU HAVE A TWO-FLOPPY SYSTEM: Insert the "startup" DOS disk in drive B and the "bootup" DOS disk in drive A then type: `COPY A:MODE.COM B:` `ENTER`	`1 file(s) copied`
7c		IF YOU HAVE A SINGLE FLOPPY SYSTEM: Insert the "startup" DOS disk in drive A and type: `COPY A:MODE.COM B:` `ENTER`	`1 file(s) copied`

Reprinted with permission of Hewlett-Packard Company.

— Instructions Checklist —

PUT YOURSELF IN THE PLACE OF THE USERS OF YOUR INSTRUCTIONS.

IDENTIFY THE PROCEDURE CLEARLY.

HIGHLIGHT THE ACTION STEPS.

KEEP ACTION STEPS SHORT.

BEGIN EACH ACTION STEP WITH A VERB.

SUPPLEMENT ACTION STEPS WITH ADDITIONAL INFORMATION OR RATIONALE, WHEN HELPFUL.

NUMBER THE STEPS WHEN SEQUENCE IS CRITICAL.

INCLUDE RELATED ACTIVITIES, CLEARLY SEPARATED AND IDENTIFIED WITH HEADINGS.

MOTIVATE THE USERS.

USE A WRITING STYLE THAT IS PLAIN BUT NOT CLIPPED.

BREAK PROCEDURES INTO MANAGEABLE STAGES.

USE ILLUSTRATIONS, DIAGRAMS, COLUMNS, AND VISUAL CUES TO SIMPLIFY THE PRESENTATION OF INFORMATION.

HOW DO I BUILD
A PERSUASIVE PROPOSAL?

Your firm has received a Request for Proposal from a company or government agency that you would very much like to make a client. How do you tailor a proposal that stands out from those of first-rank competitors?

Or you are a department head and have an idea that can improve productivity in your department by 20 percent, but you need permission and financing from top management. How do you get the backing you need?

Or a national foundation is making money available to nonprofit organizations to help fund special projects. How do you win that grant?

Though the documents produced in these three situations may vary some, essentially they are the same. All three will propose a solution to a problem or offer a program to fill a need. To win approval from the client, foundation, or management, the proposal will have to be persuasive as well as informative. This chapter tells you how to build a persuasive proposal. First, we'll look at some general concepts for developing the proposal and then at how to write the various components of a persuasive proposal.

FOUR STEPS TO CREATING A PROPOSAL THAT SELLS

The desire to sell your idea and your organization drives everything that goes into your proposal. In some instances, a problem will be brought to you in the form of a Request for Proposal (RFP). Then your task is "simply" to show the client you have the best solution and can deliver it in the most efficient manner possible. (For simplicity's sake, we will refer to all decision makers in proposal situations as "the client.") In other instances, such as that of the department head mentioned earlier, the "client" (upper management, usually) may not realize there is a problem. So you must first convince them that a serious problem exists. Then you have to convince them that you can solve it. In some instances, usually in internal situations, your proposal may not address a problem but show that a significant gain can be made if the company applies the change you are proposing.

Your proposal, then, must do three things. It must demonstrate that

❒ You understand the client's need.

❒ You know how to fill that need.

❒ You are capable of delivering what you propose.

Doing these things obviously requires the right information, often of a technical and detailed nature. But in presenting that information, in educating the client, never lose sight of your need to persuade, to sell.

Step 1: Analyze the Requirements and Needs

The first step in the selling process, before you write anything, is to study the RFP or grant application. Whether you are responding to an RFP from a company on a specific project or to a foundation's open offering, don't just read it. Study it. Pore over it carefully, highlighter in hand, to be sure you catch all the requirements and concerns of the client, as well as subtle intimations of attitude, fears, and ambitions.

Note on your "to do" sheet the technical and production requirements, the evaluative criteria to be used, and the supporting information expected, such as resumes. Listing all the requirements will not only ensure your providing them in your proposal; it will also guide you in *developing your strategy* for approaching the problem and building the proposal.

When the proposal format is prescribed, as it often is with government and foundation proposals, follow the prescription closely, especially with regard to:

- ❐ the information requested
- ❐ the order in which it is to be given
- ❐ the wording in headings and subheads
- ❐ the typographic format (e.g., single- or double-spaced)
- ❐ the number of copies submitted

By following the organization's format you simplify the client's task in appraising your proposal. And anything you can do to make your proposal easy to read wins points for you. If, on the other hand, the client cannot find certain information—because it is not in the prescribed order or is under a differently worded heading—you can lose points.

Even when the format is not prescribed, try to stick close to the language and organization of the RFP.

Step 2: Highlight the Benefits

To persuade, stress the benefits the client will receive. (In the case of foundation grants, stress the benefits society or your constituents will receive.) Try to focus on the particular benefits you know the client is looking for or is likely to respond to. You can uncover what those benefits are from the RFP, from the grant application, from talking with the client and representatives, from discussing the client with colleagues, from reading about the client. In other words, find out all you can about the client and her concern about this particular issue.

For example, assume the solution to the problem in the RFP is a relatively routine installation of an automated accounts payable system. But you find out that the client has plans for automating the operation totally over the next few years. Show in your proposal how you can install the accounts payable system so that it can easily be integrated to other systems at any time the client wishes. Touching on that *"hot button"* of the client may give you the edge over other proposals.

Another example of playing to the needs of the client would be in the internal situation. Assume, for instance, that management is reluctant to spend any money now for special projects. You also know that a particular vice president would like very much to reduce head count wherever possible. So in making your proposal, you show not only that your proposed change can improve productivity in your department, but also that the change will eliminate the need for some staff. In fact, you cite that staff reduction is the primary benefit to be derived.

You must, of course, be able to document the benefits you offer in proposals because credibility is critical to persuasion. Stay away from superlatives and unsupported generalizations. Use concrete detail and quantify whenever possible. And choose your information carefully, with an eye not only toward solving the problem, but also toward selling the client on your solution and on you.

Step 3: Start from a Strategy Statement

A major element in a winning proposal is a clear, distinct statement of your solution to the problem. That statement dictates all the material you present throughout the proposal. The client should recognize your strategy immediately and see it as the unifying thread in all the detail you present.

Design that strategy on a number of things:

❏ *The end result the client seeks or you think your management will agree to.* Remember, in selling, the key element is not the product but the buyer's want or need.

❏ *The ways through which this end can be reached.* Don't stop at the first solution that comes to mind. You want as much information as you can get on attacking the problem.

❏ *Your strengths and weaknesses in bringing about that end result.* Decide from among the possible approaches how *you can best reach the end.* For instance, assume your client, a professional services firm, wants to generate publicity to enhance its image and visibility. There are many ways to do that, but your organization has been most successful with media releases based on survey data. You find the news media agreeable to printing stories dealing with survey data, and you have gained wide visibility for other clients in this way. In your proposal, stress this means of reaching the client's goal, as it is a strength you can deliver on. Build your strategy and proposal on it.

☐ *Your competitors' strategy.* Realize that different approaches to solve the problem may be proposed by your competitors. Consider these. For example, if we continue the "publicity" proposal, some competitors may be suggesting a newsletter campaign, others a series of roundtables, and so on. Acknowledge such approaches in your planning and in your proposal, to show you understand the field and range of possibilities. Then rule them out, giving reasons why you think your approach would *best* serve the client's needs. In other words, without saying so explicitly, indicate to the client why your approach is better than those of others proposing on the project.

Naturally, this tactic will work only if you believe in what you are saying. If you propose a survey/news release approach *only* because that's all you do, you may have a hard time convincing the client you have his interests in mind.

Step 4: Dig Deep for Information

Your proposal is as good as the information it is based on, so dig deep and in a variety of places. Start with the RFP. Even if it is skimpy, poorly organized, and difficult to read, do not overlook the RFP. Each time you go through it you may pick up additional insights into the client's need as well as her "mind-set."

If you have opportunities to talk with the client before getting the RFP, pay attention to not only what she says about the project but also about what led up to this, what might follow, what changes have been occurring in the organization. If you have a question about something in the RFP, call to ask about it. Do so cautiously, however, because all questions the client fields and clarifications she gives will have to be disseminated to the other bidders as well. So do not ask questions that might reveal to outsiders what your approach will be.

Review all literature on the client, such as annual reports, brochures, newsletters, Dun & Bradstreet reports. If it is a high-profile company, check back issues of business periodicals.

And check your own company's files for documents on the company. It is possible someone else has done work for them at one time, which can help you in some way. In addition, check your company's files for proposals similar to the one you are writing. Avoid the temptation, however, to just cut and paste. That will only weaken your proposal. But you may be able to find useful ideas and approaches, benefits, and details you had not thought of.

THE BUILDING BLOCKS IN A PERSUASIVE PROPOSAL

The components may vary from one proposal to another. Government agencies have strict formulas and often require some information that organizations in the private sector do not. Projects of a technical nature may require apparatus such as diagrams and charts that other projects may not. Some proposals may run one hundred or more pages, while others may be just three or four.

For our purposes here, however, we will touch upon the kinds of information most likely to be required in most proposals. The titles of sections may differ, but basically the information is the same.

Cover Letter

Almost all proposals are delivered with a short cover letter of one or two pages. Start selling the client in your cover letter. Give a concise statement of the problem, your solution, the primary benefit the client will derive, and your approach. For example:

> To help you gain the visibility you seek, we are proposing a series of media releases based on survey data.

Give an overview of what is included in your proposal, in the order in which it appears. Express your interest in and enthusiasm for the project. Include the name and address of the person in your organization who will serve as contact on this proposal. This cover letter is more than a formality. It introduces the client to your thinking, preparing him for what is to follow, and, it is hoped, whetting his appetite for it.

Executive Summary

This component is for the executives who must sign off on such projects or want to know what's going on in the company without having to know all the little details. The summary should impress the client, make him want to know more. The summary hits the need, solution, and benefits. It gives in the most cursory terms the approach and rationale. The summary also gives your qualifications for handling the project. This summary, therefore, gives the essence of the proposal in brief (a few paragraphs for short proposal, a few pages for a long one).

Write the summary in nontechnical language, even when the project is very technical. Technical people may assess the merits of the detail, but the decision maker may not be a technical person. That individual will rely greatly upon the recommendation of subordinates but still wants to be able to understand for himself the gist of the solution. So use a writing style and visual cues that make reading easy.

Though the cover letter and executive summary come first, you probably should write them last. Wait until you have finalized your strategy and know your approach thoroughly, so you can safely and accurately summarize them.

Problem, Solution, Approach, Rationale

Some proposals may call for this information in separate sections with different headings; others may call for it in one section. Whatever the format, it is at this point in the proposal that you explain in detail your understanding of the problem or need and your approach to it. Let's see how.

PROBLEM

Define the problem and the need for a solution. Document the need, even in instances when you are responding to an RFP that explains the need. Show in your own words that you understand the situation. You can document the need in a number of ways.

QUANTITATIVE DOCUMENTATION. Show evidence of need in the form of data such as orders not processed, results of surveys, stacks of written complaints from customers, falling revenues, high turnover. Make statements such as *sales have dropped 15 percent in the last year* or *just two of the ten people in that position have all of the qualifications called for.* Tables and charts make impressive presentations of quantitative documentation.

QUALITATIVE DOCUMENTATION. Define the need with logical arguments, such as *without the proper qualifications, managers can easily lead their subordinates into serious errors.*

INADEQUACY OF EXISTING PROGRAMS. Indicate why the programs in place are incapable of meeting the need. Show an awareness of the current situation and how your proposed project can build on anything that may have been done to this point.

Here's an example of how a hospital defined its need when applying to a foundation for a grant:

A critical problem has arisen at GH revolving around the role of the nurse manager. Specifically:

1. Patient care suffers because the nurse manager now spends an inordinate amount of time (25% to 40%) on administrative/clerical duties.

2. Changes in the health care environment in general, and at GH in particular, have placed more demands on the nurse manager. Among these changes are shorter lengths of stay, more acute patients, staff shortages, the changing composition of the work force, and limited resources.

3. Upper management at GH expressed its expectation for nurse managers to become more "proactive" in making decisions in their units. (See attached Exhibit A, "Directive to Nurse Managers, 2/9/9_.") For nurse managers to comply with this directive, they must have the professional presence, training, capabilities, and time for such decision making.

SOLUTION

After defining the problem and documenting the need, give your solution to the problem. This solution may be seen in some proposals as *the primary end or objective of the project.* Offer observable, verifiable outcomes wherever possible. Use action verbs to introduce these objectives, words like *increase, reduce, select, formulate, establish.* The solution or objectives should offer a result that is measurable. For example:

> These problems can be resolved by restructuring the role of the nurse manager. This restructuring will achieve these objectives:
>
> 1. Reduce by at least 30% the time the nurse manager spends on administrative/clerical duties, enabling her to provide the leadership being called for by management and the high-quality nursing care patients in the unit are entitled to.
>
> 2. Elevate the status of the nurse manager, in terms of the kinds of duties she performs, to correspond to the expectations and demands being placed on the position.

Approach

Next, show *how* you intend to achieve the objective and solve the problem. This portion of the proposal is the heart of your sales pitch. Through the detail of your approach, you win or lose. Spell out the steps you would take to solving the problem and the rationale behind your approach. That is, explain why you have chosen this approach rather than the others. Cite instances where the proposed plan has worked. Quote research on the subject. Show that you know the field.

First give the steps in your approach in broad-based terms and then in more minute tasks or activities. Show a consistent relationship between the objectives and the activities. For example:

> *Objective 1:* Reduce by at least 30% the time the nurse manager spends on administrative/clerical duties, enabling her to provide the leadership being called for by management and the high-quality nursing care patients in the unit are entitled to.

Activities to achieve this objective:

1. Update the computerization of the administrative/clerical tasks now being done by the nurse manager.

   Install the software package "Nurse Manager 3.7." In consulting with other hospitals, we find that nurse managers at GH are using a primitive software program for capturing much of the data they need. "Nurse

Manager 3.7," used in all six of the hospitals we consulted, will enable our managers to capture the same data, in fact even more data, in half the time.

2. Provide clerical assistance to handle clerical chores. Hire a part-time clerk. Our review shows the nurse manager spends between 45 and 60 minutes per day doing routine filing, typing, and calling that can be done equally as well by a per-hour temporary worker.

Don't make the error of being too general in describing your approach, of assuming that the client will know from your objectives how you intend to achieve them. For example, moving from the foundation grant to a private sector proposal, note how the writer moves from general to specific:

Our approach to assessing your primary competitors will involve three steps:

1. Define customer requirements.

2. Assess the capabilities of your competitors to meet these requirements.

3. Compare those capabilities with your own.

After explaining what you mean by each of these steps, tell how you will accomplish each. For example:

Actions we will take within each step are:

Step 1:   Define customer requirements:

    a. Review your customer research files.

    b. Construct quantitative measures of criteria to facilitate comparisons among competitors.

    c. Review the criteria with your management and gain acceptance of them before proceeding to the next step.

    d. Identify competitors to be surveyed.

You can give still more detail, explaining, for instance, how you intend to identify the competitors to be surveyed. Of course, you must use judgment and not bury your readers in detail. But the more logical and persuasive you are in this section, the better chance you have of winning.

In explaining your approach, also spell out:

❐ How you will organize the work (work steps or activities)

❐ The people who will do it (staffing)

❐ The qualifications they have for the tasks they will be assigned to

❐ Special equipment, tools, methodologies you will use

❐ How you will control the quality and cost of the work

❐ What you will deliver to the client (deliverables such as a report, a set of guidelines, a list of recommendations)

❐ Timetable of when activities will be done

Try to anticipate the questions the reader might have while reading your proposal. Then answer those questions. Put yourself in the shoes of the client and raise the doubts, fears, and objections he might raise. Then deal with them.

Qualifications or Credibility Statement

In this section of the proposal you demonstrate your dependability and competence as an organization. You assure the client that you have the qualifications, that you have successfully done similar work for other organizations, and that you possess the resources to do it again for him. Project summaries and the types of organizations for which you did the projects are most impressive. This project summary need not be long or identify the name of the client. For example:

Corporate Diversification Study for an International Financial Services Company:

Evaluated diversification options by establishing diversification criteria, examining the profitability prospects of merger candidates, and estimating a likely range of acquisition costs for each candidate.

In the case of an internal situation or foundation grant, you give a similar assurance to the decision maker that you know how to do what you are proposing.

Fees and Budget

In the case of an internal or foundation proposal, you must specify what the project will cost. In addition, decision makers in such cases want to know how you are going to spend their money. Spell out in as much detail as possible where the money is going—so much for equipment, so much for outside consultants, so much for advertising, and so on. The more detailed you are, the more convincing you can be that you know exactly what you are about. Lump-sum figures or too large a "miscellaneous" figure can worry people. And, to assuage these fears, show how you will keep track of money spent and how frequently and in what manner you will report to the decision maker where each dollar goes.

When proposing to a company or agency, your concerns are slightly different, but you still must convince the decision maker that you are not about to squander her money. Give evidence that the budget you have developed was soundly conceived. A breakdown of expenditures, particularly for outside services such as surveys and printing, can raise the client's level of confidence in you.

Optional Material

Depending on the length and type of proposal you are writing, you may include other components, such as those described here.

TITLE PAGE

In longer proposals, and in many foundation and government proposals, a title page is often required. Work carefully in fashioning the title. Choose words that clearly state the goal of the project, that can lead your reader into your thinking, or that mention the primary benefit the client is seeking. For example, instead of "Computerization Proposal," choose something like "Proposal to Speed Order Processing through Computerization."

TABLE OF CONTENTS

For longer proposals, you may want to or be expected to include a detailed Table of Contents. Include chapter or section titles, as well as subheads showing major elements within each. Do the Table of Contents in outline form, using the same heads and subheads as in the text of the proposal. Show page numbers in the Table of Contents for easy reference. The Table of Contents, like the cover letter and executive summary, presents an overall picture of your thinking. With well-worded headings and subheads, the Table of Contents conveys your sense of coherence and direction. It can be a most important weapon in your selling arsenal.

APPENDIX

When you have reference material in the proposal, some of it will fit nicely with the text. For example, if a chart can simplify an explanation of costs and benefits, merge the chart in with the text for easier reading. If, however, you have other charts that are less vital to the flow of an argument but might be of use to some readers, put these in the appendix.

RATE YOUR PROPOSAL

Organizations that solicit proposals have a set of criteria by which they evaluate the proposals submitted and weigh one against the other. So anticipate the response of your client and measure your proposal against his criteria or against these:

Clarity	The reader can follow the train of thought, which is presented with a logical flow. Sentences are short and ideas are explained with details and examples. The reader's questions and objections are anticipated and answered.
Completeness	The proposal addressees all components of the RFP, does not assume too much knowledge on the part of the reader, and spells out all the critical information. It explains what needs explaining.
Consistency	A common theme runs throughout the proposal. The statement of need leads to the goal, which leads to objectives, which lead to tasks and activities.

Understanding of the problem	The proposal does more than state the problem as identified in the RFP. It refines the problem, putting it into a context that shows a true understanding of its ramifications and of the obstacles standing in the way of its solution.
Viability of the solution	The solution as proposed addresses the problem realistically in terms of the client's needs, resources, and intentions. The solution does not oversimplify or overcomplicate the solution to the problem.
Ability to deliver	The proposal shows evidence of your qualifications. These qualifications are evident in the quality of the solution offered, the familiarity with the problem, the experience of the people working the project, and the track record of the organization to deliver.
Efficiency and accountability	The proposal spells out clearly the timetable, costs and benefits, and reporting methods.
Enthusiasm for the project	The wording and the attitude behind the proposal indicate you are truly interested in doing the project and will work on it with enthusiasm. The client feels you will commit the resources and effort to delivering what is proposed.

— Proposal Checklist —

Make the Proposal a Selling Document.

Analyze the RFP for Requirements and Attitudes.

Highlight the Benefits the Client Hopes to or Will Receive.

Start from a Strategy Statement.

Research the Matter Thoroughly.

Write a Cover Letter that Starts the Selling Process.

Write an Executive Summary in Nontechnical Language.

Document the Need Quantitatively and Qualitatively.

Explain Your Approach to Solving the Problem.

Provide a Statement of Qualifications Demonstrating Your Competence and Dependability.

Show You Are Fiscally Responsible for Moneys and Budgets.

Include a Title Page, Table of Contents, and Appendix as Necessary.

Measure Your Proposal Against a Strict Set of Evaluative Criteria.

Problem No. **12**

How Do I Balance Detail and Brevity in My Audit Reports?

You are the VP of Audit, and senior managers are complaining because you are giving them too much to read. They want to know what's going on, but they don't want to have to wade through the deadly detail of lengthy audit reports to do it.

As the person in charge of Audit, you have to come up with a way to get your auditors to produce reports that are substantial but easy to read.

HOW TO PLEASE TWO MASTERS—THE SKIMMERS AND THE DETAILERS

By their very nature, audit reports are detail oriented. They must be, because their purpose is to explain in writing the findings that were made by the auditor. Often these reports must also be persuasive, as they will recommend actions to improve or safeguard the organization. But too often the detail obscures the very points it is intended to make, and readers cannot easily distinguish the forest from the trees.

And upper-level managers need to do just that. They need reports they can skim, so they can learn quickly the state of the many entities in the company. These managers want reports that highlight problems needing their immediate attention.

At the same time, operations managers and line personnel need audit reports that describe exceptions and problems in detail. These readers need reports that provide recommendations with enough substance to be helpful and persuasive.

So what's an auditor to do when facing these radically opposed demands of two different sets of audiences?

This chapter explains how to design the report format and set content requirements to meet the needs of both the *skimmers* (upper management) and the *detailers* (operations and line personnel). The chapter also identifies a number of expression problems that often mar audit reports, and offers techniques for avoiding these problems.

Start Strong

In many audit reports, the first paragraph is used for rather incidental details—the address of the unit being audited, its type, and so on. To put this information first may seem logical, since the reader must know what is being audited. But this kind of information just kills any interest a reader might bring to the report. This information keeps you from starting strong.

Consider moving this detail *out of the report proper* and putting it up above with the other "logistical" details—*to, from, date.* In doing so, you can even expand the level of data that could be included, adding information such as the capacity of the unit, the number of employees, and so on. Readers can read this information if they choose to, or jump right into the text of the memo. For example:

*in first
paragraph*

At the request of the Operations Department, a field audit was performed at the ABC facility on 123 Main Street, in Brooklyn, New York, on December 10, 199_.

*in
logistics
section*

TO:

FROM:

DATE:

RE: Field audit at ABC facility, 123 Main Street, Brooklyn, New York, December 10, 1999_; 12 employees; hours: 9–9; 7 days/wk

Let Form Follow Function

The form of any document is dictated in part by how the document is to be used. The audit report—like most detailed business documents—has readers who will want to skim the document. A summary up front meets their needs.

Placed at the beginning of the report, the Audit Summary presents an "Overview" and "Auditor's Comment." The Overview gives the *type and number of exceptions* covered in the report and the *degree of risk* associated with each. The Auditor's Comment summarizes for management the *auditor's bottom line thinking* on the unit. Here's what the audit summary might look like:

AUDIT SUMMARY

Overview: The three exceptions found and the degree of risk associated with each are:

Exception	Risk
1. Excess cash on premises	Serious
2. Shipping cartons blocking an exit	Serious
3. More overtime hours scheduled than permitted	Moderate

Auditor's Comment: These exceptions suggest that things are getting out of hand at this unit. The manager may need more help or more training, or both.

At a glance, then, senior managers can quickly assess the success of the unit and its manager. They know if the unit has many or few problems. They know what the problems are and how serious they are. Based on what they see in the Summary, senior managers can decide if they should read the detail and investigate any of these matters further.

On the other hand, line personnel use the Summary to focus in on the findings of the audit. The Summary provides them with a useful introduction to the detail that follows. Knowing that upper management will have been apprised of these particular findings, line personnel may give the audit report more attention.

Establish Content Requirements

Although many audit reports are lengthy, the content in them does not necessarily inform. Many reports omit the *cause of the problem or its impact on the company*. Sometimes the reader may be able to deduce these from the narrative, but in many instances that would be difficult, especially for senior managers not familiar with the nitty-gritty of every operation. *Recommendations*, too, find their way into some reports but not into others.

For greater consistency and usefulness, set up content requirements for treating the exceptions. Consider these content requirements:

❐ The *nature* of the exception and *the number of occurrences*

❐ The *effect* or *impact* of the exception on the company

❐ The *criterion* on which this exception is based

❐ The *facts* or *specific details* of the exception

❐ The *cause* of the exception

❐ The *solution* recommended to prevent a repetition of this exception

Many companies feel these six elements are necessary for the audit report to bring about a change, for operations and line personnel to learn anything from the report and be persuaded to act on it.

This set of content requirements places demands on auditors. For starters, they are asked to make judgments, such as how serious the problem is. You can hold a meeting to address the most common exceptions and label these as "serious," "moderate," or "minor." The entire department, then, will be working from the same guidelines in labeling the judgments they make.

In addition, auditors must search for the cause of the problem and propose a solution. Generally, auditors accept the challenge of those added responsibilities, viewing it as an opportunity to show more fully their understanding of the company and its operations.

Here is what the detail portion of an audit report based on these content requirements might look like:

short, indicative heading
nature of the exception and number of occurrences

effect or impact on the company

criterion on which the exception is based

facts or details of the exception

cause of the exception

solution recommended

EXCEPTION 1: $14,800 in Undeposited Cash

$14,837 in money collected was found undeposited at the location on one occasion.

Undeposited cash must always be viewed as a serious risk. Both the company and location personnel are at risk when money is not deposited.

Company policy requires money to be deposited each day. If an emergency makes a deposit impossible, the manager should make the deposit on the next day. He should document the incident in the Manager's Log Book and notify his supervisor of it.

The undeposited cash represented collections from January 5 to January 10. On none of these days did the manager tell his supervisor he had not deposited his receipts or write that fact in his Log Book.

To determine the cause of this exception, we asked the manager why he did not deposit the cash or file the reports. He said that his assistant manager was on vacation and he could not leave the unit unattended to go to the bank.

We find this explanation acceptable to a point. The manager could not leave the unit unattended. But he could have made the problem known to his supervisor.

We recommend that the supervisor explain to this manager that, under similar conditions, the supervisor will take the deposit to the bank. The manager should notify the supervisor of the situation on the first day. He should also note the problem in his Log Book.

By following the guidelines for content requirements, the auditor provides all the pertinent detail in a logical flow. Rather than constraining the auditors, the guidelines help those writing the reports to organize and make best use of the volume of detail. They do not have to struggle trying to weave it into a long, continuous narrative.

How To Initiate a Change in Format and Requirements

As the person in charge of audit reports in your company, you may be unhappy with the format and requirements of your audit reports. Those presented here will provide a framework for change that can be followed as is or modified to suit your needs. Draft your own revised format and set of requirements and ask others—management, line personnel, and auditors—to critique the draft. With feedback from all levels, you can come up with the format and requirements that work best. The result will truly be an example of form following function, because it will meet the needs of the involved parties. By the time the final format and content requirements are adopted, most of the people who would use them will have already bought into them.

How To Express Audit Information Clearly and Persuasively

With the format and content settled, take a look at expression. Many audit reports are marred by expression that muddies the presentation of information, is not persuasive, and even can antagonize the readers who should be moved to action. Here are some of the most common problems of expression in audit reports.

CLICHÉS. Many audit reports depend heavily on clichés. As a result, descriptions of exceptions are vague, and recommendations offer little real direction. Auditors can learn to replace these clichés with fresh, precise statements. For example:

> *Cliché:*   This activity *impedes audit practices.*
>
> *Precise:*   This activity *makes it impossible to track cash disbursements.*

Impedes audit practices is far too general to be helpful. Perhaps only the auditor knows what this phrase means in any particular instance. Line personnel might even respond to such a statement with: "I don't do things for the sake of audit practices." Eliminating the cliché and being precise makes the finding much more meaningful to everyone.

Here are other examples of audit clichés that are empty calories. Note how the precise replacements provide substance that means something to the readers:

Cliché:	The monthly summary did not *conform to company standards*.
Precise:	Key elements were missing from the monthly summary, including vacation days and overtime hours.

Cliché:	The practice *exposes the company to risk*.
Precise:	The practice can result in legal action taken by customers against the company.

LONG, OBSCURE SENTENCES. Readers lose focus when too many ideas are jammed into one sentence, or when one idea is buried under too many words. *To emphasize each point, write short sentences (eighteen to twenty words, on average.) For example:*

Long, obscure:	The sample was selected from the work orders completed during the three months prior to the start of the audit and focused on those work orders generated for locations where there were over $1,000 in work order charges.

Short, emphatic:	The sample was selected from the work orders completed during the three months prior to the start of the audit. The sample focused on those work orders generated for locations where there were over $1,000 in work order charges.

Splitting that long sentence in two ensures the reader's grasping each point on the first read.

PASSIVE VOICE. By relying heavily on the passive voice, auditors often leave an important element out of their recommendations—the people to implement them. This omission seldom occurs with the active voice. Note the difference:

> *Passive:* The manager *should be taught* the correct procedures for handling these transactions. (taught by whom?)
>
> *Active:* The district manager *should teach* the manager the correct procedures for handling these transactions.

When auditors use the active voice, they are less likely to omit the doer of the action, *even inadvertently*.

CHARGED LANGUAGE. The tone of an audit report has much to do with its effectiveness. Some overzealous auditors use language that can offend the people they have audited. When this happens, those people are not very receptive to audit recommendations.

Auditors would do well, therefore, to choose their words carefully, avoiding expressions such as: *take the blame for, is guilty of,* and *flout* company policy. Eliminate all phrasing that seems to be critical or is placing blame. Focus on the action not the person. Instead of using charged words like *flout*, use more neutral phrasing like *does not adhere to* company policy. While the company wants its auditors to be diligent in rooting out problems, it wants those problems corrected. But antagonizing people with charged language can only exacerbate problems.

TOO MANY IDEAS. Clear, convincing audit reports need unity of thought. Paragraphs should present one idea at a time, developing the idea fully. In too many reports, paragraphs dance around two or three ideas but never really develop any one of them, as in the following example:

too

many

ideas

> Our review of the work order sample showed time lapses extending beyond one week between request and completion dates as well as ten "negative" time lapses where the work was completed before the work order was issued. Most of these negative time lapse orders were related to ongoing installations for which the original work order had been closed out. In some of these, new work orders were generated to account for subsequent charges.

The first sentence introduces two ideas. The one dealing with *time lapse work orders* is totally ignored in the rest of the paragraph; the other idea—negative time lapses—is developed somewhat. But because of the presence of the first idea, its development is less than effective. This paragraph, then, confuses the reader because of its lack of unity. For the same reason, the writer does not make the most of the information he has uncovered in the audit.

Writers can overcome this serious flaw—lack of unity and development of thought—by getting into the habit of *using topic sentences*. These sentences state one main idea for the paragraph. With the topic sentence up front, the writer can focus all supporting sentences toward that idea. In the revision that follows, each main idea is developed in a paragraph of its own:

one

idea

in

each

paragraph

Our review of the work order sample showed time lapses extending beyond one week between request and completion dates. Work Order #123 involved installation begun 16 days after the request. Work Order #456 resulted in a 12-day delay. Work Order #789 took 14 days from request to completion, though the work itself was finished in two hours.

In addition, we noted ten "negative" time lapses where the work was completed before the work order was issued. Most of these negative time lapse orders were related to ongoing installations for which the original work order had been closed out. In some of these, new work orders were generated to account for subsequent charges.

With each main idea singled out in a topic sentence, the writer can more readily develop that idea before moving on to the next one. Readers benefit from the clarity and fullness of the finding. (For more instruction, see "Topic Sentences" page 166.)

ABRUPTNESS. Complementing unity of thought is continuity. When writers make an effort to link sentences and bridge paragraphs, ideas flow smoothly and readers can easily follow the flow. Note how the simple repetition of a key word creates an interlocking chain of thoughts:

Audit asked each staff member to complete the *questionnaire* for the period January 2 to January 30. The *questionnaires* were then returned to Audit for *review*. *In the review*, Audit assigned the responses to *eight categories*. Those *eight categories* are...

This kind of repetition provides the continuity readers need to follow the thoughts. For continuity, writers should also use connectives such as *in addition, however, as a result, similarly*. (For more instruction, see "Continuity" page 177.)

POOR GRAMMAR. Errors in mechanics can mar an otherwise well-written report. Auditors would do well to brush up on some writing conventions that seem troublesome for many writers, not just auditors. Among these are the misuse of the comma, run-on sentences and sentence fragments, and lack of agreement between subjects and verbs. (You can find instruction in these and other points of mechanics.)

— AUDIT REPORT SHELL —

TO:

FROM:

DATE:

RE: (address, type of location; type of deal; capacity; scope of audit)

AUDIT SUMMARY

Overview: Give the number of exceptions and degree of seriousness of loss or risk for each.

Audidor's Comment: Make a statement that summarizes for management *your bottom line thinking* on this location. This statement might give a general understanding of your comfort level with this location, of patterns that should be watched, of matters that should be looked into, of provisions that should be made.

EXCEPTION 1:   (short but indicative heading)

A. The <u>nature of the exception</u> and <u>the number of occurrences</u>.

B. The <u>effect</u> or <u>impact</u> of the exception on the company.

C. The <u>criterion</u> on which the exception is based.

— AUDIT REPORT SHELL —
(continued)

D. The <u>facts</u> or <u>specifics</u> for the exception.

E. The <u>cause</u> of the exception.

F. The <u>solution recommended</u> to prevent a repetition of this exception.

EXCEPTION 2: _____

   Repeat A through F

EXCEPTION 3: _____

   Repeat A through F

— MODEL AUDIT REPORT —

TO:	C.B. Jackson, Dir. Operations
FROM:	The Audit Department—I. M. Watchung
DATE:	February 13, 199_
RE:	Field audit at the ABC facility, 123 Main Street, Brooklyn, New York, December 10, 1999__12 employees; 9__9; 7 days/wk

---

AUDIT SUMMARY

<u>Overview</u>:

The two exceptions found and the degree of risk associated with them are:

<u>Exception</u>	<u>Risk</u>
1. $14,800 in Undeposited Cash	Serious
2. Out of Uniform Violation	Minor

<u>Auditor's Comment</u>:

In light of the kinds of exceptions found in this report, management should pay close attention to this manager's performance and attitude over the next few weeks.

EXCEPTION 1: $14,800 in Undeposited Cash

A. $14,837 in money collected was found undeposited at the location.

B. Undeposited cash must always be viewed as a serious risk. Both the company and location personnel are at risk when money is not deposited.

C. Company policy requires money to be deposited each day. If an emergency makes a deposit impossible, the manager should make the deposit on the next day. He should document the incident in the Manager's Log Book and notify his supervisor of it.

D. The undeposited cash represented collections from January 5 to January 10. On none of these days did the manager tell his supervisor he had not deposited his receipts or write that in his Log Book.

E. To determine the cause of this exception, we asked the manager why he did not deposit the cash or file the reports. He said that his assistant manager was on vacation and he could not leave the unit unattended to go to the bank.

   We find this explanation acceptable to a point. The manager could not leave the lot unattended. But he could have made the problem known to his supervisor.

F. We recommend that the supervisor explain to this manager that, under similar conditions, the supervisor will take the deposit to the bank. The manager should notify the supervisor of the situation on the first day. He should note the problem in his Log Book.

EXCEPTION 2: Out of Uniform Violation

A. On the one occasion on which we visited the location, the Manager was out of uniform.

B. In itself, this exception is no major risk. But it seems to be one more instance of this Manager's not adhering to company policy. It may, therefore, reflect a serious discipline problem developing.

C. Company policy states that at all locations, attendants and managers are to wear their name tags outside their uniforms, visible to customers, while on duty.

D. On the one occasion on which we visited the location, the Manager was not wearing a name tag on the outside of his uniform.

E. The Manager said that he thought he left his name tag at home and would be wearing it the next day.

F. The supervisor should check for this manager's name tag and other elements of proper appearance each time he visits the location.

C.:

— Audit Report Checklist —

USE A FORMAT THAT MEETS THE NEEDS OF ALL YOUR READERS.

PUT LOGISTICAL DETAIL IN THE LOGISTICS SECTION, NOT IN THE
NARRATIVE.

BEGIN WITH AN AUDIT SUMMARY, INCLUDING AN OVERVIEW
AND THE AUDITOR'S COMMENT.

IN THE OVERVIEW, IDENTIFY THE MOST SERIOUS FINDINGS AND
THE LEVEL OF SERIOUSNESS OF RISK.

IN THE AUDITOR'S COMMENT, GIVE A BOTTOM-LINE OPINION.

SET CONTENT REQUIREMENTS TO MEET THE NEEDS OF ALL
YOUR READERS:

- ❏ *The nature of the exception and the number of the occurrences*
- ❏ *The effect of the exception on the company*
- ❏ *The criterion on which the exception is based*
- ❏ *The facts or specific details of the exception*
- ❏ *The cause of the exception*
- ❏ *The solution recommended to prevent a repetition of the problem*

AVOID CLICHÉS.

EMPHASIZE EACH POINT WITH SHORT SENTENCES.

USE THE ACTIVE VOICE AND IDENTIFY PEOPLE WHO SHOULD
IMPLEMENT THE RECOMMENDATIONS.

AVOID CHARGED LANGUAGE.

PRESENT ONE IDEA AT A TIME.

STRIVE FOR CONTINUITY OF THOUGHT.

AVOID ERRORS IN GRAMMAR, WORD USAGE, SPELLING, AND
PUNCTUATION.

How Do I Write
a Winning Resume?

You have just been victimized by that devastating corporate strategy—downsizing. You have to start the job search, which means, in part, writing a resume. After twelve years with the company, you don't even have an old resume to build on. What's the best way to go about it?

Or, unhappy with the future prospects at your present job, you want to test the waters for something better. But some people say your continuous search for "something better" looks to many human resource directors as an "erratic job history." How do you get these hiring people to look beyond names and dates to see the skills you have to offer?

Or, you've seen an ad that seems to have been written just for you. But when you start your resume, the perfect match between your experience and the job requirements seems to blur. What's wrong?

In addressing the concerns described in these three situations, and in many others, this chapter shows you how to build what can be the most important document in your business career—a winning resume.

A RESUME: MORE THAN A RECORD OF EMPLOYMENT—A SALES TOOL

Although the resume does summarize your employment career, you should look on it as more than a history. Consider your resume *a selling document*. Keep reminding yourself as you develop the resume that it should do more than inform. It must also persuade. Its purpose is to persuade company officials to interview you.

Through your resume you are making a sales pitch of sorts. And in any kind of selling, the starting point is not what you have to sell but what the buyer needs, wants, or can be persuaded to buy. So you must go beyond stating your qualifications. *You must show how your qualifications fill the need of or offer benefits to the hiring company. Bear this point in mind as you learn more about building a winning resume.*

There are two basic types of resumes: the chronological and the functional. Choose the type that is suited to your job history and goals.

HOW TO CREATE A WINNING CHRONOLOGICAL RESUME

Let's look first at the more conventional one, the chronological resume. This is the form to use if you are looking for a job that is fairly closely related to your most recent one, if your job history shows a steady application of your skills to a particular field or industry, and if you are not a "job hopper."

Summary: An Employer-Focused Opening

Many human resource officers say "objectives" traditionally used at the beginning of the resume have little impact on the decision process. If your resume comes in response to an ad, they know the job you are applying for, so the objective is not necessary. If the resume comes to them cold, they might be interested in how you can help the company, not what your ambitions are. Put another way, the objective is applicant-focused; the summary is employer-focused. And as mentioned before, if you are going to sell yourself, think first of the needs of the buyer. Note the difference:

Objective (applicant-focused):   Seeking a position of responsibility
                                      in the marketing department.

— MODEL CHRONOLOGICAL RESUME —

Name
Address
Phone number

SUMMARY

Ten years experience in increasingly more responsible editing positions. Edited, developed, and coordinated production for successful series, which have gone into multiple printings.

EMPLOYMENT HISTORY

1987–Present   <u>Verbatim Publishing Company</u>
Senior Editor

Responsible for planning projects; developing budgets; supervising staff, writers, and book production.

<u>Accomplishments</u>

❐ Developed *The Writing Series,* named by English Teachers Union as "an excellent text for teaching the writing process" (now in third printing)
❐ Quickly (within six months) produced a companion workbook (now in second printing), enhcancing sales of original
❐ Brought both projects in under budget and within deadlines

1985–1987   <u>Preliminary Magazine</u>
Assistant Managing Editor

Responsible for managing editorial production for monthly magazine. Scheduled features, approved manuscripts, coordinated layout and production.

<u>Accomplishments</u>

❐ Won "Maggie" award for best overall publication in the category
❐ Developed and implemented plan to change size and look for magazine
❐ Increased advertising by 45 percent
❐ Helped build circulation from 15,000 to 43,000 in two years

EDUCATION

B.A., Literature, M.A. Journalism, Sobright College
Professional workshops in editing, acquisitions, trends in education, computer software

Summary (employer-focused):   Six years marketing experience. Created and implemented campaigns, designed materials. Increased sales 32 percent.

A short summary of your skills and experience does more for the hiring person, who is the one that must be served. The summary gives a quick glimpse of what you have done. It implies what you can do for the hiring company. If you are answering an ad, the summary should show that your skills and experience match those the company seeks. In doing so, the summary can be a powerful tool in getting you through the initial screen. The reader subconsciously says *Yes* to your summary and is likely to carry a favorable attitude as she reads through the rest of the resume.

Note how the summary in the chronological resume gives an overview in its first sentence. In its second, the summary highlights the accomplishment the applicant thinks will be most impressive to the hiring company.

Therefore, the key points to try to get into the summary are:

❐ Years of experience
❐ Highly specialized training
❐ Industry knowledge
❐ Skills listed in the ad as requirements
❐ An accomplishment or example of past success

Before You Write, Read the Ad Closely

When responding to an ad, pull from the ad the qualifications being sought. List them. Check off the requirements you can satisfy. Try to get as many of those requirements as you can in the summary without making it too long. For example:

Electronic technician—Instrumentation distributor requires indiv for repair of analog/digital instruments. Component-level troubleshooting capabilities and 1 year exper. a must. A bkgd in repair of analytical instruments and Assoc degree in electronics or BS in chemistry a plus.

REQUIREMENTS

<u>Must have</u>	<u>A Plus to Have</u>
repair a/d instruments	*bkgd in repair of analytical*
component troubleshoot	*AA in electronics*
1 year experience	*BS in chem*

Summary: Electronic technician with two-plus years diagnosing and correcting problems in analog/digital instruments. AA in electronics, with coursework toward BS in chemistry.

Is it silly to "parrot" the same words from the ad? Not at all, because the first person to read and act on your resume may not be very familiar with the job or the field. Your resume may be read by a clerk in the personnel office who was given a hundred resumes, a list of requirements, and the instruction to "rule out any resume that does not have all of the requirements." So if your phrasing is different from that on the list, or you do not highlight the fact that your background matches the qualifications in the ad, your resume can get kicked out, even if you are the most qualified applicant in the bunch.

Here's another example of a person working from the ad to the requirements to the summary:

Legal secretary for prominent law firm. Private secretary to partner. Litigation skills required. Well-organized, superb working conditions in luxurious offices.

This ad is ambiguous, as many are. Does the last sentence mean that the working conditions are well organized, or that the employer wants a person who is well organized? In either case, it can only help the candidate to mention that he is organized.

REQUIREMENTS

<u>Must have</u>

Private secretary
Work for partner
Litigation skills
Organized

Summary: More than three years as private secretary for senior
                      law partner. Well organized and professional, with
                      extensive experience in litigation.

The word "professional" in this summary meets concerns implied in
"*prominent* law firm," "*private* secretary to partner," and "*luxurious* offices." The
people placing the ad seem impressed with themselves, so the successful candidate must convey an equal amount of confidence and sophistication.

Although the summary appears first in the resume, you may find it easier to write it last, after you have spent time with your skills and experience and
can more effectively highlight the most impressive material in the summary.

Employment History: Not Just Names and Dates

In listing your employment experience, begin with your most recent position and work back. If you have had many positions, it is not necessary to list
all of them. For example, someone who has been in the business world for
twenty years need not go back as far as a first job out of school, unless that is
significant. On the other hand, try not to create gaps in the middle of the
sequence that can set the hiring person to wondering about you.

For each job you list, give:

Dates, beginning and terminating
Name of company
Your job title
Your responsibilities
Your accomplishments

The sample shows you how to lay these out on the resume. If you need to
conserve space, place the job title on the same line as the company and date.
For example:

1987–present   Verbatim Publishing   Company Senior Editor

Of more importance, however, are responsibilities and accomplishments.
Let's discuss these.

RESPONSIBILITIES

Responsibilities is not job title. Do not assume that the hiring person will know what you do if you write down "secretary," or "electrical engineer," or "department manager." Similar job titles may carry different duties from one company to another.

Spend some time thinking about the things you do on the job. To develop a complete list of your responsibilities—from which you will select the most appropriate for the resume—consider:

❏ *Functions of each job* you have held, such as planning, supervising, budgeting

❏ *Related tasks*, such as interacting with upper management, assessing needs

❏ *Equipment used*, from the simplest to the most complex

❏ *Software you know*, such as Wordperfect and Lotus

❏ *Materials produced/used*, such as budgets, schedules, performance reviews, newsletters

❏ *People you report to, work with, and who report to you*, as a way of uncovering more of your duties and indicating the level of responsibility you hold

❏ *Job description*, is available it should give many of your most important responsibilities, but do not limit yourself to this

❏ *Daily routine*, for a week, keep track of what you do every day

❏ *Periodic duties*, such as monthly updates and schedules, quarterly news-briefs, annual meetings or reports

By considering these elements for each job you have had, you should develop an extensive list of *specific things you have done*, which are more meaningful on a resume than simply titles or general descriptions. Note the difference:

Responsibilities (General): Responsible for customer service in NY/NJ area.

Responsibilities (Specific): Responsible for customer service in NY/NJ area. Provided installation/repair service to 300 customers. Trained apprentices. Interfaced with management on CS issues.

The general statement assumes that *customer service* means the same thing in every company, and that is not true. The specific statement leaves no doubt as to what the major responsibilities are. And it offers an opportunity *to sell*, to impress the hiring person with *what you do*. Yet it takes up only one more line in the resume than the general description does.

Here's another example:

Responsibilities (General): Responsible for all training activities.

Responsibilities (Specific): Responsible for all training activities:

— Created training materials and conducted workshops for nontechnical areas, such as sales, customer service

— Maintained department budget

— Hired staff and outside consultants

If you have the space, use a bullet-point list like this to make each responsibility stand out. If not, paragraph form is acceptable, but highlight the words *responsible for*.

USE VERBS

In listing responsibilities, think in terms of action verbs, not nouns. Note the difference:

Nouns: Responsible for general office management.

Verbs: Responsible for *maintaining* schedules, *purchasing* materials, *assigning* space, *monitoring* expenses.

By using action verbs you stress the fact that you are a *doer*, which most organizations look for. Here is a list of commonly used verbs designating duties people may undertake at work.

administered	built	controlled	established
aided	calculated	coordinated	evaluated
analyzed	catalogued	counseled	executed
applied	communicated	diagnosed	guided
arranged	computed	directed	hired
assembled	conducted	documented	implemented

indexed	negotiated	prepared	revised
instructed	operated	processed	scheduled
interfaced	ordered	purchased	screened
inventoried	organized	reported	supervised
maintained	participated	researched	taught
managed	personalized	resolved	trained
monitored	planned	reviewed	wrote

ACCOMPLISHMENTS

Listing job responsibilities tells the hiring person what duties your jobs entailed. It does not tell *how well you performed those duties*. People who do the hiring work on the theory that past success is the best indicator of future success. So by putting accomplishments before the decision makers, you tell them you have succeeded in the past and can be successful for their company too.

Note how accomplishments raise the level of the candidate's impressiveness:

Job Title: Director of Training

Responsibilities: Responsible for all training activities. Create training materials and conduct workshops for nontechnical areas, such as sales, customer service. Maintain department budget. Hire staff and outside consultants.

Accomplishments:

❐ Doubled the number receiving training each year without increasing the budget

❐ Created sales training workshop which is now a model for the industry

❐ Reduced turnover by 68 percent over two years

Accomplishments on a resume highlight your success in carrying out your responsibilities. When you select accomplishments to match the needs of the hiring manager, you stand an even better chance of getting through the initial screen to the interview stage.

In listing accomplishments:

❐ address the hiring company's needs

❏ use verbs to show what you have *done* and *can do for them*

❏ quantify your accomplishments, such as:

  – reduced turnover by 70 percent
  – cut equipment costs by 25 percent

❏ give specific detail, such as:

  – revised the reporting process, making reports shorter but more informative

Here's another example of how you can strengthen your qualifications by moving from job title to responsibilities to accomplishments:

Job Title:	Assistant Manager, Customer Service
Responsibilities:	Responsible for customer service in NY/NJ area. Provided installation/repair service to 300 customers. Trained apprentices. Interfaced with management on CS issues.

Accomplishments:

❏ Re-signed 92 percent of my customers to extended contracts

❏ Developed three apprentices into crack service reps

❏ Streamlined service reports, reducing completion time by 33 percent

❏ Introduced three new lines of service to the business

HOW TO MAKE YOURSELF CREDIBLE

To present your accomplishments most impressively, state the action with a verb, and in some way quantify it or clarify it with detail. Numbers and detail make you more credible. In the chronological resume, for example, the candidate quantifies success with, *"Now in third printing,"* and gives details such as "under budget and within deadlines."

Here are some guidelines for presenting your accomplishments:

Action	Detail
trained others	results? why you?
received awards	which? why? from whom?
instituted new procedures	how? why? results?
increased sales	by how much? how?
saved company money	how much? how?

received promotions	when? why?
identified problems	how? results?
reduced inventory	how? results?
increased efficiency	how? results?
managed office	how? results?

HOW TO WRITE A FUNCTIONAL RESUME THAT GETS RESULTS

The functional resume downplays employment history and highlights skills and experience. The functional resume is useful to the person who has large gaps between jobs, who has changed jobs frequently, or whose recent jobs are unrelated to the job now being sought, as when someone wants to make a drastic career change. Names of companies worked for and the dates are given in the functional resume, but *after* experiences, skills, and accomplishments are shown.

The reasoning behind this organization is to keep the person doing the hiring from disqualifying the candidate before reading the "meat" of the resume. That is, some personnel people may dismiss immediately any resume showing an employment history with more than the average number of job changes. There may have been legitimate reasons for those switches, but the candidate never gets the chance to explain. But if the resume leads with strengths—skills and accomplishments—the hiring person may be so impressed that, when she sees the spotty work history, she may choose to overlook it now and raise the issue at the interview.

The writer of the model functional resume may have felt that four companies in five years may not look good to a personnel officer. So the writer used a functional resume—to hold back on that information until after the officer has read of his skills and accomplishments.

SUMMARY: A SHORT WAY TO SAY ALOT

The summary in the functional resume is the same as in the chronological resume, except that it may cover a broader range if you have had jobs of very different types. Rather than using titles of the jobs you've held, use a more generic term like "self-starter" or "seasoned professional." Have the ad, job requirements, or company needs dictate what goes into the summary.

— MODEL FUNCTIONAL RESUME —

Name
Address
Phone number

SUMMARY

Self-starter with successful experience working with people. Adapted to new situations and contributed to productivity and profitability quickly. Maintained large budgets, achieved savings in purchases, trained others.

WORK EXPERIENCE

Office Manager

Responsible for all aspects of managing the office of a $100 million manufacturing company and a $15 million consulting practice. Made decisions for office equipment purchases, scheduled administrative staff, trained and evaluated office personnel.

Accomplishments

- ❏ Reduced cost of equipment purchases by 15 percent by shopping and negotiating
- ❏ Introduced PCs to office staff
- ❏ Developed performance goals/evaluation procedures for office staff
- ❏ Reduced absenteeism by 47 percent
- ❏ Streamlined timesheet system, improving expense recording

Sales Associate

Responsible for assisting customers on the sales floor with purchase decisions, exchanges. Trained other associates.

Accomplishments

- ❏ Received "good service" award six times
- ❏ Bettered my sales quota every quarter
- ❏ Trained associates who went on to become "employees of the month"
- ❏ Suggested new procedures to management, resulting in tighter security

EMPLOYMENT RECORD

1994–present	XYZ Manufacturing Company
1993–1994	Tacky Retail Stores
1992–1993	Stop Watch Consultants
1990–1991	Schlock Retailers

EDUCATION

BS, Management, State College, 1990

WORK EXPERIENCE: IT'S WHAT YOU DID THAT COUNTS

In this section you give job titles, responsibilities, and accomplishments, following the same guidelines as given for the chronological resume. The only difference is that in the functional resume you group together similar work experiences had in different companies. For example, in the model functional resume, the responsibilities and accomplishments given under "office manager" reflect work done as office manager at two different companies. The same is true for the information given under "Sales Associate."

With the information presented in this way, you stand a better chance of the personnel officer assessing your skills and accomplishments.

Employment Record: When and Where You Did It

Here you name the companies for which you worked, and give the beginning and terminating dates. Without this history, the hiring manager may feel—logically—that you have something to hide. Seeing this history, that manager may conclude your record is too erratic and disqualify you anyhow. On the other hand, if your skills and accomplishments are impressive enough, that manager may give you a chance to explain your history.

WHAT TO SAY ABOUT EDUCATION, HOBBIES, PERSONAL AND MILITARY HISTORY

Most of the other information people typically crowd their resumes with is not critical to most situations and does not have to be included unless the ad specifically asks for it.

Education may be more important in the resume of a person with limited work experience than one whose work history implies a certain level of schooling. In the chronological resume example the applicant cites workshops attended, to indicate she is current with what is happening in the field.

Hobbies mean little unless they in some way relate to the job sought and can enhance your candidacy. For example, if you are applying for a position as a sales rep for a sporting goods manufacturer, it might help to say that you are an avid tennis player and daily jogger.

Age, sex, family status, and *military history,* by law, should not discriminate against you, so you may leave these out. If, however, the job sought requires

— CHRONOLOGICAL RESUME —	— FUNCTIONAL RESUME —
Name	
Address	Name
Phone Number	Address
	Phone Number

Chronological Resume:

Summary:

Outlines experience

Shows basic qualifications

Employment History:

Job 1

Dates, Company
Job Title
Responsibilities
Accomplishments

Job 2

Dates, Company
Job Title
Responsibilities
Accomplishments

Education:

Hobbies, Interests:

Personal:

Military:

Functional Resume:

Summary:

Outlines experience

Shows basic qualifications

Employment Experience:

Experience Category 1:
Job Titles
Responsibilities
Accomplishments

Experience Category 2:

Job Titles
Responsibilities
Accomplishments

Employment History:

Dates, Companies

Education:

Hobbies, Interests:

Personal:

Military:

significant travel and you feel that being single might give you an edge over people with families, include your status.

Include *references* only if specifically asked for. And don't give *salary requirements,* even when asked for. Skirt this issue by saying *"flexible"* or *"vary with opportunity for growth and details of benefits package."* Too high or too low a figure can disqualify you.

FINE-TUNE YOUR RESUME: A CHECKLIST

You should not expect to build a good resume in one sitting. It takes much thought and work. After putting your resume together following the principles given here, review it with these points in mind:

1. Buzzwords—terminology current in the field—are effective in a resume. They show you are up to date. But clichés are not. They are empty and may be seen as a sign of an unoriginal thinker or someone trying to fill up space on the page.

2. Use verbs in giving your responsibilities and accomplishments.

3. Be specific, giving numbers and the kind of detail that raises your credibility.

4. Be brief. Although this chapter suggests putting a great deal of information in the resume, such as responsibilities and accomplishments, you must try to do that succinctly—in one page if possible, certainly no more than two.

5. Create an appealing page. Lay out the information so it is inviting to read. Be sure key elements, such as responsibilities and accomplishments, stand out. Use capitals, boldface, underlining, and other visual cues to make it easy for readers to see what you have done and can do for them.

6. Omit the pronoun "I" from the resume. Instead of saying "I maintained the budget. I conducted interviews," write: "Maintained the budget. Conducted interviews."

7. Use a fresh typewriter ribbon or printer cartridge to produce a clearly printed resume. Use standard business stationery, nothing cute or fanciful.

THE COVER LETTER: AN ESSENTIAL INGREDIENT

A cover letter accompanying a resume is expected today. But don't make it just a formality, because that's not the way it is looked upon by human resource directors. Make your cover letter an important piece in your selling package. It should preview the resume, arousing interest in you as a candidate. You can generate interest by following the same philosophy as in the resume—show you know the company and highlight the specific skills you have that the company is seeking or can benefit from.

Keep the cover letter to one page, customizing each letter to the specific company or ad. A form letter will antagonize the reader and reduce your chances. Address the letter to an individual whenever possible, rather than the generic "Dear Personnel Director." Do not use "Dear Sir" as your salutation unless you know your letter will be received by a man. When you don't know who will receive the letter, address it as "Dear Sir or Madam" or "Dear Director." Don't offend with sexist language or implications.

Three Parts of a Great Cover Letter

Think of the letter as having three parts, each with a separate function:

Opening: tell your purpose and how you have come to know of the company, such as

- ❏ Response to an ad
- ❏ Suggestion from a contact
- ❏ Research you've done into the company

Body: show you match their needs, indicating

- ❏ Your skills, work habits, experience
- ❏ Benefits to the company

Closing: express your eagerness to meet, and say you will call

Let's look at a sample cover letter.

— MODEL COVER LETTER —

Ms. Barbara Dumas
Director, Human Resources
ACB Company
123 Boulevard
Anywhere, NJ 07676

Dear Ms. Dumas:

Recently I learned from your controller, Bill Kennedy, of ACB's expansion plans. At Bill's suggestion I am writing you to suggest that my experience in a similar corporate expansion could help your Human Resources Department manage the personnel aspects of this expansion.

As Assistant Director of Human Resources at XYZ, I drafted the basic plan for expansion. I implemented many aspects of it, including recruiting and hiring new employees, and coordinating integration of new staff with the experienced. Management singled my efforts out as being "instrumental in the success of the expansion."

My resume is enclosed and details my activities in this expansion, which are likely to be what your organization will be going through. I will call you in two weeks to see if you think we should talk further about how I might help ACB complete a successful expansion.

Thank you for your consideration.

Sincerely,

The model cover letter mentions the contact, shows knowledge of the company, and gives an overview of the candidate's experience in the first paragraph. The second paragraph highlights the applicant's experience as it relates to the company's needs at the moment. The last paragraph repeats the key theme of this person's candidacy—how his experience in expansion projects can help the company. He also says he will follow up by phone.

— Resume Checklist —

CHOOSE THE TYPE OF RESUME THAT FITS YOUR EXPERIENCE.

PROVIDE AN EMPLOYER-FOCUSED SUMMARY OF YOUR
EXPERIENCE RATHER THAN AN APPLICANT-FOCUSED
OBJECTIVE.

READ THE AD CLOSELY AND TAILOR THE SUMMARY TO IT.

SPECIFY RESPONSIBILITIES, USING ACTION VERBS.

QUANTIFY AND DETAIL ACCOMPLISHMENTS FOR CREDIBILITY.

USE THE FUNCTIONAL RESUME IF YOU HAVE AN UN-
CONVENTIONAL JOB HISTORY.

IN THE FUNCTIONAL RESUME, GROUP WORK EXPERIENCES
BY TYPE.

IN THE FUNCTIONAL RESUME, INCLUDE AN EMPLOYMENT HISTORY
OF COMPANY NAMES AND DATES.

KEEP THE RESUME TO ONE PAGE, IF POSSIBLE.

USE VISUAL CUES TO HIGHLIGHT IMPORTANT AREAS.

CUSTOMIZE A COVER LETTER FOR EACH COMPANY YOU
APPROACH.

IN THE COVER LETTER, HIGHLIGHT THE MATCH BETWEEN
YOUR BACKGROUND AND THE COMPANY'S NEEDS.

Part 2

COLLECTING INFORMATION,
ORGANIZING, GETTING STARTED,
AND WRITING CLEARLY
AND FORCEFULLY

WHERE CAN I FIND
AND HOW DO I COLLECT
THE INFORMATION I NEED?

*Y*our firm has received a Request for Proposal from a company you know little about. How can you find the information you need to tailor your proposal to the company?

Management of your company is seeking to diversify and wants a report describing various types of businesses and their potential for synergy with the work of your company.

You have been asked to write an article for the professional association you belong to or to give a talk at your college. While the subject is one you know well, you want to research it further to be sure you are current and thorough.

In each of these and other instances, you have to find the information you need and collect it in a form that enables you to weave the information easily into your document.

EIGHT LIKELY SOURCES OF KEY INFORMATION

Research can be an enlightening experience or a frightful waste of time. The difference depends on how you conduct your search.

You can simplify that search by identifying the sources you think are most likely to help you, and then begin systematically to look into them. Here are the most likely sources to consider for most business research problems.

1. People

Begin with the people you work with and then fan outward to colleagues, friends, and others. Ask not only for information on the topic but also for suggestions as to where you might look for it. Conversations may not always give you the information you are looking for, but they often open up new areas of thought you had not considered.

In addition, in contacting some of the sources for materials described in the paragraphs that follow, you can often get a wealth of information from a conversation with people in those offices. In other words, do not overlook the channel of information as a potential source as well. That is, in asking a company librarian to send you an annual report, you may also get some useful background information from a conversation with that librarian.

2. Company Documents

Check your company files. Consider memos, letters, proposals, projects, reports and any other types of documents your company might keep. Cross-reference the files, looking under names of companies, industry, and names of individuals.

Should you find anything in those files, try to track down the individuals associated with the topic. You might get lucky and uncover someone in the firm who has extensive knowledge of the company or topic you are researching. When it comes to research, there's no sense in hacking through forests of data when someone has already cut a clear path to what you need.

3. Corporate Communications Offices

If you are researching a particular company, you might go directly to that company's Public Relations Department or communications officer. You should be able to get at least an annual report, if not a good deal more. Many large companies can send you back issues of their customer newsletters and white papers, which can tell you much about what the company does and how it operates.

4. Trade Groups and Associations

If you are looking for information about an industry, seek out its trade group or association. These organizations often produce a magazine and generally are willing to share back issues. Ask for programs of the conferences and seminars they have run in the last few years. From these you may gain insight into the key issues and get the names of individuals in the industry who seem conversant with those issues.

5. Libraries

Consider the range of libraries available to you. There's your *local library*—both where you live and where you work. Many cities have branches devoted exclusively to business and subscribe to more business reference books and magazines than a general-use library would. In addition, find out if the *trade association* for the industry you are researching has a library. Most will open them to the public as a professional courtesy.

Consider, too, the *libraries at publishers* that produce magazines and newspapers in the industry you are researching. I once was researching the bankruptcies of a number of retail companies and found invaluable information in the back issues of newspapers and magazines specific to retailing. I found these issues in the publisher's library, which graciously gave me access to its stacks.

And don't forget college and university libraries. Many community colleges often have extensive holdings in business-related materials.

HOW TO MAKE THE MOST OF THE LIBRARY'S RESOURCES

Libraries can prove to be frustrating mazes if you don't know your way around them. The traditional card catalog, which keeps a record of every holding in the library, has now been computerized in most libraries. Besides giving the standard information of the printed cards, the computer can often give you the holdings of other libraries associated with the one you are in. Through reciprocal arrangements, your library can get the material you need from one of its sister libraries.

The reference section contains many of the general sources of information you might need, such as *Moody's Industrial Manual; Standard & Poor's Register of Corporations, Directors and Executives; & Dun's Directory of Service Companies.* The reference section also contains bibliographies, which can point you toward sources to look into.

The *periodical section* contains the various newspapers, journals, magazines, and trade papers that may hold what you are looking for. The first stop in the periodical section should be its indexes, which can tell you all the articles treating your subject and the names and dates of the publications in which those articles appeared. *Business Periodical Index, Reader's Guide to Periodical Literature,* The Wall Street Journal *Index,* and The New York Times *Index* are the primary sources to check.

And when all else turns up nothing—or perhaps even before you start wandering around aimlessly—ask the librarians for help. Most are more than willing to assist serious researchers. Your request might be a refreshing break for them from a routine day. Librarians, especially reference librarians, often look upon a request as a challenge, as a means of keeping sharp and enhancing their own familiarity with the library's holdings.

6. Government Agencies and Publications

Local, state, and federal governments collect a broad range of data and publish hundreds of information-filled reports, brochures, and pamphlets. In addition, a number of agencies are equipped to handle queries over the phone. Two sources you might begin a search with are:

Federal Information Center
P.O. Box 600
Cumberland, MD 21502-0600
(800) 347-1997

Superintendent of Documents
Government Printing Office
North Capitol and H Streets, NW
Washington, DC 20401
(202) 512-0000

Obviously, with such a huge resource as the federal government, you may not connect on your first phone call. But with perseverance, you may eventually be put in touch with the agency that can give you just what you need.

7. Electronic Databases

If you have access to electronic databases, you may have volumes of pertinent information at your fingertips. Electronic databases have grown tremendously in just a few years, and millions of records are added to them each day. While many companies subscribe to the on-line databases most useful to their own business, many public and college libraries also offer a variety of electronic databases to their customers.

There are four major on-line libraries—BRS, CompuServ, DIALOG, and ORBIT—as well as hundreds of other, highly focused services and databases. As with everything else in research, there are directories describing the offerings in each service. Take some time to study these directories and locate the services that are most likely to be of help to you. Because you pay for all time on-line, electronic databases cost you money as well as time. So be very deliberate in using these databases.

8. Desktop Reference Materials

Don't overlook the information closest at hand—the reference books sitting on your desk or in your office library. Among these are:

a good dictionary
a desktop encyclopedia
an almanac
a telephone book
a directory of people in your professional association
a handbook related to your field

Perhaps the most useful desktop reference source of all is *The New York Public Library Book of How and Where to Look It Up*, published by Prentice Hall. In this one volume you will find thousands of sources, all clearly described. The book lists sources in six categories: reference books, telephone sources, government sources, picture sources, special collections, and electronic databases. Within each category, sources are listed by subject, alphabetically.

HOW TO RECORD INFORMATION FOR READY RETRIEVAL

You can see that the sources described here will generate information in many different forms—spoken, printed, and electronic. How you record this information is important if you are to make the most of it in writing your document.

For example, you cannot handle smaller pieces of information—such as you might get in a phone call or from a one-line entry in a directory—as you would larger pieces of information, such as columns of statistical data. So let's look at how you work with both.

Use File Cards for Tidbits

File cards are the traditional—and still the best—way to record a variety of small bits of information from many sources. The file card is valuable because it serves two needs—recording the information and using it later in the writing.

Assume, for example, you are researching "corporate alliances" and come across a short magazine article on the topic. On one page the article touches on four different aspects—types of alliances, reasons for them, trends, rates of success and failure. You put those four pieces of information on four separate cards. When you are writing your paper, you can pull the note you need when you need it. After you've used it, you put that card aside, and now work with fewer cards.

But if you photocopy the page, or record your notes on a sheet of paper, you have to wade through the entire page to find the data you want when writing. And after you've used that information, you still have to keep the sheet if you want to use the other information later. Often you will find yourself flipping back and forth looking for bits of information.

Using cards, then, either 3 × 5 or 4 × 6 inch, you can collect disparate bits of information separately and work with them much more easily. What's more, you can move those cards around at ease, thereby grouping related bits of information regardless of their many origins. You can even build your outline simply by grouping and ordering your note cards.

In recording information on note cards, be sure to identify the information. Write a SLUG, or identifying title, at the top of the card, indicating the aspect or type of information held on the card. For example:

Slug

> ALLIANCES - TYPES OF
>
> ---
>
> 1) full control - 100% ownership
>
> 2) 50-50 joint venture
>
> 3) sponsorship - e.g., Monsanto sponsors research at Harvard
>
>
>
> **Source** Doorley, "Strategic Alliances," 1991 Conference Exec. Summary, The Planning Forum

Notice that in addition to the SLUG and the information, the card includes the source of the information. Even if you are writing an in-house report and do not have to footnote material, you want to be able to verify the source if called upon to do so. Particularly with statistics, people are quick to challenge, with such questions as: "Where did you get those numbers?" Or people may ask you a related question, such as: "How large a sample did they use in this survey?" If you don't have that information on the card, you can easily go back to the source to find it, if you have identified the source.

You will also notice that the card does not contain too much information. Some people waste a great deal of time copying passages word for word or paraphrasing line by line. You can make better use of your time if you read a passage, determine what's useful in it, and jot down the gist of the idea in a few words—your own words.

When you feel the weight of the writer's own words would help your case, copy small segments word for word. Be exact and use quotation marks so you'll know, perhaps weeks later, that these words are a direct quote.

Follow these steps regardless of the source—people, books, on-line databases.

Identify Each Piece of Information

Some of the material you collect will be in the form of reports, letters, photocopied pages, columns of numbers, and other documents that you cannot or do not want to transfer to cards. Organize this information as you would file cards by putting a SLUG at the top of each. If you pull a page from a larger document, be sure to identify the source.

— Information Checklist —

CONSIDER PEOPLE FIRST TO GET INFORMATION AND SUGGESTIONS FOR SOURCES OF INFORMATION.

SEARCH YOUR COMPANY FILES AND TRACK DOWN PEOPLE IN THE COMPANY WHO HAVE BEEN ASSOCIATED WITH THE TOPIC.

LOOK TO COMMUNICATIONS OFFICES, PUBLIC RELATIONS DEPARTMENTS, AND TRADE ASSOCIATIONS.

CONSIDER LIBRARIES—LOCAL, BUSINESS, SCHOOL, COMPANY.

USE TOOLS SUCH AS INDEXES TO FOCUS YOUR SEARCH.

ASK HELP FROM LIBRARIANS TO POINT YOU IN THE RIGHT DIRECTION.

TURN TO GOVERNMENT AGENCIES AND PUBLICATIONS FOR CERTAIN KINDS OF INFORMATION.

USE ELECTRONIC DATABASES BUT REMEMBER THAT THE METER USUALLY STARTS RUNNING AS SOON AS YOU SIGN ON.

DO NOT OVERLOOK DESKTOP REFERENCE SOURCES.

USE FILE CARDS FOR RECORDING SMALLER PIECES OF INFORMATION FROM DISPARATE SOURCES.

IDENTIFY THE INFORMATION ON EACH CARD AND THE SOURCE IT CAME FROM.

HOW SHOULD I ORGANIZE MY MATERIAL TO BUILD A STRONG, SMOOTH-FLOWING REPORT?

You've brainstormed and used other techniques for generating ideas on the topic. You've talked to people and researched the topic extensively. You now have file cards, stat sheets, newspaper clippings, and a motley collection of reports, memos, letters, and other materials containing information related to the topic you are reporting on.

How do you organize all this information?

CREATE A BLUEPRINT

Writing is a dynamic process. Once you put pen to paper, the writing often seems to take on a life of its own and seemingly goes its own way. Such writing can sometimes be imaginatively brilliant, but it can also take you off on a tangent, never to return to your prescribed topic. You therefore have to bridle your vivid imagination somewhat to string your thoughts together deliberately, so your readers can comprehend them.

Before writing any paragraphs or sentences, then, build a plan for your document. That is, create some graphic representation of the information you hope to include in the document and the order to present it in. If you think I'm leading up to an outline, you're right. An outline of some sort—formal or of your own type—is an excellent schematic format for planning a document.

With an outline, you can:

- ❏ See at a glance what information you have.
- ❏ Easily recognize what information is missing.
- ❏ Arrange and rearrange elements easily.
- ❏ Try various arrangements of the pieces before settling on the order that works best.

For a short memo or letter, you probably do this kind of organizing in your head. But for a paper even a few pages long, you are better off planning on paper in outline form. You can better assess the material you have and decide on the best order for presenting it.

The outline is analogous to the floor plan. You can, if you want, move all the furniture in your living room from place to place to see what fits where. But if you have a floor plan drawn to scale, you can save a lot of energy and time by laying out the furniture on the plan first. Of course, once you actually place the furniture, you may want to move a piece or two for better effect. But at least the bulk of the pieces will be carried and positioned only once. The same is true of an outline. Once you have written your document, you may decide to rearrange portions of it. But the larger share of the document will stay as is because you thought about positioning before you started to write.

Outline to Get a Handle On Relationships

An outline lists *categories of information*, showing the major concepts and aspects of supporting detail. An important facet of the outline is the ease with which it shows this relationship among concepts, primary ideas, and supporting details. The traditional way of showing this relationship is through a system that uses both numbers and letters as well as indenting. For example:

major concept   I. Plan Goals and Objectives for Corporate Growth

primary idea   A. Goals   *where there's an A, there's a B*

supporting   1. In performance figures   *where there's a 1, there's a 2*
information
in descending   a. Sales
                         b. Profits

level of   2. In market share

detail   3. In company image

primary idea   B. Objectives

                      1. Develop a timetable

                      2. Determine feasibility of reaching goals

major concept   II. Implement the Plan

               A. Assess our capability to implement the plan, etc.

After building an outline such as this, you can assess your information. You may realize, for example, that you don't have anything under "determine feasibility of reaching goals." You realize, too, that the reason for the omission is that you don't have any information on that topic. So you have to go and do some more research.

The outline also helps you critique the planned order. For instance, the sample outline shows goals "in performance figures" first. But you know that before the company can improve performance, it will have to improve its image. So you may decide to treat image before performance. Adjust the outline by putting "in company image" as number 1 instead of number 3.

Furthermore, the outline may call to your attention another glaring omission. You can't jump from "Plan" in I to "Implement" in II. There's an important step in between—management review of the plan. So you slot "Management Review" as II, and move "Implement" to III.

These changes are easy to make in outline form. They are less easy to make after the document has been drafted, because the omissions and the need for rearrangement will not be so obvious.

HOW FORMAL MUST THE OUTLINE BE?

If the idea of the roman and arabic numerals and the upper- and lowercase letters bothers you, don't use them. Create your own means of showing the relationship between categories of information. You may, for example, use a series of bullets. Use a single bullet for a concept, two bullets before primary ideas, and more bullets before lower levels of detail.

Whatever method you use, distinguish the general from the particular in some way, so that when you move an item you move everything that is to go with it. In addition, you want to be able to see at a glance just how much information you have to support an idea and to what level of detail you go. A list of single bullet-point items cannot provide you with a true understanding of what you have.

HOW TO BUILD YOUR OUTLINE

Build your outline *after* you have done your research or brainstorming, not before. Some writers create an outline first, then go out and hunt for information to fill it. That process is constricting. That is, people overlook or reject information that *might be* useful because it does not fit the outline. For example, in researching personnel matters in a company, you may speak to someone who says, "by the way, did you know the company was once affiliated with Smyrna Electric?" "No," you answer, "but history isn't part of my report," and you end the discussion. Unfettered by a rigid outline, you might pursue that detail and uncover some pertinent material.

Of course, you may want to build a *preliminary* outline, just to give your research some degree of focus. But don't let that preliminary outline become a straitjacket on your research.

In building the outline, then, work *from* the information you have generated and collected. Use the SLUGS on your file cards and information sheets to group your information into related categories. Determine concepts, main ideas and supporting information. Then write these as headings and subheadings in your outline.

Choose a Pattern of Organization

What's the best order in which to present material in a business document? That depends on your subject, purpose, and audience—especially your audience. The outline enables you to examine your material in this context so that you present the information in the order that works best for the audience. Let's look at the most common patterns of organization.

KNOWN TO UNKNOWN

After working with a subject for a while, you know it inside out. But what do your readers know about it? How much background do they need? What information in your plan would go over their heads without this background?

One effective pattern of organization starts with what readers already know and builds on that knowledge to tell them what they don't know. Many proposals begin this way, for example. They describe the particular problem at hand, then move to the writer's solution to the problem. A letter offering a decision on an issue might follow the same pattern. The writer begins with a review of the facts and details and moves from there to an analysis and the decision.

TIME

Some topics dictate your treating them in chronological order. Tracing the history of a company, issue, or product, for example, you will more than likely write a narrative of related events starting with the first and proceeding to the current.

LOGIC

In some reports, a history may comprise only one portion, and you have to decide where to place the history in the overall scheme. If that history is fundamental to the rest of the paper, and readers are not familiar with the history, you'd place it up front. If, however, everyone knows the history or it is not crucial, you may place it toward the end of the paper.

In other words, you decide on an order that is most logical for the presentation of your information, for conveying the main points. If, for example, your report is comparing two alternatives—such as suggested locations for expansion—you might treat one location first, evaluating it on all relevant criteria. Then you'd show the second location in regard to the same criteria. Or you may plan the report around the criteria. Present the first criterion and show how both locations fare against it. Then present the second and evaluate both on that. And so on. Your decision will vary with the amount and type of information you have. The order should rest, however, on which will be more effective for the readers.

Reports Are Not Mysteries

Regardless of the order you choose, bear in mind that a business document should present its major points, findings, or recommendations up front. In an introduction or executive summary, give the essentials of the report. Readers then can ease into the detail more intelligently.

For example, assume your task is to offer an opinion on a recommended procedure. Your report might be a detailed statement of the analysis that leads to your recommendation. But don't force people to read the entire report before they know your recommendation. Lead with that recommendation and then give the reasons that led to it.

The executive summary serves as the perfect vehicle for this kind of preview or overview.

— MODEL OUTLINE —

The Feasilibility of Moving Corporate Headquarters to East Podunk
Introduction: The Task Before the Committee
Executive Summary

I. Benefits of Relocating
    A. Financial
        1. Lower occupancy costs
        2. Lower employee wage costs
        3. Lower real estate taxes
        4. Reduce operating expenses

    B. Improved Operations
        1. Proximity to engineering staff
        2. New facility and equipment

II. Drawbacks of Relocating
    A. Costs of relocating staff or hiring new staff
    B. Quality of the work force in the area
    C. Training and retraining needed

III. Committee's Recommendation
    A. Make the move
    B. Reasons for this recommendation
        1. Cost-benefit analysis
        2. Political climate
        3. Concern about the unions

IV. Tables, Charts, and Other Supporting Data
    A. Occupancy cost comparisons
    B. Wage comparisons
    C. Real estate tax comparison
    D. Cost-benefit analysis

— Organizing Checklist —

PLAN YOUR DOCUMENT IN SOME GRAPHIC REPRESENTATION.

CREATE AN OUTLINE TO SHOW RELATIONSHIPS BETWEEN CATEGORIES OF INFORMATION AND THE ORDER IN WHICH YOU WILL PRESENT THE INFORMATION.

CRITIQUE YOUR OUTLINE FOR GAPS IN THE MATERIAL AND PROBLEMS IN THE ORDER.

BUILD THE OUTLINE AFTER YOU HAVE COLLECTED ALL YOUR MATERIAL.

CHOOSE A PATTERN OF ORGANIZATION THAT BEST SUITS YOUR PURPOSE, SUBJECT, AND AUDIENCE, SUCH AS FROM KNOWN TO UNKNOWN, IN TIME ORDER, OR IN THE MOST LOGICAL SEQUENCE.

WHEN THE WRITING GETS TOUGH, HOW DO I GET STARTED?

You've been working on this report for three hours and all you have to show for it is a basket filled with crumpled paper.

Or you've been thinking for more than a week about how to write this performance evaluation to a valued member of your staff who you know is highly sensitive to criticism. At times you think you've found the right approach, but as soon as you write a few words, you know "that won't work."

Or you've been staring at the blank screen on your word processor so long you're beginning to see movement in it. But there's no movement in the proposal you should be writing.

Or you know what you want to say in a request for additional staff, and you know you can say it well, if only you can get this first paragraph off the ground. After a dozen or so tries, however, it's still not what you want. And this bloody first paragraph is keeping you from proceeding further.

These are the kinds of frustrations writers endure when they cannot get started. Poets might call this inertia a lack of inspiration. Other professional writers might call it writer's block. The person who works in an office and writes simply to move the business along calls it an exasperating waste of time and energy.

FIFTEEN WAYS TO JUMP-START YOUR WRITING

When you are having trouble getting a document started or moving it along, try one or more of the techniques described here.

1. Read Company Documents

Getting started doesn't necessarily mean scribbling away or hammering the keyboard. The best start may come in your learning more about the subject you are to write about. One way of doing that is by reading.

For example, if you are agonizing over how to write a difficult performance evaluation, you might review other evaluations in your file. Or look at those of a colleague. Or you might review the company manual on this subject. Even if you cannot find a model that reflects the situation you are facing, you may find language or suggestions that you can use.

If you are writing a proposal, read material on the client's company. Read more closely the company's Request for Proposal, highlighting concerns that it stresses or that you can capitalize on. Read your own company's promotional literature.

In preparing for that request you want to make for additional staff, read over the notes or reports of past months that have brought you to the conclusion that you need more help. Some of the detail there may be critical to your argument. You may decide to begin your document with a list of instances in which the company lost money, time, or business because of your department's limited resources.

2. Peruse Your FYI File

If you keep an FYI file or a collection of articles, brochures, clippings, and other published and unpublished documents related to your work or industry, thumb through it. You may find some useful information here, current buzzwords, and important issues that you can incorporate into your document. For example, as a manager you may have saved articles on evaluation and dealing with staff disharmony and discordant voices in a department. Notice particularly the leads to the published pieces. They may give you an idea for starting your document.

3. Speak into a Tape Recorder

Another way of getting started is to talk your thoughts into a tape recorder. This approach isn't going to give you a first draft, because this recording is likely to be very disjointed, without the kind of logical flow a written document needs.

But by speaking into a recorder you will be converting your thoughts into words, thereby putting them into a form you can work with more easily. Play the tape back, and jot down notes about what you want to keep and what you don't. Catch phrases that you find effective and those that miss the mark.

Having gone through these exercises, you will probably be in a better frame of mind to write.

4. Explain Your Main Idea Succinctly

We sometimes have trouble in getting started because we are not certain of what we want to say. A way of crystallizing your thinking is to write your main idea on a 3 × 5 index card—one side only. Given such limited space, you know you cannot deal with minor details or peripheral thought. You must get to the main point or thesis.

Begin with a thought starter as basic as: *The main point I want to make is....*

The psychology involved here is that you are not facing a blank page. So you know you are not expecting to write the entire document. Given this less demanding challenge—at least in terms of length—you may have less trouble putting your ideas into words.

Remember, however, that stating your thesis succinctly at this stage of the writing can be a difficult task. Writers often are not sure of what they want to say until they have worked with it through one or two drafts. But when facing a block, you might try this approach. It can focus your thinking. This thesis statement could in fact become your opening paragraph—a clear, bold statement of your idea. For example:

The main idea of this memo is that the company is losing money, time, and projects because my department has been understaffed for so long. Additional staff will reverse this situation.

Use a few cards, until you've stated the main idea you hope to convey.

5. *Apply the Rule of Three*

Jot down three of the most important points you want to make. Like the previous approach, this activity is not demanding too much of you—just three short lines will do. And identifying three points may be easier than zeroing in on one main idea.

For example, three points to be made in writing the performance evaluation are:

1. Your creative contributions are highly significant.

2. Your attitude toward colleagues can be upsetting.

3. You are a mature professional and should take this criticism in the spirit in which it is given—for the good of the department and your own professional advancement.

With points such as these, the writer can begin to develop any one, and thereby be off and running.

6. *Doodle*

Get your hand moving while your mind works. Doodling can be an outlet for "mind static" that gets in the way of creative thought. Doodling is obviously less disciplined and mental an approach than applying the rule of three, but it may be the approach that works for you today.

7. *List Ten Questions a Reader Might Ask*

Put yourself in the place of your reader and list ten questions about the issue, service, or product the reader should or will be asking. Then answer them. For example, if you are writing to a supervisor asking for additional staff members, *be* that supervisor for a moment and ask the tough questions he or she would ask, such as:

❑ How many people do you think you need?

❑ How many can you get by with?

❑ How much will they cost?

❑ Will the benefits of additional staff outweigh the costs?

Then write your answers to these questions. You may eventually present your entire document in this question-answer format.

8. Visualize People Physically Reacting to What You've Written

Sometimes you may need a little extra incentive to do your best work, particularly when it comes to writing. That incentive may come in the form of your own mental picture of your audience after they have read your document. Do you visualize their tossing it aside and giving it little thought? Or do you visualize their reading it seriously, nodding their heads in agreement, calling you in to discuss it? What would you have to do to make the second scenario come about? What kinds of information, expressed in what way, would generate the response you would hope for?

Knowing these kinds of things, you may be in a better state of mind to plunge in. You may be more inclined to begin the document with a statement and tone designed to achieve the reaction you want. For example, if you want your supervisor to sit up and take notice, you might begin your request for more staff in this way:

Mr. G, I think we've been penny wise and pound foolish. And our penny-pinching is squeezing life out of the organization.

9. List All You Know About Your Audience

Your audience determines much of what you say and how you say it. By listing what you know about your audience, you may hone in on both your content and expression, thereby finding your starting point.

For example, in writing the request for more staff, think about the supervisor who must approve or deny the request. What drives that supervisor? Is it the need to increase sales? Improve quality? Cut costs? The prime interests of your readers may be an angle you can work in addressing the issue of more staff.

For example, if quality is a concern of your supervisor, you might begin with a statement such as:

> More than once in the past month you have said that you are not satisfied with the quality of the widgets we have been turning out. I agree with you. We should be turning out better widgets and could be turning out better widgets. But to do so we need more staff. Let me explain why.

10. *Put Your Purpose in Writing*

If you are having trouble getting started, it may be because you are not too sure of what you are about. Though you feel you know your purpose, write it out on paper. Doing so will help crystallize for you exactly why you are writing.

This technique is much like technique four, but instead of setting down your main idea, you are dealing with purpose. The two are not synonymous. A unique purpose in writing a performance evaluation, for example, might be:

> To help a good, sensitive staff member overcome a flaw that is affecting departmental morale, and to do so without offending him.

You must know what you want to accomplish before deciding the content to use in accomplishing it. Knowing that purpose from the outset can help you begin the writing.

11. *Begin with "I'd Just Like to Tell You That..."*

Sometimes writers tie themselves up in knots looking for a clever, profound, or otherwise unusual beginning. Taking the opposite tack may be what you need to do if you are having trouble getting started. That is, imagine you are speaking to your audience in person and saying: *I'd just like to tell you that....* Write those words and follow with what comes naturally to mind. You may be pleasantly surprised to find they give you a running start. For example:

> I'd just like to tell you that you are doing a fine job, but your contribution is being marred by one thing—your attitude toward some of your colleagues in the department...

Later you can go back and delete the "I'd just like to tell you that" and fashion a more fitting opener. But to get you out of the blocks, you might try this approach.

12. Write Anything to Prime the Pump

Some writers have found that writing anything can lead them to writing something meaningful. And when they say *anything,* they mean just that. They may even write *I don't know why I can't get started with this memo.*

The physical act of putting words on a page primes the pump, gets the thoughts flowing, and eventually may draw out the thought or two needed to unleash a flood of ideas. It might happen like this:

> I don't know why I can't get started with this memo. It's not that difficult a piece. I should be able to say this fairly easily. All I want to say is that I appreciate the job he is doing for the department but that his attitude toward a few people in the department is creating disharmony among the troops.

13. Complete a P-A-M Chart

If you are the highly organized type, a chart detailing what you know about your purpose, audience, and message may be your way into the document. For, while you may have trouble with sentences and paragraphs, you may be more comfortable with bulleted lists. Simply create a chart like the one here, and fill in the appropriate information.

Purpose	Concerns of Audience	Message
To win the OK to add staff	Mr. G. —concerned with quality, lost sales	1. Product is not top quality. 2. We've never replaced AC, our top-notch quality assurance monitor. 3. When I serve in that role, supervision of other things suffers. 4. Quality can be restored if we hire a quality assurance monitor.

You can, of course, make this chart as detailed as you like. The more concerns or characteristics of your audience you cite, for instance, the more detailed your message box is likely to be. By including message points directed to each aspect or concern of the audience, you may be outlining your entire document.

But even with a skimpy P-A-M chart, you have laid out you thoughts on paper and in your own words. You have something then that you can build a preliminary opening paragraph around.

14. Build a Brainstorming Cluster

Begin with a task or subject, and put that in a circle in the center of a blank page. From there, write words and phrases that have even the remotest connection to the subject. Expand the network as one thought triggers another. When you're finished, connect those that are most closely related.

As in a brainstorming session with colleagues, the purpose of this activity is to generate ideas *in quantity*. Don't judge these ideas at this point, but simply jot down as many as possible. Some that you will later rule out may trigger off others that you will use.

A brainstorming cluster for the staff addition request might look like this.

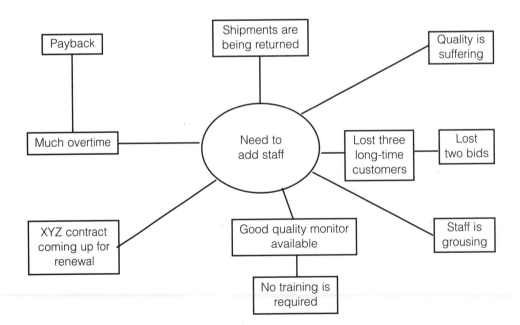

This form of brainstorming may not look like writing but it is. You are putting words to paper, generating thoughts, and tying them together. You are gaining control over your subject and will be in a stronger position for getting started.

15. *List All You Know About the Subject*

With a list you need not qualify, evaluate, or interrelate information. Just jot down everything that comes to mind. Then review your list and group ideas that relate. This technique is much like the brainstorming cluster but may be more acceptable to the linear minded.

16. *Skip the Beginning*

Instead of wasting time with a beginning that will not take shape, skip it. Move to another section of the paper that seems more accessible. A section that deals with facts and figures may lend itself more easily to writing than one that requires persuasion, judgment, or consolidation of thoughts. Writing a "nuts 'n' bolts" section first may, in fact, give you the understanding of your topic that you need to write an even more effective opening.

— Getting Started Checklist —

READ COMPANY DOCUMENTS.

PERUSE YOUR FYI FILE.

SPEAK INTO A TAPE RECORDER.

EXPLAIN YOUR MAIN IDEA ON AN INDEX CARD.

APPLY THE RULE OF THREE.

DOODLE.

LIST TEN QUESTIONS YOUR READER SHOULD ASK, THEN
ANSWER THEM.

VISUALIZE PEOPLE REACTING TO YOUR DOCUMENT AND DO
WHAT'S NECESSARY TO STIMULATE THE REACTION YOU WANT.

LIST ALL YOU KNOW ABOUT YOUR AUDIENCE.

WRITE OUT YOUR PURPOSE.

BEGIN WITH, *I'D JUST LIKE TO TELL YOU THAT*....

WRITE ANYTHING TO PRIME THE PUMP.

COMPLETE A P-A-M CHART.

BUILD A BRAINSTORMING CLUSTER.

LIST ALL YOU KNOW ABOUT YOUR SUBJECT.

SKIP THE BEGINNING.

HOW CAN I MAKE THE MOST OF MY GOOD IDEAS?

You've been thinking for a week about this report. You have a number of good ideas and information to support them. But when you write the report, it somehow doesn't seem as impressive on paper as it was in your mind? What's happened to those powerful ideas?

Or your boss returns your analysis of equipment needs with the simple directive, "Beef up the rationale." How do you "beef up," without just spreading on layers and layers of fat?

FOUR WAYS TO CAPITALIZE ON GOOD IDEAS

The failure to capitalize on good ideas is one of the most serious flaws in business writing. People waste some of their best thoughts by:

- ❐ Burying them in a tangle of distracting information
- ❐ Presenting them without the supporting information readers need
- ❐ Not relating them to the thoughts that precede and follow

To make the most of your ideas and the information you have, feed those ideas to readers in digestible bites, enabling them to grasp one idea at a time. Give them the details, examples, definitions, and other supporting information they need to understand each idea. And build bridges for your readers, so they can easily link one idea with the next and follow your thought process from beginning to end.

In other words, in developing your ideas, work for unity, enrichment, and continuity of thought. Let's take a look at how to do that.

Create Unity: One Idea at a Time

Your writing becomes "reader friendly" when you present ideas in unified paragraphs. *Unified paragraph* is actually a redundancy because a paragraph, by definition, is *a group of sentences developing one idea*. It consists of a topic sentence and supporting sentences.

THE TOPIC SENTENCE, OR THE UMBRELLA STATEMENT

The topic sentence:

- ❐ Is limited to a single idea, the main idea of the paragraph
- ❐ States the main idea in general terms
- ❐ Points the writer and reader toward particulars

For the greatest clarity, place the topic sentence first in the paragraph. The reader learns immediately what the paragraph is all about. Seeing the idea in general terms, the reader can grasp the concept, the big picture, and then be in a better position to make sense of the detail that follows.

Placing the topic sentence first is analogous to a fitness instructor's stating the objective of a set of exercises before leading his charges through the steps. Knowing the goal, they are better able to see the reasoning behind the various exercises.

A topic sentence, therefore, is an umbrella statement, an idea stated in general terms. For example:

❏ The past year has been a rocky one for the stock market.

❏ The company has fallen behind its competitors in the use of technology.

❏ This division places interpersonal skills above all others.

❏ We offer eight ways through which you can generate new business.

Each of these sentences presents a general idea. Each focuses the reader, pointing her toward particulars, such as:

❏ Specific difficulties in the stock market during the year

❏ Examples of technology that competitors have which the company does not

❏ Reasons for giving priority to interpersonal skills

❏ A run-down of the eight ways

The Supporting Sentences, or the Ribs

The supporting sentences:

❏ Provide the particulars

❏ Define, explain, illustrate, verify, describe, narrate, show cause and effect of that main idea

The supporting sentences are all closely related to the main idea, thereby achieving the unity needed for comprehension. The supporting sentences can present a wide variety of information in an array of methods, but the common factor must be their *oneness* with the main idea in the topic sentence.

Oneness sounds so basic you might think it doesn't even have to be mentioned. But unless you consciously work toward paragraph unity, chances are your paragraphs will come across to readers as a jumble of detached thoughts.

Here's an example of a paragraph that does *not have the unity* readers need to comprehend fully:

> As the bridges between the executive office and the staff, middle managers can make the difference between a well-run company and a chaotic one. Managing people is most important in companies with a long chain of command. While the technical expertise of managers must differ along the line, the basic people management skills apply universally.

This paragraph is rather confusing because it has no core. While it talks about management in every sentence, the reader is at a loss to know *the point* of those sentences. The first sentence talks about the difference good management can make. The second is about the importance of middle managers in a larger company. The third speaks of people management skills. The writer had an idea but never quite crystallized that thought in his own mind. Had he begun with a topic sentence, he might have been able to tie this information together to make a meaningful and comprehensible point. Not having done that, he leaves the reader confused.

Here's another example of a paragraph that lacks unity, but for a different reason.

> Company resources are wasted by processing computer reports that are not used. Reports printed but not used include Bankcard Master and Unmatched Bankcard. Reports requiring format revision to improve efficiency include Journal Vouchers with missing audit data.

This paragraph has more going for it than the previous example. It has a good topic sentence that introduces a single idea in general terms—*resources are wasted by reports that are not used.* The sentence points toward particulars, and the reader expects to learn about reports not being used. The second sentence provides such information, naming two such reports. *But the third sentence in the paragraph destroys the unity.* That sentence does not deal with unused reports; it deals with format revision. That's another idea and should be put in another paragraph.

   This paragraph illustrates how easily writers can drift away from unity. As the mind is thinking about reports and wasted resources, it slips into another aspect of that subject. That kind of slip can confuse readers. That's what happened in the following example. See if you can spot what is destroying the unity in the paragraph:

> Leadership changes aided the company's collapse. Communication throughout the company was also a problem. The founder's brother-in-law, Sam Nepotamkin, served as president from 1982 to 1988. These men had never really liked each other but were tied together through the wife/sister, which neither really liked either. Nepotamkin's successor was Mabel Frump. When the expansion program ran into trouble, Frump was replaced by Sidney Stylish at the end of 1991. Inventory problems were quite evident during these years and management should have recognized the credit disaster developing. As sales and profits worsened, company veteran R. J. Fullhouse was summoned from retirement to try to turn things around.

This paragraph is typical of what you will find in many business documents. The writer begins with a single idea—*leadership changes aided the collapse*—presented in a good topic sentence. Some of the sentences support that idea, giving specifics of those changes. But amid that related detail, the writer throws in some unrelated material. The reference to communication and inventory problems and the credit disaster should probably be in topic sentences for paragraphs of their own. And the chatter about the wife/sister is totally irrelevant to the main idea and should be cut altogether.

This kind of paragraph confuses readers and deceives writers. "Did you mention the inventory problems?" the boss might ask. "Yes, I did," the writer will say. He did mention them, but never in a way that would be meaningful to a reader. The idea of inventory problems, which could be important to the report, would go undeveloped and be totally wasted. Yet in the writer's mind, that idea was "covered" in the report.

Now let's look at some examples of unified paragraphs. Note how the first sentence introduces the main idea in general terms and how each of the supporting sentences relates directly to that main idea, developing that idea fully:

> *We chose the ABC compactor for handling trash and garbage disposal on board our vessels for a number of reasons.* First, the ABC Compactor meets our requirements for capacity, construction, warranty, and past marine sales. Second, it is in use on U. S. Navy vessels, U.S. Coast Guard vessels, and hospital ships. And, third, it is the least expensive of the compactors that meet all our needs.

The topic sentence says *we have chosen the ABC compactor for certain reasons.* That's one general idea. It points readers toward particulars given in the supporting sentences—what those reasons are. The supporting sentences do not tell anything about when the compactor will be installed, or how, or by whom. Those are details for other paragraphs. This paragraph is unified around the single idea of *why this compactor was chosen.* From the start, the reader knows what to expect and can easily follow the progression from general idea to particulars.

Here's another example of a unified paragraph:

> *Market research is not a recent development but has been around for a long time.* In fact, evidence of market research dates back to the fourteenth century when textile manufacturer Johann Fugger established a market research network by having strategically placed relatives exchange detailed letters on trade conditions and finance throughout Europe. In this way Fugger, operating from Augsburg, could make accurate trading decisions based on current knowledge of the supply and demand for money and goods throughout the continent.

The topic sentence introduces the main idea—in general terms—*that market research is an old concept.* The reader senses from the topic sentence that the paragraph will deal with the history of market research. And that is exactly what is treated in the supporting sentences. These sentences say nothing about why our company should get into market research, or how we can do it, or what its drawbacks might be. If the writer wants to get into those aspects of the subject, she does so in other paragraphs.

Imagine, however, if the supporting sentences were given without the topic sentence. The reader could be confused. All the while he's reading about fourteenth century manufacturers and letter exchanges, he's wondering, "What's the point of all this?" By telling what the point is in the topic sentence, the writer enables the reader to separate the forest from the trees.

SHORT AND SIMPLE: THE KEY TO EFFECTIVE TOPIC SENTENCES

We've seen how the topic sentence helps readers, giving them the main idea and enabling them to get the point of the details. But the topic sentence also helps the writer, by focusing his attention on one aspect of the subject. If you get into the habit of starting paragraphs with topic sentences, you will produce unified paragraphs and develop ideas more fully.

To write an effective topic sentence, keep it short and simple. Compound sentences—those with two or more ideas—can cause the writer to write about one of the ideas and ignore the others. For example, read the following sentence and decide what you would follow it with:

> **Poor Topic Sentence:**   The new process is designed to personalize a program for each individual, and it consists of three phases.

If you are like most writers, you probably said you'd follow this sentence with a description of the three phases. But in doing so, you'd be ignoring the idea of *a personalized program.* You would be wasting an important aspect of the program but not even realize it. To avoid this kind of inadvertent omission, limit your topic sentences to a *single* idea.

> **Strong Topic Sentence:**   The new process is designed to personalize a program for each individual.

Similarly, avoid qualifiers in topic sentences. These can distract the reader from the main idea and propel the writer away from it. For example:

> **Poor Topic Sentence:**   Your organization requires an approach that is responsive to its unique qualities, *especially today when conditions in the economy are so unstable.*

The italicized qualifier can divert attention from the main idea—the required approach. It may set the writer off on a tangent whereby he writes about the unstable conditions in the economy rather than of the required approach.

Therefore, to ensure you stay the course and write unified paragraphs, keep your topic sentences short, simple, and unadorned.

> **Strong Topic Sentence:**   Your organization requires an approach that is responsive to its unique qualities.

Add Richness with Full, Robust Ideas

If you are fortunate enough to have a colleague edit your writing, one of the most frequent notations that person might write in the margin of your documents is, "What do you mean by this?" Writers often expect too much from their readers, assuming that the readers have all the insight into the subject they have.

Provide the kinds of supporting information your readers need to fully understand each main idea. Consider enriching the ideas in your topic sentences with *details, definitions, examples,* and *repetition.* Only then can you be certain your readers know exactly what you mean.

Let's look at these methods of enriching your thoughts and building more comprehensible paragraphs.

SHOW AND TELL THROUGH DETAILS, DEFINITIONS, AND EXAMPLES

DETAILS. Good ideas are often ignored or misunderstood because they are left in the abstract. Readers cannot perceive their full meaning unless they are put into concrete situations with specific details.

Note, for example, how a key idea in the following passage is glossed over, leaving readers with a major question:

> *Weak:*   Management felt the company was ready for expansion. So it laid out a plan to open 48 new units over 18 months. During the first year, 16 new units were opened, and construction began for 16 others. But that is as far as the expansion got, as costs far exceeded estimates.

(Question: What made the company feel "ready for expansion"?)

> *Clear:*   Management felt the company was ready for expansion. *Profits had been consistently good, all systems were state of the art and expandable, and a corps of experienced but young managers was eager to grow further with the company.* So management laid out a plan to open 48 new units over 18 months.
>
>   During the first year, 16 new units were opened, and construction began for 16 others. But that is as far as the expansion got, as costs far exceeded estimates.

The details explaining *ready for expansion* may be part of the writer's knowledge of the background, but not necessarily of the reader's. Rather than have readers wondering about that issue, include the information to be sure they keep pace with you. In providing that detail, you may find yourself having to divide what was one paragraph into two, as in the example. That's fine. In fact, in doing so you can clearly see yourself enriching your ideas.

DEFINITIONS. Sometimes misunderstanding arises when the writer uses a term he is quite familiar with but which may be foreign to the reader. Even when you have only the slightest doubt as to whether the reader knows the term, define it. In the following example, the reader may be stopped dead by the term that is not defined. As a result, her understanding of everything that follows will be less than complete:

> *Weak:* Financial statements must be written so that they can be easily interpreted by *end-users.* Management seeking investment capital must present its business in a form that is understandable to all people interested in it.

(Question: Who are the endusers?)

> *Clear:* Financial statements must be written so that they can be easily interpreted by end-users—*banks, investors, company management, industry analysts,* and *regulatory agencies.* Management seeking investment capital must present its business in a form that is understandable to all the people interested in it.

With the definition, readers are capable of following the thought process.

Here's another example of a paragraph in which an omission can cause confusion. What information do you think should be provided?

> *Weak:* Contrary to public perception, productivity is higher in the United States than in the other major industrialized nations. A recent study shows that productivity in the United States exceeds that of West Germany, Japan, and Britain.

Before a reader could continue reading and make sense out of this passage, he'd have to know what *productivity* means, not in a loose sense, but as it was defined and measured by the study. So a more meaningful paragraph would include that definition:

> *Clear:*   Contrary to public perception, productivity is higher in the United States than in the other major industrialized nations. *Productivity is the ratio of goods and services produced to the resources used to produce them.* A recent study shows that productivity in the United States exceeds that of West Germany, Japan, and Britain.

EXAMPLES. Like details and definitions, examples enrich ideas, helping readers put abstract ideas in a concrete context. *For example* and *for instance* are the most useful catalysts in writing. Note how examples in the second paragraph below give a richer, more exact meaning to the abstract idea in the first paragraph.

> *Weak:*   Companies often rely too much on their accounting systems as a way of managing the business. They think that every important business event affecting the company is recorded in an accounting transaction. But that is not always true.

> *Clear:*   Companies often rely too much on their accounting systems as a way of managing the business. They think that every important business event affecting the company is recorded in an accounting transaction. But that is not always true. *For example,* if a key executive leaves the company, no accounting record will be made of that departure. It is, however, a significant business event affecting the company seriously.

The example enables the reader to fully understand the concept by bringing it into the concrete, where the reader can more easily work with it.

TEST YOUR "DEVELOPMENT-ABILITY"

Which ideas should be developed further to improve comprehension of the following passages? How would you develop them fully?

1. I have outlined a five-point checklist for customer inquiries. I hope that this outline will help you. The five points are the following:

2. The widget industry is becoming more competitive. As a result, established companies have taken to some very questionable practices.

3. Companies often reward each department on meeting its own efficiency and productivity objectives. Consequently, some departments develop a department-selfish attitude.

Some suggestions for developing ideas in the foregoing passages and improving their comprehension are

1. In 1, give details of how the checklist might help the readers. Those details might make them more receptive to the checklist.

2. In 2, details of *more competitive* and examples of *questionable practices* would help the reader. As the passage stands now, the reader is expected to take the writer's word for these statements without any proof.

3. In 3, a definition or examples of *department-selfish attitude* would almost be necessary.

Repeat Key Ideas to Ensure Understanding

Surprising as it may sound, readers do not hang on our every word. They may *read* every word but still overlook key ideas or fail to grasp their significance. To be sure your readers seize every important point, repeat key thoughts. *Change the wording some, but convey the same idea.* If readers don't get your message in one sentence, they should get it in another.

Note how repeating a key idea in the following example makes sure that readers grasp it.

> Performance objectives are critical to evaluating the success of a training program. *Unless you know the specific objectives of the program, evaluating its success is impossible.* Where appropriate, pretests and post-tests might be used to measure the success of a training program, particularly when detailed knowledge is the subject. Where more subjective issues such as "attitude" are the matter of the training, interviews with supervisors and customers can determine the success of the program. Where "selling technique" is the course content, sales figures can be used in measuring the success of the program.

The second sentence repeats the idea of the topic sentence, putting it in other words.

It's a good practice to *repeat in the last sentence* of the paragraph the main idea stated in the topic sentence. For example:

> A *chief cause of employee turnover is lack of commitment.* For employees to gain that commitment, supervisors must define goals for employees and stress their importance in the company mission. Employees will feel more a part of the company and see purpose in their jobs. *Without this feeling of self-worth and a sense of belonging in the operation, employees are more likely to go looking elsewhere to find them.*

The idea of the topic sentence is repeated in the last sentence, tying up the idea nicely to be sure the reader gets the point.

Test Your "Comprehension-Ability"

How would you improve the comprehension of the following paragraphs by repeating the key idea?

1. Despite the costs, turnover does at times have positive aspects. For example, turnover provides the opportunity to replace below-average performers with above-average performers. When such a switch is made, productivity can increase greatly.

2. Effective training programs are well organized. That is, they show a logical sequence in the material treated, as well as a sense of balance. Provisions are made so participants have ample opportunity to ask questions, make comments, exchange concerns and strategies, and engage in hands-on applications or simulation activities.

Some suggestions for improving these paragraphs through repetition would include:

1. In 1, conclude the paragraph with a statement that repeats the topic sentence in some way, such as: *So not all turnover is bad for the company.*

2. In 2, follow the topic sentence with a sentence that repeats for clarification the idea of *well organized,* such as: *They are planned with a concern for content as well as delivery and student participation.*

Provide Continuity by Linking Ideas

For readers to understand your ideas, they must be able to follow their progression. *Use transitions to link one idea with the next.* Link sentence to sentence and paragraph to paragraph.

Note how transitions link the sentences and paragraphs in this example:

> On-the-job training is an investment that pays handsome dividends. First, an improvement in employee skill results in lower wage costs. *Second,* the skillful, more productive workers feel happier about their jobs, and this feeling reduces supervisory problems. Morale, *then,* is better, and the company always benefits from good morale.
>
> *In addition,* training keeps employees up to par with the new equipment and processes. *As a result,* fewer abuses of the equipment are experienced, and repair bills are lower. *And* because trained employees use new equipment more efficiently, the company recoups its investment more quickly.

The italicized words and phrases link the ideas by showing the relationship between them. The words *first* and *second* indicate that the "dividends" mentioned in the first sentence are to follow. The word *then* suggests a causal relationship, indicating that as a result of what was said before, the following happens. *In addition* links the second paragraph with the first, indicating that what follows will continue the line of thinking of the paragraph before.

Connectives Show the Relationship

The words and phrases in the examples are called connectives. Connectives are words and phrases used specifically to link ideas and *show the relationship* (continuation of an idea, shift in thinking, illustration, etc.).

Note the following connectives and the direction in thought they signal. Use these connectives to tie your sentences and paragraphs together, enabling your readers to move easily from one idea to the next.

To indicate addition to or continuation of an idea: again, also, and then, besides, equally important, finally, first, furthermore, in addition, likewise, moreover, next, third

To indicate cause and effect: accordingly, as a result, consequently, hence, in short, then, therefore, thus

To indicate comparison: in like manner, likewise, similarly

To indicate concession: although this may be true, even though, I admit

To indicate contrast: and yet, at the same time, but, however, in contrast, in spite of, nevertheless, on the other hand, still

To indicate special features or examples: for example, for instance, incidentally, in fact, in particular, specifically, that is, to illustrate

To indicate summary: in brief, in conclusion, in other words, in short, on the whole, to sum up

To indicate time relationships: afterwards, as soon as, immediately, in the meantime, meanwhile, since, thereafter, thereupon, when

USE A SENTENCE, CLAUSE, OR PHRASE TO CONNECT IDEAS. Writers can also connect sentences by repeating a word, phrase, or clause from one sentence and using it in the next. The wording may change slightly, but enough similarity exists to build the bridge. For example:

> A second symptom of an uncontrolled MIS department is increased demands by *user departments* for data processing in their daily activities. These *users* want more and more services and become frustrated by the lack of control over MIS activities related to their areas. This *frustration* may be the result of several problems.

Note how a key word or idea from one sentence is repeated (in modified form) in the succeeding sentence.

Paying attention to transitions keeps you from wandering off the subject and forgetting about paragraph unity. If you cannot insert a transition between sentences, chances are the sentences are not close enough in thought to be in the same paragraph.

— Idea Development Checklist —

PRESENT ONE IDEA AT A TIME.

INTRODUCE THE MAIN IDEA OF EACH PARAGRAPH IN A
TOPIC SENTENCE, WRITTEN IN GENERAL TERMS.

RESTRICT THE TOPIC SENTENCE TO A SINGLE IDEA WITHOUT
QUALIFIERS.

DEVELOP THE MAIN IDEA WITH PARTICULARS IN THE
SUPPORTING SENTENCES.

RELATE ALL SUPPORTING SENTENCES TO THE MAIN IDEA.

GIVE READERS THE INFORMATION THEY NEED BY PROVIDING
DETAILS, DEFINITIONS, EXAMPLES.

STRESS KEY IDEAS BY REPEATING THEM IN A MODIFIED FORM.

LINK IDEAS WITH TRANSITIONS, SENTENCE TO SENTENCE AND
PARAGRAPH TO PARAGRAPH.

How Can I Write Clear, Emphatic Sentences?

Your supervisor has sent back the draft of a report you wrote last week. You thought it was a sterling document, and were waiting anxiously for her to concur. Instead, you find scrawled across various pages:

"Too long and wordy"

"Get to the point"

"Muddled. Clear it up!"

FIVE STEPS TO WRITING SENTENCES WITH IMPACT

How do you include all the detail and qualifiers necessary and still be to the point? Is this supervisor asking for too much?

No, she's not. This supervisor is asking for *less*. She's asking for writing that cuts out the fat while strengthening the muscle. She wants to *emphasize* the key thoughts, not bury them in a sea of unnecessary words. She wants to be sure the writing keeps the attention of the readers, and doesn't bore them or weigh them down.

When trying to make your writing more direct, clear, and emphatic, the place to begin is the sentence. If you can make each sentence clear, leans and emphatic, you are well on your way to writing a report that is readable and digestible.

No writers deliberately set out to make their writing unclear. But many do not know how to recognize sentences that are longer than necessary, or how to whittle them down to size. This chapter gives you the *five steps to writing clear, emphatic sentences.*

1. Keep Each Sentence Short

Long sentences are a major source of difficulty in reading. (See Problem No. 22), "Is My Writing Readable?" And long sentences can confuse. They not only contain more words, but they often contain more ideas. With too many ideas in a single sentence you run the risk of readers' not grasping each one. Short sentences are clearer. And they emphasize each main point. As a rule, if you keep your average sentence length to 18 to 20 words, you'll be right on target.

Note how muddled the ideas are in the first example that follows, and how each idea is clear and emphatic in the second.

Muddled:	Upgrading our PC setup will require assessment of our needs, determination of software compatibility, and selection of hardware, and the upgrade must be done without disrupting the normal work routine. (1 sentence, 30 words, 2 ideas)
Clear, Emphatic:	Upgrading our PC setup will require assessment of our needs, determination of software compatibility, and

selection of hardware. *The upgrade* must be done without disrupting the normal work routine. (2 sentences,
29 words, 23 ideas)

In the revision, the idea about *not disrupting the routine* receives emphasis.
It is not buried amid the details of the upgrade requirements.

To the writer, each idea in a long sentence may be crystal clear. But to the
reader coming upon the document cold, some ideas may be lost. Serve your
ideas in digestible bites, to give readers the opportunity to savor each one.

To recognize overly long sentences quickly, without having to count
words, look for sentences that run more than two or two-and-a half lines long.
In such sentences look for *sentence extenders,* words that lead to cramming more
ideas into the sentence. For example, *and, but, as, which, since, although, because,*
and similar words often cause writers to extend sentences beyond a manageable
length. Watch out for these words. When you see them, try to break the sentence in two. Very often you can do this simply by inserting a period and cap-
italizing the first letter of the new sentence. For example:

Muddled:	It is important that managers in the areas affected by the upgrade realize there will be some disruption *because* there will be a short learning curve required as staff members become familiar with the new equipment and software.
Clear, Emphatic:	It is important that managers in the areas affected by the upgrade realize there will be some disruption. *There* will be a short learning curve required as staff members become familiar with the new equipment and software.

Sometimes you may have to delete and add a few words, or even restructure the sentence:

Muddled:	We understand that, according to the agreement we have with XYZ, all invoices should be sent in triplicate, with a detailed listing of items purchased, the number of each item shipped, and the cost per item.

Clear, Emphatic: We understand that, according to the agreement we have with XYZ, all invoices should be sent in triplicate. *Include* a detailed listing of items purchased, the number of each item shipped, and the cost per item.

By making two sentences out of the one, the writer emphasizes the content more effectively. Readers will be more likely to note both points of the message: *that invoices should be sent in triplicate and the information that must be sent with the invoice.* If everything is put in the one sentence, readers may not grasp all of it.

In isolation, none of the "muddled" examples in this section is totally incomprehensible. But placed in a paragraph, with other sentences like it, such sentences do become a serious challenge for even the most alert reader. The same point, in fact, can be made throughout this chapter. Compound the difficulty of each isolated example throughout the document, and the writing becomes most uninviting and obscure.

2. Avoid Wordiness

Wordiness can kill more than a reader's afternoon; it can also kill his or her interest in the document and its author. Documents that even *look* too long are often put aside.

If you know the expressions that *lead* to wordiness, you can hunt for them in your writing and cut them out. These expressions are of two types: nouns made from verbs and multiword phrases. Let's examine each.

Avoid Nouns Made from Verbs

Examples of nouns made from verbs are *evaluation* from *evaluate, understanding* from *understand, development* from *develop, definition* from *define.* While there is an appropriate time for using these noun/verbs, a careless use of them can make sentences wordier than necessary. For example:

Wordy: A number of key operating issues require *resolution* before the company can achieve *realization* of its goals. (nouns from verbs)

Lean: The company must *resolve* a number of key operating issues before it can *realize* its goals. (verbs)

Wordy: We held a *discussion* on the *expansion* of the use of the Quality Improvement Program. (nouns made from verbs)

Lean: We discussed *expanding* the use of the Quality Improvement Program. (verbs)

Use the Verb Not the Noun/Verb

analyze	not	make an analysis of
calculate	not	in the calculation of
apply	not	in the application of
evaluate	not	conduct an evaluation of
develop	not	involve the development of

Many of these nouns made from verbs end in *-tion, -ance, -ence,* and *-ment.* View these endings as danger signals.

Noun/verbs often lead to *a string of prepositional phrases* (*of, with, by,* etc.) These phrases often make sentences wordy. For example:

Wordy: An analysis *of* the situation led *to* our understanding of the underlying problems. (Prepositional phrases are spawned by the noun/verbs *analysis* and *understanding.*)

Lean: We *analyzed* the situation and *understood* the underlying problems. (The verbs *analyzed* and *understood* preclude the need for prepositional phrases, shortening the sentence.)

Wordy: We will show a comparison *of* weekly performance against budget *through* a graphic representation *of* the figures. (The noun/verbs and prepositional phrases add length.)

Lean: We will *compare* weekly performance against budget in a graph. (The verbs preclude the need for prepositional phrases, shortening the sentence.)

AVOID MULTIWORD PHRASES

When Charles Dickens began writing fiction, his works were serialized in magazines, and he was paid by the word. Maybe that's why his novels are so long. In business, brevity, and length, is the goal. We often add length to documents inadvertently by using multiword phrases that could easily be replaced by shorter phrases or even by a single word. For example:

Wordy: *In the event that* the contractor does not meet these deadlines, we expect a payment *in the amount of* $1,000 for each day of delay.

Lean: *If* the contractor does not meet these deadlines, we expect a payment *of* $1,000 for each day of delay.

In revising your drafts, look for these long phrases and replace them with shorter alternatives. For example:

Wordy	Lean
in order to	to
for the purpose of	to
in light of the fact that	because, since
in association with	with
in the near future	soon
during the course of	during
subsequent to	after
due to the fact that	because
at this point in time	now

DOUBLETS. Another type of multiword phrase combines two words with overlapping meanings. You might call these redundant phrases "doublets." For example, we often speak of *basic fundamentals,* but would a *fundamental* be anything but *basic? Fundamental* by itself is sufficient. Other examples of doublets are:

Doublet	Lean Alternative
absolutely complete	complete
key essentials	essentials
future outlook	outlook
exactly identical	identical
meet together	meet
my personal opinion	my opinion

Doublet *(cont'd)*	Lean Alternative *(cont'd)*
each and every one	each one
just recently	recently
temporarily suspended	suspended
repeat again	repeat
true facts	facts

3. Prune and Simplify

While certain words and phrases can lengthen sentences unnecessarily, there is an even more serious cause of wordiness—our penchant for saying things in complicated ways. Some writers think they are impressing readers with such style. But most writers just don't take the time to look for a simpler, clearer way of expressing an idea. Instead, they settle for sentences that are not only longer but also muddled. For example:

Wordy, Muddled: The company will use internal personnel as the primary source for filling promotional positions to the extent consistent with other objectives such as availability of personnel and mandatory reinstatement.

Lean, Clear: The company will promote from within whenever possible.

As you can see, the revision involves more than changing a word or two. It requires an attitude that says: *What do I really want to say? How can I say it as simply as possible?* Thinking this way, the writer can cut out much of the fluff and pretension that muddy up so much business prose.

Here are other examples:

Wordy, Muddled: Use this test to measure the accuracy of the estimates, particularly *for those in which* the cost of equipment is involved.

Lean, Clear: Use this test to measure the accuracy of the estimates, particularly *when* the cost of equipment is involved.

The savings here may be only three words, but if you can save three words in every sentence, you would be shortening—and strengthening—the document significantly.

> *Wordy, Muddled:* Listed below are major internal barriers that we have identified as impediments to our ability to deliver quality service.

> *Lean, Clear:* Listed below are major internal barriers to our ability to deliver quality service.

Barriers and *impediments* are redundant here.

> *Wordy, Muddled:* In our opinion, we think that many of the functions now performed manually by staff people can be automated and be done by computer.

In our opinion and *we think* are redundant. *Performed manually* implies the functions are performed by people. *Automated* and *done by computer* are redundant.

> *Lean, Clear:* We think many of the functions now performed manually can be done by computer.

Beware of *which* and *that* clauses. Very often these are not needed.

> *Wordy, Muddled:* Each office will be responsible for correcting its work orders that have been created with incorrect codes.

> *Lean, Clear:* Each office will be responsible for correcting its work orders with incorrect codes.

Look for opportunities to express your thoughts in fewer words, *without sacrificing substance or clarity or ease of reading.*

4. Add Momentum with the Active Voice

Though the active voice is more natural to the English language, many people mistakenly turn to the passive voice when they write for business. Note the difference between the two:

| *Passive Voice:* | Staff hours *are calculated* by the dock foreman on actual work load. |
| *Active Voice:* | The dock foreman *calculates* staff hours on actual work load. |

In the active voice sentence, the subject acts.

ACTIVE VOICE

Subject	Verb	Object
The director	ordered	an investigation.
Actor	Act	Receiver of Act

In the passive voice sentence, something is *done* to the subject.

PASSIVE VOICE

Subject	Verb	Object
An investigation	was ordered	by the director.
Receiver	Act	Actor

Active voice verbs give motion to the sentence, are more lively, and generally are more concise. For example:

| *Passive:* | It *has been decided* by management that a second set of controls is needed. |
| *Active:* | Management *has decided* that a second set of controls is needed. |

By using the active voice here, the writer puts *management* in a more active position. The writer also eliminates the clumsy and wordy *it has been decided*.

Note how the active voice casts a light on the doer and conveys a stronger connotation of action in the next example:

| *Passive:* | Referral procedures *will be learned* by the operator. They *will also be reevaluated and streamlined,* if possible. |
| *Active:* | The operator *will learn* the referral procedures, *reevaluate, and streamline* them, if possible. |

In this case, the writer has been able to consolidate two sentences into one, using the one subject for the three active voice verbs.

Writers who habitually use the passive voice run the risk of omitting the doer of the action when that information is important. For example, in an audit or in outlining duties, you may leave out critical information by using the passive voice:

Passive: Notices should be sent to these delinquent customers after 30 days.

Readers may not know who should send the letters. No one, therefore, may do it. By using the active voice, the writer makes clear who should be doing the action:

Active: *The ledger clerk* should send notices to these delinquent customers after 30 days.

In some instances the passive voice is acceptable, even preferable to the active voice. If, for example, identifying the doer of the action would show a lack of tact, the passive voice would be appropriate:

Active: We regret that *our office manager erred* in sending you the quote for this project.

Passive: We regret that *an error was made* in sending you the quote for this project.

5. Use Clear, Conversational Language

Conversational language lowers the fog and makes reading easier. Business writers, however, often feel the need to use *grandiloquent expressions, archaic language,* and *telegraphic phrasing* that impede readers and raise the fog. Let's look at each type.

Eschew Grandiloquent Expressions

Grandiloquent: We were positioned on the proverbial estuary minus the proper means of locomotion.

Conversational: We were up the creek without a paddle.

Grandiloquent: Please confirm in writing when these changes *will be effected.*

Conversational: Please confirm in writing when these changes *will be made.*

Grandiloquent	Conversational
a multitude of	many
expend	spend
obviate	prevent
remittance	payment
in lieu of	instead of
establish	set up
rectify	correct
endeavor	try
inception	start, beginning
attributable to	caused by
pursuant to	following, after
aforesaid	mentioned above
we deem it advisable	we suggest, we advise you

Mark Twain, a great writer and student of the human condition who also kept an eye on his financial condition, once said: "I never write *metropolis* for seven cents a word because I can get the same price for *city.*" Twain's comment may be a good reminder to use the conversational rather than the grandiloquent in your business writing.

SHUN ARCHAIC LANGUAGE

Readers tend to lose interest in correspondence sagging with the weight of archaic language and stock phrases, particularly at the beginning of the document. For example:

Archaic:	Payment will be made within 60 days, *per* an agreement with XYZ, Inc.
Conversational:	Payment will be made within 60 days, *according to* an agreement with XYZ, Inc.
Archaic:	The customer is questioning *the below-mentioned* bills.
Conversational:	The customer is questioning *the bills mentioned below.*

Archaic	Conversational
as per your request	as you requested
enclosed please find	I have enclosed
per your memo	according to your memo
We are in receipt of your letter of…	We have received your letter of
Herewith are forwarded…	Here are…
Regarding yours of June 6…	Regarding your letter of June 6
Pursuant to our conversation…	As we discussed…

AVOID TELEGRAPHIC PHRASING

In the interest of brevity, some writers drop words like *an, the, us*. While gaining little, these cuts make letters read like telegrams. This kind of telegraphic writing can raise the fog or just make the writing tedious enough to be annoying. For example:

Telegraphic:	Will advise regarding outstanding claim.
Conversational:	*We* will advise *you* regarding *the* outstanding claim.
Telegraphic:	Suggest we inform each department head of results.
Clearer:	*I* suggest we inform each department head of *the* results.

These little words are needed for smooth flow and should not be the target of your word pruning. Hunt for bigger game.

REVISION: THE BEST WAY TO KEEP YOUR WRITING ON TARGET

Of course, in the heat of composing, you may not be able to think about sentence length, unnecessary words, or the passive voice. And out of habit you may mindlessly drop time-worn expressions and phrases into your writing. But after you have written your draft, after you have wrestled with the content, go back over the draft looking for opportunities to improve the expression. Revise each sentence with cold, calculating objectivity. Measure each sentence against each item in the checklist that follows. Change each sentence as needed to make each as lean, clear, and emphatic as possible.

The time you spend revising sentences for clarity and emphasis may be just what you need to change your supervisor's comments from *"Too muddled. Clear it up!"* to *"Nice job!"*

— Clarity and Emphasis Checklist —

KEEP THE AVERAGE SENTENCE LENGTH AT EIGHTEEN TO TWENTY WORDS:

    ❏   *Look for sentence extenders that lead to cramming.*

OMIT UNNECESSARY WORDS:

    ❏   *Look for nouns made from verbs.*
    ❏   *Look for multiword phrases.*

PRUNE AND SIMPLIFY.

USE THE ACTIVE VOICE.

USE CLEAR, CONVERSATIONAL LANGUAGE.

STRENGTHEN SENTENCES IN REVISION.

HOW CAN I PUT
SNAP INTO MY WRITING?

You've just read a report from a colleague and you're impressed by the way it seems to jump right out at you. When you read a report of your own, however, it seems to just plod along like an overloaded truck. What gives a piece of writing vitality, or snap?

This chapter demonstrates a number of techniques you can use to put snap in your writing.

ADD ZEST WITH ACTION VERBS

Action verbs enliven sentences. Verbs such as *decide, enforce, escalate, plummet, rescind,* and *scramble* show action. These kinds of verbs drive sentences to swift, emphatic ends. In contrast, verbs such as *is, were, has been,* and *will be* do not show action. These are called *verbs of being,* because they simply show that something exists. They do not show action. Note the difference:

Verb of being:	Working conditions *are* in need of a complete review.
Action verb:	Working conditions *cry out* for a complete review.
Verb of being:	Stock prices *were* low in the morning but then *were* higher at the day's close.
Action verb:	Stock prices *fell* in the morning but then *rallied* at the day's close.

At times you will need the verb of being. But sentences with such verbs sound flat compared to those with action verbs. In revising a document, consider replacing every verb of being *(is, are, was, were, will be)* with an action verb.

Sometimes you may have to do more than replace one verb with another; you may have to restructure the sentence. For example:

Verb of being:	This procedure *was* not acceptable to the regional office.
Action verb:	The regional office *rejected* this procedure.

In this instance the writer could not make a one-for-one substitution but had to rearrange the sentence to get the action verb in. But by looking for a way to replace the verb of being with an action verb, the writer shortened the sentence, strengthened it, and converted it from passive voice to active voice. In Problem No. 18, you saw the importance of using the active voice instead of the passive. By switching from the verb of being to the action verb you can energize sentences in a number of ways.

CREATE AN IMAGE WITH CONCRETE VERBS

Besides looking to replace verbs of being with action verbs, seize opportunities to replace abstract verbs with concrete or pictorial verbs. An abstract verb conveys *an idea*. A concrete verb conveys *an idea and an image of it*. The concrete verb creates a picture for the reader to envision, thereby making the reading easier and more entertaining. For example:

Abstract verb:	The lecturer *explained* each point to the audience at great length.
Concrete verb:	The lecturer *drilled* each point into the audience.

Though *explained* is an action verb, it does not create an image for the mind of the reader as *drilled* does. *Drilled* makes the reader see the lecturer force-feeding the audience, leaving no doubt as to how the action was performed. At the same time, *drilled* also results in a shorter sentence, quickening the pace. Here's another example:

Abstract verb:	*Include* the names of vendors, by order of sales volume, in the report.
Concrete verb:	*List* the names of vendors, by order of sales volume, in the report.

Here the revision gives a clearer directive, specifying with the concrete verb exactly how the names are to be given—in a list.

To substitute a concrete verb for an abstract verb, you might try a few techniques. First, ask yourself how you would say the sentence if you were speaking it rather than writing it. Sometimes the word that comes more naturally in speech is the concrete verb. Second, look for an action that can be seen within or behind the abstraction. For example, if you are writing about sales increasing, visualize the action within the word *increase*. You may see a chart with a jagged black line climbing from left to right. You may then think of replacing *increasing* with *climbing* or *rising*.

The thesaurus is a good source of alternatives. For example, *Roget's International Thesaurus* offers these concrete alternatives for the abstract verb *increase: extend, expand, inflate, thicken, raise, boost, hike, jump, rise, shoot up.* Not all these would fit the context of *sales increase,* but a number of them would. Choose the one that best suits your subject, purpose, and audience.

Here are other examples of abstract words often used in business writing and a number of pictorial verb alternatives:

make one	meld	*reorganize*	restructure
	fuse		shake up
	solidify		realign
relate	connect	*analyze*	break down
	link		dissect
	string together		segment
exceed	surpass	*disassociate*	sever
	transcend		uncouple
	overshoot		fracture
establish	set up	*support*	bolster
	embed		buttress
	lodge		cushion

The alternatives in each group are not necessarily synonymous and interchangeable in all situations. Each carries a different shade of meaning. You must use judgment, therefore, in finding the right pictorial verb for each situation.

PINPOINT THE ACTION WITH SPECIFIC VERBS AND MODIFIERS

For many actions, the English language offers a variety of verbs to signify the degree to which the action is performed or the way it is performed. For instance, there are different ways of *descending,* such as *slip, drop, plummet, plunge, decline, slump.* Try to find the verb that most pinpoints the action.

When you don't choose verbs carefully, you may wind up using additional words to shore up a general or imprecise verb. You'll write phrases such as *the value descended sharply,* rather than *the value plummeted.* Sentences carrying extra baggage lack the snap of sentences with specific verbs without the qualifiers.

Note how the following sentences with specific verbs are livelier than those with general verbs and modifiers:

General verb and adverb: The editing changes *made* the point very *clear.*

Specific verb: The editing changes *crystallized* the point.

General verb and adverb: Negotiators *worked very hard* to settle the contract dispute.

Specific verb: Negotiators *labored* to settle the contract dispute.

General verb and adverb: Management *described in general terms* its position on maternity leaves.

Specific verb: Management *outlined* its position on maternity leaves.

To replace general verbs and modifiers with specific verbs, try saying the sentence aloud, picturing the action behind the idea, and checking a thesaurus.

SPICE UP YOUR DOCUMENTS WITH SIX LITERARY TRICKS

Besides using the best verbs, you can also add snap to your writing by sprinkling a variety of literary devices throughout your document. The devices, or writing techniques presented here might at first seem to be tools of novelists and poets. But, in fact, these devices help to enliven many business documents as well. Let's take a look.

Alliteration (power-packed)

Alliteration is repeating initial consonant (not vowel) sounds in two or more neighboring words or syllables, as in *tricks of the trade* and *wild and wooly.*

Alliteration creates a pleasing repetition and musicality that strike a responsive chord in the ear, even when read silently. Because of that audio appeal, the phrase and the idea are more likely to be grasped by the mind. Advertisers, of course, have worked this technique for years with great success. You may also see it in business documents in expressions such as:

*d*etermined *d*ecision makers	*c*ash and *c*arry
*b*uilding *b*oom	*f*ully re*f*undable
*p*erformance and *p*erspective	*t*ime-*t*ested

Using alliteration sparingly, you can highlight important points in a business document, as others have with expressions such as *a position of prominence, self-starters, and more sizzle than steak.*

Rhetorical Questions (*How did I get this great career?*)

The rhetorical question does not expect an answer. The writer supplies it. In effect, rhetorical questions are the writer's way of anticipating and acknowledging the readers' questions and addressing them. When readers sense that the writer is on the same wave length as they are, they read with greater attentiveness. Rhetorical questions should be short and direct:

How can we accomplish this?
Why is this the best alternative?

Rhetorical questions can be effective transitions, moving the reader from one major thought to the next. Place rhetorical questions at the beginning of paragraphs, or write them as headings and subheads. Instead of introducing the section with a subhead that makes a statement, ask a question. For example:

How can we offer so much for so little?
How will this affect the staff?
What is the next step?
Where has this been done before?

For more examples, scan a number of magazines. You should see many subheads written in the form of rhetorical questions.

Imagery (glass ceilings and golden parachutes)

Imagery is the term for creating images or pictures in the mind of the reader to convey an idea. People paint word pictures frequently in the course of a business day. In fact, some word pictures have been such effective and efficient transmitters of ideas, they have become clichés: *bottom line, red ink, inside track, lackluster performance, top drawer.*

Ideas can be conveyed with more snap, however, when the word pictures are fresher. For example:

> The *linchpin* in our proposal is our experience.
>
> We don't mind your *metering the flow* of information, but please don't *turn off the spigot* altogether.
>
> Too much management stability can lead to a *hardening of the business arteries.*
>
> The mainframe is the *source* for information *tributaries* throughout the system.

Earlier we saw how effective concrete verbs can be in creating images of actions. The same kind of image-making can be done with other parts of the sentence as well.

Abstract:	We can overcome the obstacles easily.
Word picture:	We can clear these *hurdles* easily.
Abstract:	The office received many applications.
Word picture:	The office received a *wave of* applications.

Picture the action behind the idea and find words to paint that picture.

Parallel Construction (systems that work and people that care)

Parallel construction is expressing related ideas in similar arrangements of words, phrases, clauses, or sentences. One of the most famous uses of parallel construction is Julius Caesar's *I came, I saw, I conquered.* Each of the three short clauses has a subject (I) and a verb.

Here's another example of parallel construction, this one using three prepositional phrases:

…government *of the people, by the people, and for the people.*

Business writers use parallel construction when they write sentences, such as:

> Do they have *the insight, the drive, and the courage to be a success?*
> We *hire the best people, pay the best salaries, and show the best results.*

Parallel construction (the phrasing is similar, or "parallel") is great for pulling key thoughts together. In addition, the faint musical aspect flowing from the repetitiveness adds to the auditory impact, which enlivens the reading.

Antithesis (*We want channeled aggressiveness, not unbridled arrogance.*)

Antithesis is expressing *contrasting* ideas in similar arrangements of words, phrases, clauses, and sentences. Antithesis is parallel construction but with a twist. It highlights opposing ideas, rather than related ideas, through the similar phrasing. Remember Marc Antony's, *I come to bury Caesar, not to praise him.* And Lincoln's: *…the world will little note nor long remember what we say here, but it can never forget what they did here.*

You might inject antithesis into a business document in this way:

> Our approach is structured, but not inflexible.
> It isn't what you know, but who you are.

The antithetical phrasing brings the two concepts into sharp contrast, making the point vividly for the audience.

Humanization of Large Numbers (*a mere pennies a day*)

Large aggregate numbers often make little impression on readers. Told, for example, that *126 million tons of garbage are generated each year,* readers may not blink an eye. The numbers may just be too large for the readers' perspective. They may respond, "Well, it's a big country." Breaking the large aggregate number to a more personal comprehensible unit, however, may have greater effect. For example:

Every man, woman, and child in this country generates three pounds of garbage a day.

Note similar differences in the use of numbers in these examples:

Aggregate:	There are 960 muggings in New York City every day.
Broken down:	In New York City, a person is mugged every 90 seconds of every day.

Aggregate:	The state could recoup $91 million with this plan.
Broken down:	The state could recoup $91 million with this plan. That could pay a year's salary for 2000 teachers or cover tuition for a year for 25,000 students at the state university.

All these literary techniques have been around for a long time and continue to be used because they work so well. You may feel a little uncomfortable with them at first. But try them and see how they help to put snap and vitality into your writing.

— Snap-in-Your-Writing Checklist —

FOCUS ON THE VERBS YOU USE.

USE ACTION VERBS, NOT VERBS OF BEING.

USE CONCRETE VERBS, NOT ABSTRACT VERBS.

USE SPECIFIC VERBS, NOT GENERAL VERBS WITH MODIFIERS.

USE ACTIVE VOICE VERBS, NOT PASSIVE VOICE VERBS.

USE LITERARY DEVICES OR TECHNIQUES:

- ❏ *Alliteration*
- ❏ *Rhetorical questions*
- ❏ *Imagery*
- ❏ *Parallel construction*
- ❏ *Antithesis*
- ❏ *Humanization of large numbers*

HOW CAN I MAKE
MY WRITING PERSUASIVE?

*Y*ou've been asked to spearhead a committee in your office dedicated to a necessary but unpopular task. How do you convince others to work with you?

Or you have researched a number of alternatives and must report on your findings. A major part of your report is your recommendation of one of those alternatives. How can you be persuasive in that recommendation?

Or you are entered in a Walk-a-thon for charity and want people in your office to support the effort with contributions. How do you persuade them to offer a dime or dollar for every mile you walk?

These and many other business tasks require more than information. They require a set of techniques that can break down resistance, enkindle an interest, and move people to action. This chapter shows you how to do that—how to persuade in writing.

FIND THE COMMON GROUND AND CREATE A WIN-WIN FRAMEWORK

The objectives of persuasion are:

☐ To get people to accept your proposition

☐ To act on it

The objectives in persuasion are the same, whether you are selling vacuum cleaners, seeking aid for orphans, or recommending the purchase of a new bookkeeping system. Read the two short requests below and decide which is more likely to persuade you to accept the proposition and act on it:

A.   So that I can process benefits claims more easily, please follow these new procedures in submitting claims:

B.   So that your benefits claims can be processed more quickly, please follow new these procedures in submitting claims:

Both statements ask the reader to do the same thing—follow the new procedures in submitting claims. But the reasons for doing so differ. Statement A says that if you follow the new procedures, you will be helping the claims administrator. Asking busy people to do more work or learn a new procedure just to help you is not likely to get a strong response—a favorable one, that is.

On the other hand, statement B says that if you follow these procedures, you will help yourself—your claims will be processed more quickly. B, then, would probably generate a more positive response because it addresses the issue *from the perspective of the reader.*

By nature we are all selfish, primarily interested in our own welfare, jobs, families. Appeal to our vanity, sense of security, desire for success, love and happiness, and you've got us in the palm of your prose.

When you want readers to accept your idea, take some action, or follow your directive, *find the slant that focuses on their self-interest.* Find the common ground, some point or element in your proposition that benefits both you and them. Highlight the benefit to them.

For instance, in persuading customers to buy a new product, would users be persuaded by your telling them of all the work that's gone into the product? Or would they want to know how it is going to make them more successful?

Here's another example. Assume an office worker wants greater job responsibility, to advance her career. Would the argument that follows persuade the supervisor to assign to her the desired responsibility?

> Now that JB has retired, I think it's time I be given the chance to take on many of his recruitment and staff development responsibilities. I believe I'm entitled to a shot because I have been in the department four years and have been doing the same job for most of that time. Having these added responsibilities is critical to my career development and ultimate advancement.

This statement gives *the writer's reasons* for wanting the added responsibilities and they probably sound persuasive to her. But we cannot expect to be given things just because we want them or feel we have a need for them. Such short-sightedness does not persuade. If, however, the writer were to try to see the situation from the reader's perspective, she might be able to find some common ground. That is, she might uncover reasons that make her proposition attractive to the reader, while satisfying her own needs. That statement might look like this:

> Since JB retired, much of his work in recruitment and staff development has fallen on your shoulders. May I suggest that I handle some of those duties for you. I have the background and, with your direction, could do a good job. You could then devote more time to the upcoming budget, without worrying about these other matters.

By finding the common ground and slanting the statement toward the needs and concerns of the supervisor, this statement creates a win-win framework. It:

❏ Shows how the supervisor's personal workload can be reduced

❏ Addresses the concern every supervisor has that the duties be placed in qualified hands

❏ Creates a mild sense of urgency by suggesting that with budget planning on the horizon, the supervisor will have even less time to handle these added responsibilities

In this statement, then, the writer has taken what she wants and phrased it in terms of what benefits the reader. Finding that common ground is the starting point in persuasion.

PLAY ON EMOTION

When focusing on the reader's concerns, consider the emotional forces driving them. For example, are your readers highly competitive leaders who cannot stand the thought of being second in anything? Or are they frustrated from being overworked and underpaid? These two audiences obviously would require two different approaches. The competitors will jump at the chance to do something if they think it will improve their standing. The frustrated, on the other hand, will do nothing unless they feel it will ease their burden.

In writing to persuade, therefore, try to determine and play on the emotion or temperament of the audience—in general, at the moment, or in regard to a particular issue. In persuading management to try a new approach to an old problem, will you be more successful appealing to their sense of pride in being innovative or to their sense of fear in being left behind by more daring competitors? In asking for donations to a charitable organization, should you appeal to your coworkers' sense of compassion or to the embarrassment they would feel in not contributing?

Let's look at an example. Assume a bookkeeping department is about to be converted to a computerized system. You are writing a memo to prepare the bookkeepers for the training they are to begin on Monday. Note how the two openings that follow differ. One takes into consideration the emotions of the bookkeepers as they approach this project. The other opener does not. Which will be more persuasive in getting the readers to accept the new system and to adopt it willingly?

A.   Training for the conversion to our computerized bookkeeping operation begins on Monday. These sessions will enable you to learn how to use the computer efficiently and effectively, with a minimum of error and lost time in the transition. Please be prepared to devote a full four hours a day to this training over the next two weeks.

B.   As you know, the bookkeeping department will convert from a manual to an automated system at the end of this month. Some of you have expressed concerns about being able to learn the new system. Let me put those fears to rest. Once you've gone through the training and have worked with computers for a few weeks, you will never want to go back to the old system.

Training for the conversion to our computerized bookkeeping operation begins on Monday...

The first opening makes no attempt to assuage the fears the bookkeepers could be expected to have. The impersonality of this memo would probably reinforce those fears. People in that emotional state are not about to buy into anything. They will approach the training apprehensively, perhaps even with strong resistance. The second opening, on the other hand, appeals to the emotions of the readers. By addressing their fears, the opening channels the feelings of the readers toward the writer's purpose—preparing people for the training. Playing on the emotions of the readers, the writer has a greater chance of persuading them to accept the idea of the new system and to throw themselves heartily into the training.

Here are two more examples. In both cases the writer *does* appeal to the emotions of the audience. But in each case the appeal is different.

A.   Here at Scintillating Services, we have always tried to maintain a pleasant working environment, the kind that professionals deserve. That environment, however, has been upset by the untidy conditions in the office kitchen. I realize that in the rush of our work we may forget to wipe up a spill, but that sort of thing has been happening too much lately. May I call upon your professionalism and sense of fairness to others to clean up after yourself in the kitchen.

B.   Here at Scintillating Services, we have always tried to maintain a pleasant working environment. But that environment has been upset by the untidy conditions in the office kitchen. If people don't do a much better job of cleaning up after themselves, we'll just have to close the kitchen and turn it into a storage closet. The choice is yours.

Memo A appeals to the professionalism of the readers, while memo B appeals to baser emotions. We cannot say one is instrinsically more persuasive than the other. An appeal to professionalism may persuade some readers; an appeal to people's fear of losing something or their desire to keep it may be needed in others.

SUPPORT THE APPEAL WITH CONCRETE EVIDENCE

Although persuasion relies heavily on emotional appeal, the writer must support that appeal with evidence to the intellect—accurate facts, sound reasoning, examples, and details. Opinions, too, can be persuasive evidence, but they must be based on logic and supported by facts, testimony, and other details.

For example, in a report advocating a particular action for the department, the writer might provide the following evidence:

- ❏ A list of advantages of the action
- ❏ Names of competitors employing the action
- ❏ A cost-benefit analysis

This type of information might be considered "hard" evidence, quantifiable data and verifiable facts. Hard evidence is generally the most persuasive. If, however, your evidence is not "hard," show thoroughness and logic in making your case. For example, if you are trying to persuade someone that you should be given a particular project though you've had no experience in that area, you may:

- ❏ Explain in detail your understanding of the project
- ❏ Show how your experience, though unrelated, has prepared you for this project
- ❏ Itemize skills that you have developed elsewhere that are needed on this project

In other words, though you cannot give quantified data or verifiable facts to support your position, present an argument that is based in logic. If, for example, your claim is that *our scintillator is the best on the market,* you cannot support that claim by saying *it is better than all the others.* That's double talk. The statement merely restates the claim. A more logical process might state that you use the best materials available in producing your scintillator, have thoroughly researched it, and have tested it in twenty states. This kind of evidence is not hard, such as a feature-by-feature comparison against competing scintillators would be. But it does have a logical base. People can accept a lack of hard evidence in certain situations. They are not likely, however, to accept your simply playing word games with them. That may work in mass market consumer advertising, but it hardly works with seasoned business people.

SEQUENCE THE MATERIAL TO MEET THE NEEDS OF YOUR AUDIENCE

What might the most suitable order be? It is the one that works best for this audience with this subject at this time. Generally, a persuasive document might follow this pattern:

1. Alert readers to a need or appeal to their emotions, or both.

2. State your proposition, make your request.

3. Present an argument or piece of evidence readers are most likely to agree with.

4. Proceed to more difficult points.

5. Make a call for action.

Let's look at each of these elements because there is flexibility in this order.

(1) THE HOOK

Elsewhere in this book we suggest that business documents begin with a clear statement of purpose. We have said that in starting a memo or letter, for example, you identify your subject in the first paragraph and state clearly the reason for which you are writing. That recommendation may still hold in some kinds of persuasive writing, but very often it may not. You may need to "hook" the readers first, before letting them know what you want from them. In such cases, hold off your proposition or request until you have drawn them in and whet their appetite by addressing their needs and making an appeal to their emotion.

(2) The Proposition

You may want to state your proposition or make your request at this point in the document. Having drawn the reader in by addressing his needs and playing to his emotions, you may assume he's ready to hear your proposal. State it and proceed into the evidence.

You may, however, want to hold off stating your request or proposition until *after* you have given all or at least some of your evidence. In some situations you may feel the reader will "turn off" too quickly if you state your request or proposition here. You may want to "give him a little more line" to make sure he's securely on the hook. In such cases, state your claim later in the piece.

(3) The Evidence

Remember that in persuasion you are often trying to break down resistance. That's tough to do if right out of the blocks you begin with the point your audience is most resistant to. You may have more success beginning with an argument the reader is most likely to agree with. It may not be the most important point you want to make, but if it gets him saying, "OK, I can go along with that," you are breaking down that resistance, putting him in a frame of mind that will keep him reading.

(4) The Clincher

If the reader has stayed with you this far, he's interested. Now you can broach the more difficult points, the arguments he is likely to resist most strongly. For example, assume you are proposing a new approach to an office procedure. You anticipate your boss's objections will be the following:

Any change that costs money is out of the question

Don't fix what's not broken

People have trouble adapting to change

Change means delays and we can't afford delays

Of these objections, which is the boss most adamant about? If it's cost, then in addressing his anticipated objections, you might do well to leave the cost issue to last. In other words, until now you may have been feeding the reader information he finds very palatable. Now, however, you introduce the parts about his giving up something to get all the things you've promised. As in all writing, persuasion requires knowledge of the reader. Anticipate how your reader will react to each point and position your information accordingly.

(5) THE CALL FOR ACTION

Do not overlook the call for action. Never assume readers will do what you want without your explicitly asking. "Tip" O'Neill, who spent his entire adult life in the U. S. Congress, said that no matter how close people are to you, they still expect you to *ask* for their vote. This point is so much more true when you are trying to persuade someone to act on your recommendation, make a purchase from you, or contribute to your charity.

ADOPT A TONE SUITABLE TO YOUR AUDIENCE AND YOUR MESSAGE

Tone is that intangible in a piece of writing that conveys your attitude toward your readers and your subject. Tone in business documents can range from authoritative to friendly to alarming. The tone you convey should, of course, vary with your audience and message. Earlier we saw two memos regarding the conditions in the office kitchen. The tone in the memo appealing to the professionalism of the group might be called *conciliatory;* the tone of the other might be considered *scolding* or even *threatening.*

How do you achieve tone? Certainly the things you say will affect tone. To say, for example, *if you don't pick up after yourself we will close the kitchen* no doubt conveys an authoritative, even scolding tone.

Your choice of words, too, can convey tone. Note, for example, the difference in tone caused by a single word change in the following sentences:

This was a *bold* decision on the part of management.

This was an *innovative* decision on the part of management.

This was an *unusual* decision on the part of management.

The word *bold* in the first sentence carries an excited tone. At the other end, the third sentence carries a matter-of-fact tone, because of the word *unusual*. The middle sentence is somewhere in between in tone, because of the word *innovative*, which is stronger than *unusual* but less charged than *bold*.

When focusing on tone, be careful not to overdo it. If, for example, you are making an appeal for donations to an orphan's fund and describing the plight of the children, don't set such a depressing tone that people will stop reading. If you want to set a friendly, lighthearted tone, don't be so lighthearted that readers see it as phony and cut you off. In setting the tone for a document, you want, above all, to come across as trustworthy. If you go to any extreme, readers will discredit you and turn a deaf ear to your pleas.

POLISH MAKES PERFECT: REVISE AND REWRITE

Persuasive writing usually requires that you pull out all the stops. Examine the document and revise it for sentence clarity, thought development, transitions, and choice of words. Use literary devices, visual cues, and strong action verbs. (Each of these elements is treated elsewhere in the book.) In short, because persuasion is one of the most difficult forms of writing, you must use the full arsenal of weapons available to you.

— MODEL PERSUASIVE PIECE —

Situation: The hospital has had a shortage of nurses, creating complaints of too many patients per nurse and too much overtime. The purpose of this memo is to persuade nurses to get involved in a new recruitment program.

reader's needs	When was the last time you had two consecutive days off? Or spent an entire holiday with your family? Double shifts and overtime have raised everyone's frustration level to intolerable heights.
appeal to emotion; tone	While these conditions have caused others to bolt for greener pastures, you have stayed on the front line, diligently delivering top-notch professional care. And I appreciate that.
subhead	*Help Is on the Way*
hard evidence	We finally have approval for a recruitment plan that I think will work, that will enable you to work a more humane schedule again. It's called Front Line. It's been used in many hospitals like ours. In 92 percent of those, Front Line has generated at least 50 percent increase in recruitment. In only six months!
reader's needs *visual cues*	Front Line works because it's nurses recruiting nurses. Now wait. Before you start screaming, hear me out. You're probably saying, "I'm overworked now and you want more time from me!" **No, we're not asking you for more time.**
	Here's the Offer
highlight key points	1) If you become involved in Front Line you will not be asked to work any overtime you do not choose to work.
	2) You will be paid at your regular rate for every hour you devote to Front Line.
	What's to Gain?
proposition	If you're close to burn-out and think something has to be done to get more help, come to the information meeting to get details on Front Line. By coming to the meeting you are not committing to anything.
common ground	But we think you'll see Front Line as the way to make nursing at GH a truly professional experience. You have nothing to lose and much to gain—like some **weekends off.**
call for action	To learn more about how Front Line can make your life more livable, please sign your name on the attached sheet indicating the information session you will attend.

— Persuasion Checklist —

FIND THE COMMON GROUND BETWEEN YOUR OFFER AND THE READER'S NEEDS.

APPEAL TO THE READER'S EMOTIONS.

PRESENT EVIDENCE TO THE INTELLECT.

PRESENT THE MATERIAL IN THE MOST SUITABLE ORDER.

ADOPT A SUITABLE TONE.

USE ALL THE TECHNIQUES FOR BEING CLEAR, INTERESTING, AND FORCEFUL.

How Do I Make
the Tone Of My Writing
Work for Me?

*Y*ou are writing to a manager in another department to complain about that department's delaying delivery of your staff's reports. Because the manager is a "colleague," you do not want to be abrasive. Still, you want to let him know you are not happy and want to see a change.

Or you are writing a thank you memo to your staff for a beyond-the-call-of-duty effort. How do you phrase the memo to convey your feelings without sounding maudlin?

Or you are writing to a group of staff members to respond to a proposal they have made. You have many good reasons for rejecting the proposal, but you don't want to crush the initiative of the writers. How do you give the reasons for your rejection without coming across as dogmatic?

In each of these writing situations, and in many others, you would be concerned with tone. Let's examine what tone is and how to use it to your advantage.

TONE: THE "BODY LANGUAGE" OF WHAT YOU WRITE AND SAY

Tone is an aspect of writing or speech that is easier to identify than define, as is evident in the following dialogue:

"Why are you so upset? What did she say?"

"It isn't so much what she said but how she said it."

Tone rings loudly in speech. We know almost at an instant when a speaker is being sarcastic, condescending, enthusiastic, or hostile. We do not even have to see the speaker's face to detect tone. Over the phone we can identify the speaker's level of formality or informality, her sincerity or lack of it. The tone comes through clearly in the person's voice. Even using the same words we can convey different tones. Think, for example, of:

Good morning.	(said *matter-of-factly* in a simple greeting to a stranger in the elevator)
Good morning.	(said *sarcastically* to the employee who arrives for work an hour late)
Good morning?	(said *angrily* in response to the greeting of the teenage child who was brought home by police the night before)

Though the words remain the same, the tone changes. And as the tone changes, so does the meaning. For example, the meaning behind the sarcastic "Good morning" is: "You're late. It's almost noon." The meaning behind the irate parent's "Good morning?" is: "What's good about it? How do you have the nerve to say 'good morning' after that stunt you pulled last night?"

As in speaking, tone permeates writing. For example:

Hostile:	No one can tell me that people who work at home—so-called telecommuters—put in a full day's work. I may have been born at night but it wasn't last night.
Friendly:	I have my doubts, Jack, about telecommuting. I just find it hard to believe that people will put in a full day's work. Doesn't it seem contrary to human nature not to slack off even some?

Impersonal:	The issue of casual dress has been brought to my attention and has received my careful thought. At this time, however, this practice of casual dress seems inappropriate for this office and has been rejected as an option.
Personal:	I've considered your request for permission to dress casually in the office. After thinking about it carefully, I have to say No at this time. I think casual dress would be inappropriate for us right now. Sorry, guys.
Indifferent:	If, after you have read our proposal to outsource your mail room operations, you would like to discuss it further, you can reach us at (289) 555–1234.
Enthusiastic:	We hope that after reading our proposal you will agree that we are the firm to run your mail room operations for you. We are eager to meet with you personally to discuss further how we might meet your outsourcing needs.

Just about any emotion that a writer feels can creep into the document—anger, fear, confidence, whimsy, sincerity, warmth, bitterness, respect, admiration, strength, weakness, enthusiasm, indifference. Any attitude the writer has toward the subject or the reader can come across—deliberately or inadvertently. Therefore, tone can strengthen your message or sabotage it.

HOW TO ACHIEVE RESULTS BY PUTTING THE RIGHT TONE INTO ALL YOUR COMMUNICATIONS

Writers have to be conscious of tone for two principal reasons. First, the wrong tone can alienate or confuse the reader. For instance, if you take a whimsical tone in a letter or memo by beginning with a harmless joke, your readers may misread the joke and take you seriously. Or your readers may think you are a bit too cavalier about a serious subject. Or what you think is humorous may be perceived as sarcasm and therefore backfire on you.

Second, if you capture the right tone, you have another weapon working for you—the power of the emotional push. Particularly when you want to persuade, an appeal to the emotions can reinforce a logical presentation to the intellect. The right tone can strengthen that emotional appeal.

How to Control Tone

To put tone to work for you and to prevent its inadvertently undermining your efforts, you have to control it. You control tone in writing primarily by making judicious choices in words, sentence structure, and figurative language. Content, of course, enters into tone, but writers often modify what they write after they have taken a look at the way it reads. In other words, the ideas may change somewhat after the writer realizes the tone of those on the paper is inaccurate or inappropriate. At that point they make changes in wording and sentence structures, which often lead to changes in content as well.

Let's look at each of these main ingredients of tone.

Word Choice

The words you use do much to establish your tone. For example, note how the same message carries a different tone in the two sentences that follow simply because of a change in the words used.

> *Formal:*   Enclosed please find the report requested by your office.
>
> *Informal:*   Here's the report you asked for.

The second sentence is more informal because of its more conversational language. The contraction *here's* is certainly more conversational than *enclosed please find.* And *you asked for* is more conversational and informal than *requested by your office.* Pronouns also help to create a more informal, more personal tone. The change from *your office* to *you* personalizes the tone greatly.

In presenting these pairs of sentences, we are not suggesting that one tone is better than the other. The writer has to decide the appropriate tone in each situation. Here's another pair of examples showing two different tones:

> *Authoritative:*   To achieve this quarter's sales goals, I expect each sales rep to set and meet a daily quota.
>
> *Modest:*   To achieve this quarter's sales goals, it might be a good idea for each sales rep to set and meet a daily quota.

The switch from *I expect* to *it might be a good idea* changes the tone. The shift here is from an almost demanding tone to one of strong urging.

The change in tone reflects a change in the attitude the writer wishes to convey to the readers. But that in fact is what tone does—it conveys attitude. Identifying the tone in your writing can help you identify the attitude you are showing to your readers. You can then decide if that is the attitude you want to express. In modifying the attitude through the tone, you will often change the content as well.

Here's another example:

Bitter:	Obviously, you just cannot do the job I expected from you.
Disappointed:	I'm sorry things did not work out the way we had hoped.

You might be hard-pressed to objectively determine when the bitter tone would be more effective in the situation created in this pair of sentences. But this pair shows that the things we write in haste or in a fit of anger may well be written another way, if we choose to. So before mailing that "clears-the-air" letter, cool off a bit, reread it, and check the tone. You may want to soften it some while still making your basic point.

SENTENCE STRUCTURE

Longer, complicated sentences generally convey a formal, impersonal tone, unless, of course, the words used are heavily conversational.

Formal:	Given the situation the company is in regarding the drop in sales and our escalating costs, it is imperative that costs savings be sought by each department.
Informal:	The company is facing a drop in sales and escalating costs. So each department should be looking for cost savings.

The second passage carries a less formal tone because it is in two shorter sentences rather than one longer one. Shorter sentences are more direct and have less formality about them. In addition to length, there is a change in the voice of the verbs. The formal passage uses the passive voice: *cost savings should be sought by each department.* The revision uses the active voice: *each department should be looking for cost savings.* The active voice usually creates a more informal tone than the passive.

Besides lending a note of informality, shorter, clipped sentences can inject an angry tone into a piece of writing. For example:

Controlled:	We cannot tolerate this situation, and we expect that you will see that the situation does not happen again.
Angry:	We cannot tolerate this situation. See that it does not happen again.

Freshen Your Writing with Figurative Language

Most business writing is literal, even abstract. When a writer uses figures of speech, she injects a freshness that can carry an air of confidence and an enthusiastic tone. For example:

Literal:	We may have a significant opportunity before us, but it will exist for only a short time.
Figurative:	We have before us a window of opportunity that will close very quickly.
Literal:	Our publication gives you information on the major companies in your industry.
Figurative:	Our publication takes you inside the major companies in your industry.

Figures of speech add color to writing and make reading easier, more enjoyable, and therefore more comprehensible. For many situations there is different figurative language to convey different tones. For example, note how the writer's attitude toward the subject's work ethic changes with the change in the figure of speech:

Critical:	She buries herself in her work.
Approving:	She has a no-holds-barred attitude toward her work.

In the following pair, the change in figurative language intensifies a disapproving attitude:

Mildly Disapproving:	He comes to the company with a somewhat checkered record.
Caustic:	A graph of his success and failures would look like an erratic cardiogram.

— TYPES OF TONE —

INFORMAL

informal metaphors conversational

active voice

short sentences personal pronouns

Sales reps today are of a different breed. If we are going to keep the good ones, we are going to have to work harder at it. This may mean abandoning some sacred cows and trying some fresh ideas. For instance, we might try some innovative compensation packages to keep people tied to the organization. Commission as we know it may give way to income based on overall account profitability. Or we may want to look at a "total service" format and base compensation on some team success formula. Things are changing and we have to change with them. Our products and services are different. Our customers are different. So our delivery has to be different. And our incentives to sales reps must be different.

FORMAL

less
conversational

passive
voice
long
sentences

no figures
of speech
fewer
personal
pronouns

It is necessary for the organization to work more diligently at retention of essential sales representatives, and as a result innovative compensation packages will have to be developed to retain quality representatives in the organization. Compensation packages may have to be modified radically, changing them from the traditional percentage of commission revenue to perhaps an overall account profitability-based package because of the differences in the kinds of products and services offered by the company and because of the changes in the clientele the registered sales representative will be required to deal with. In addition, the differences in the sales representatives themselves warrant experimentation to accommodate their attitudes, work ethic, and life-styles. It has been suggested that a team concept of compensation be experimented with for the promotion of a "total service" format.

HOSTILE

We've been getting a lot of flak about reports not getting to people when they need them. We're trying to do a job here but your people are getting in the way. They're creating a bottleneck. All you guys have to do is record and copy these reports and ship them along. I can't see why that should take so long! Let's get the lead out.

CONTROLLED

We've received some criticism about our reports not reaching their users on time. Since these reports go through your department to our users, I was hoping we could identify the problem and resolve it.

Currently it takes two days for reports to get from us through you to the users. Is it possible to reduce this transit time? Is there anything we can do to facilitate speedier handling in your department? Please call me to discuss this issue.

— Tone Checklist —

USE TONE TO CONVEY ATTITUDE TOWARD YOUR AUDIENCE AND SUBJECT.

CONTROL TONE SO IT WORKS TO YOUR ADVANTAGE AND PREVENT IT FROM INADVERTENTLY CONVEYING THE WRONG ATTITUDE.

CONTROL TONE THROUGH WORD CHOICES, SENTENCE STRUCTURE, SENTENCE LENGTH, USE OF ACTIVE AND PASSIVE VOICE, AND FIGURATIVE LANGUAGE.

IS MY WRITING READABLE?

You work pretty much alone and don't have anyone to critique your writing for you. What you write makes sense to you, but you're not sure someone else will be able to read it.

Or your supervisor has returned your report to you with the vague comment, "Too tough to read." How do you go about making such a document more readable when to you it already flows like silk off a spool?

This chapter will show you how to measure readability and identify potential readability problems. Knowing the symptoms of muddled writing, you can then apply techniques that lead to clear, readable prose.

Readability: The Key to Effective Writing

Readability is the ease with which a person can read and comprehend a piece of written material. There are two key words in that definition—*ease* and *comprehend.*

Is it your job as a writer to make it easy for someone to read what you write? It is, if you want that reader to respond in a particular way. When you consider how crowded the day is for most businesspeople, you realize that they don't want to spend any more time than necessary reading your memos or reports. When you think about all the paper that floats across the average desk every business day, you know why people appreciate written material that's easy to read. They may not all realize that one document is easier to read than another, but even unaware of the difference, people usually respond more quickly to a document that's easy to read. Their unconscious "thank you" will come in the form of a quick response to those more readable documents. On the other hand, documents that are difficult to read are often put aside for "later, when I have more time."

Besides ease of reading, an effective document is comprehended on the first reading. Readers should not have to pore over a business letter or report as if it were written in hieroglyphics. They should be able to read it much as they do a newspaper, drawing the key ideas and important details on the first read.

Check Your Readability Quotient: The Fog Index

In the late 1940s Robert Gunning created his Fog Index, which is still a reliable and easy-to-use method for determining the level of readability of your memos, letters, reports, and other business writing. To calculate the level of fog or incomprehensibility in your writing, follow these three steps:

1. Count the *total number of words* in the document (or in a few passages of about 100 words in a longer document). Exclude proper nouns from the count.

2. Count the *number of sentences* and divide the number of words by the number of sentences to get the *average sentence length.*

3. Count the *number of long words* (three or more syllables), and divide by the total number of words in the passage, to achieve the *percentage of long words.*

(Do not consider as long words combinations of easy words, such as *noteworthy,* or words made into three syllables by the addition of a suffix such as *-er* or *-ing,* like *defender* and *rewarding.*)

4. Add the average sentence length and the percentage of long words. Multiply the sum by 0.4 to attain *your readability score.*

For example:

Step 1:

$$\frac{\text{Total words}}{\text{Total sentences}} = \text{Average sentence length}$$

$$\frac{100}{5} = 20$$

Step 2:

$$\frac{\text{Total long words}}{\text{Total words}} = \text{Percentage of long words}$$

$$\frac{16}{100} = .16$$

Step 3:

Average sentence length
+ Percentage of long words (drop the decimal point)
_____

Sum
× 0.4
_____

Readability score

20
+ 16 (drop the decimal point)
____

36
× 0.4
____

14.4

WHAT'S THE SCORE?

Once you have the score, what does it mean? It means that the higher the score, the more difficulty one might have in reading the document.

What is an acceptable score? Gunning recommends we shoot for 12. He arrived at 12 by applying his formula to excerpts from a number of popular magazines. He found that no popular magazine had a Fog Index score much above 12. The conclusion is that, given a choice, people won't read anything higher than 12 on the Fog Index.

The results of Gunning's study looked like this:

Fog Index	Magazine
17	
16	
15	(no popular magazine)
14	
13	

Danger Line for Readability	
12	*Atlantic Monthly*
	Harper's
11	*Time, Newsweek*

Easy Reading Below This Line	
10	*Reader's Digest*
9	*Saturday Evening Post*
8	*Ladies Home Journal*
7	*True Confessions*
6	Comics

Source: Robert Gunning, *The Technique of Clear Writing,* McGraw Hill, 1952, 1968, p. 40.

While *True Confessions* and *Reader's Digest* my be beneath the level of the people you write to, realize that *Atlantic Monthly* and *Harper's* are rather sophisticated publications. And remember that Gunning conducted his research some forty years ago. Since then we have become a more visually oriented society. Compare the look of a newspaper today to its counterpart of forty years ago. You will see more color, artwork, headings, and even white space today. In keeping with that "reader-friendly" trend, publishers are insisting on simpler writing styles as well. Though the general population is better educated today, the readability level in most publications is lower than it was forty years ago.

APPLYING THE FORMULA

Take a few minutes now to apply the Gunning formula to the following passage or to a document of your own.

> It is necessary for the organization to work more diligently at the retention of essential personnel and sales representatives, and innovative compensation packages will have to be developed to retain quality people and tie them more to the organization. In line with that innovation, compensation packages may have to be modified radically, changing them from the traditional percentage of commission revenue to perhaps a package based on overall account profitability because of the differences in the kinds of new products and services offered by the company and because of the changes in the kinds of clientele the registered sales representative will be required to deal with. It has been suggested that a team concept of compensation be experimented with for the promotion of a "total service" format.

This passage is typical of the kind of writing found in many business documents. Its Fog Index score is quite high, around 26. Now you may say you didn't have that much trouble reading the document. Perhaps you are an exceptionally good reader. But would you have more trouble with it if the passage were in a document surrounded by many paragraphs written in the same way? That is, in isolation a passage like this may be easier to read than its Fog Index would indicate.

DIAGNOSING THE PROBLEM. In reviewing the calculation, you can quickly determine the primary culprit causing the high fog—long sentences. The 127-word passage has only three sentences, for an average sentence length of 42.3.

So if the writer wanted to improve the readability of this passage, the first thing he or she could do would be to cut the length of the sentences. Problem No. 23 shows you how to do that. The point here is that by calculating the Fog, you can see if readability is going to be a problem, and if it is, you have a start in determining the causes of the problem.

SIMPLIFY TO MAKE YOUR WRITING READABLE AND PROFESSIONAL

Some people at first balk at the suggestion that they deliberately work toward simplifying material for their readers. *"The people I write to,"* they say, *"are all well-educated professionals. If I do what you suggest, I'd be condescending, writing down to these people. The writing would sound childish."*

Their argument is valid, up to a point. It doesn't take a rocket scientist to realize that you can achieve a very low Fog Index score by writing in four-word sentences with all one-syllable words. That kind of writing *would be* childish and a tedious distraction to an adult reader. But business prose written at a Fog Index of around 12 is not childish, does not write down to adults, and will not be unprofessional. To prove the point, read the following passage:

> The organization should work more diligently to retain key personnel and sales representatives. We will need to develop innovative compensation packages to retain quality people and tie them more to the organization. We may have to modify compensation packages radically, changing them from the traditional percentage of commission revenue to perhaps a package based on overall account profitability. This change is needed because of the differences in the kinds of new products and services offered by the company. Changes in the kinds of clientele the registered sales representative must deal with also demand this change. We suggest that a team concept of compensation be tried to promote a "total service" format.

Does this passage sound any less professional than the original? Hardly. In fact, most readers think its clarity makes it appear even more professional than the original. What's the readability level on this passage? About 15. That's not the 12 we shoot for, but it's much better than the 23 of the original. The reduction in fog from 23 to 15 was accomplished largely by working on the biggest problem in the original—average sentence length. That was cut from 42 to 18. The shorter sentences help stress ideas, raising comprehension on the first read. The revision also has somewhat fewer long words—seven fewer. Neither change, however, makes the writing seem childish or unprofessional.

If you still have doubts about the professional tone of business documents written at a Fog Index of around 12, apply the formula to passages from leading business publications such as *The Wall Street Journal, Forbes,* and *Fortune.* See for yourself that these important publications strive to keep their fog low and readability high. And these are prestigious publications directed at the most sophisticated people in business. If these publications achieve high readability without writing down to their readers, couldn't you try to do the same?

Begin with the Fog Index

As we said earlier, a low Fog Index score does not necessarily result in an effective document. Other chapters in this book point out the many elements that must be married together to produce a document that is clear and forceful. But measuring the readability of your writing is a good place to start.

If you are not satisfied with a document but don't know why, check its readability. If the fog is high, you can work on long sentences and words to improve readability. If the document has a readability of around 12, then you know you must look elsewhere—perhaps to organization, thought development, continuity, for example—to find the source of the problem.

— Readability Checklist —

WHEN A DOCUMENT DOES NOT CONVEY WHAT YOU WANT, TEST ITS READABILITY:

- ☐ *Count the total number of words, excluding proper nouns.*

- ☐ *Count the number of sentences and divide that number into the total number of words to get the average sentence length.*

- ☐ *Count the number of long words (three or more syllables), and divide by the total number of words in the passage, to achieve the percentage of long words. (Do not consider as long words combinations of easy words, such as* noteworthy *or words made into three syllables by the addition of a suffix such as* -er *or* -ing, *like* defender *and* rewarding.

- ☐ *Add the average sentence length and the percentage of long words. Multiply the sum by 0.4 to arrive at your readability or Fog Index score.*

STRIVE FOR A FOG INDEX SCORE AROUND 12.

WITH A MUCH HIGHER SCORE, DETERMINE THE CAUSE— HIGH AVERAGE SENTENCE LENGTH OR PERCENTAGE OF LONG WORDS, OR BOTH.

Part 3

REVISING FOR CORRECTNESS, PRECISION, AND VISUAL APPEAL

HOW EXACTLY
DO I REVISE?

You've just finished a short report and are pleased with it. But a little voice tells you to revise it. "I've run it through spell-check; I've checked the grammar," you respond. "Isn't that enough?" "No," the voice answers. "What more do you want from me?" you cry out in despair.

REVISION: THE VITAL LAST STEP

Revision is much more than a cosmetic make-over. It is that step in the writing process that makes the document comprehensible. It's through an intensive revision that you bring clarity out of chaos, that you convert what *you* understand into language someone else can understand.

Many people do not like to revise. Some feel they should "get it right" the first time, but that's asking too much. Writing is such a dynamic process, with so much running through your mind as you write, it's impossible to weigh all the variables of content and expression simultaneously. So, instead of considering revision as "doing it over," look upon revision as the final but critical phase in a multiphase process.

FIRST YOU WRITE FOR YOURSELF

In the first phase of writing you gather material, jotting down notes, brainstorming on paper, and collecting information and thoughts on the topic. You are trying to learn as much as you can about the topic. Next, you try to organize what you have into some manageable form, some scheme that will enable you to make the key points. So you outline the material, weighing which information to include or exclude, which details to use in supporting your points, where to place the major concepts and primary ideas.

Then you start putting your ideas into sentences and paragraphs. You try to stick to the outline but as you write, new thoughts creep into your head and onto the paper. Supporting information that seemed so solid before now seems like a weak reed. What seemed like a logical connection before, now seems disjointed. So you make adjustments and plod on, sentence after sentence, wrestling with the elusive ideas, trying to make one fluid stream of thoughts from the jumble of data you had collected. You are quite surprised that the document presents such a struggle, since you knew the material very well before you started—or thought you did. Finally, though, it's finished.

Well, at least the first draft is finished. At least, you have taken a first cut at making a statement. To this point you have been focusing on the content, on the information you want to convey. To a great extent, you have been learning more about the subject as you write. In that sense the first draft is for *your* benefit, not the reader's. The first draft, then, is like the orator's rehearsal, an attempt to get the thoughts and words out in the open, to hear what they sound like, while there's still time to make adjustments.

THEN YOU REVISE FOR YOUR READER

In succeeding drafts—there may be more than one—you revise. That is, you look at your document critically. You evaluate the strength of your arguments. You challenge the validity of your statements. You try to decide if the document says what you wanted to say. And if it does not, is that statement better than what you had originally intended?

In critiquing the document you try to be objective, to view it as if someone else had written it. You try to base your evaluation on only what's on the paper, without allowing all that you know about the topic to shore up what the reader will see—the words on the paper.

First, Massage the Content

You make the adjustments called for by your challenges and findings. *You add, delete, modify, move things around.* Then you take another look at the whole document. Now, instead of looking at it from your point of view, from what you were trying to say, you look at it *from the reader's point of view.* You repeatedly ask: "Will my readers understand this point? Is this a good example to illustrate this idea to them? Will they need more details to understand this idea?" In other words, your focus has now shifted to the reader. You are reader oriented now, determining if the paper offers just what the reader needs and wants to know.

Then, Tweak the Expression

Notice that until now we've said nothing about expression. We've focused strictly on content, because content is the writer's first concern. Once you are pretty much settled on the content, you can move on to expression. Systematically test each section, each paragraph, each sentence against the standards of good writing that you want to practice. Look to see, for instance, that each paragraph has a good topic sentence and that all supporting sentences relate directly to it. Look for and insert transitions, so your reader can easily move with you from sentence to sentence and from paragraph to paragraph.

Then narrow your focus and look at each sentence, particularly those that seem long or read somewhat awkwardly. Check to see if you should split some of these in two, if you can cut out unnecessary words, change passive voice verbs to active, and replace clichés, jargon, and grandiloquent wording with fresher, more conversational language.

In addition to clarity issues, look for opportunities to enliven the writing with imagery, rhetorical questions, comparisons and allusions, a neat turn of a phrase. In other words, draw on your full repertoire to make the writing as interesting and entertaining as possible.

Next, put on your grammarian's cap and test your sentences for fragments, run-ons, subject-verb agreement, misplaced parts, and other grammatical elements that you might have a tendency to ignore from time to time.

(All of these issues are treated at length in other chapters. If you need help, turn to those chapters.)

In revising, don't overlook the larger elements. That is, give some attention to titles, headings, and subheads. Writers who have labored over a document for days often find upon publication spelling errors in the title of the report or in company names. Or they realize that captions have been misplaced under pictures or charts. Working so hard on the "little stuff," we can easily miss errors in the areas one would think are "so obvious."

Besides looking for errors, try to energize your headings and subheads by injecting verbs and other meaningful words into them. For example, instead of just "Recommendation," write "Recommendation: Make the Move." Have your headings and subheads act like headlines in a newspaper, giving the essence of the information that follows, so readers have a good idea of what they will be reading even before they read it.

In addition, double-check the data and appearance of your charts, tables, graphs and other visual aids. Very often these are the first thing readers go to, so you want to make these as powerful as possible, a draw to the text in your document.

Last, step back and look at the physical appearance of the document. Does it say "professional"? Does it look inviting and easy to read? Wide margins, white space between sections, crisp typeface, plenty of visual cues make a document appealing, whereas too much type on a page without visible breaks can be daunting. Make comprehension easier by highlighting important points with boldface, underlining, bullets, and other visual cues.

GOOD WRITING IS GOOD REVISING

Revision may seem like a lot of work and it is. But revision is important work and it can be more creative than it appears. If you consider it an integral part of the writing process, not a remedial chore, you can get as much satisfaction from revision as from your original draft.

How well you revise can be the difference between rave reviews and a ho-hum response. Some of that difference comes from knowing what to look for. The novice auto mechanic, for instance, who looks under the hood and waits for the "problem" to show itself is no match for the veteran who diagnoses problems from a list of potential trouble items. Similarly, working from the Revision Checklist in this chapter, you can systematically look for potential problem areas and make changes as needed.

Further, some of the difference between a meaningful revision and a cosmetic make-over results from attitude. Just as one homeowner simply puts on a coat of paint while another repairs and renovates, one writer may just "run it through spell-check" while another actually revises. Cosmetic changes in writing, like paint, cannot cover up a crumbling structure.

— SAMPLE REVISED DOCUMENT—

stronger
verb

fan

Begin with people you work with and then ~~move~~ outward to colleagues, friends, and others. Ask not only for information on the topic but also for suggestions as to where you might look for it. Conversations may not always give you the information you are looking for, but they often open up new areas of thought you had not considered.

head changes   ‖ Review Company Do*c*ments.

memos, letters,

spelling

Check your company files. Consider /proposlas, projects, reports, and any other types of documents your company might keep. Cross-reference the files, looking under names of

delete

companies, industry, names of individuals. ~~If your company keeps a file of proportional materials, you might look there too.~~

modify

those   *try to track down*

Should you find anything in ~~your company files, look for the~~ *associated with the subject*
~~names of~~ individuals wh~~o might still be with the company who can~~
~~add to what you find in the files.~~ You might get

spelling
add

lucky and unco*v*er someone in another office who has extensive knowledge of the company or topic you are researching.

move,
transition

for

In contacting some of the ot~~d~~ur sources listed below, in ~~addition to the printed~~ material, ~~they may send~~ you, you can often get a wealth of information from a conversation with

add

people in those offices. *That is, in asking a company librarian for an annual report, you may also get some useful background information in a conversation with that librarian. In other words, do not overlook the channel of information as a possible source.*

When it comes to research, there's no sense hacking through forests of data when someone has already cut a path to what you need.

— Revision Checklist —

Beginning

HOOK THE READER:

- ❐ *Create a sense of urgency.*
- ❐ *Focus on reader needs.*
- ❐ *Use imaginative leads.*

IDENTIFY SUBJECT AND PURPOSE:

- ❐ *Answer the reader's question, "Why am I reading this?*

Middle

CONTENT:

- ❐ *Focus on the central theme throughout.*
- ❐ *Include the most appropriate information.*

ORDER:

- ❐ *Flow from intro.*
- ❐ *Put information in the best order.*
- ❐ *Guide reader from point to point.*

Ending

IMPACT:

- ❐ *Reinforce key idea.*
- ❐ *Give significance.*
- ❐ *Make call for action.*
- ❐ *Convey feeling of writer.*

Paragraphing

USE TOPIC SENTENCES.

DEVELOP ONE IDEA PER PARAGRAPH.

PROVIDE TRANSITIONS WITHIN AND BETWEEN PARAGRAPHS.

DEVELOP IDEAS FULLY WITH DETAILS, EXAMPLES, DEFINITIONS, REPETITIONS.

Clarity

APPLY THE FOG INDEX TO MEASURE READABILITY.

CONSIDER LENGTH, UNNECESSARY WORDS, ACTIVE VOICE, ACTION VERBS, CONVERSATIONAL LANGUAGE.

BE CORRECT; DOUBLE-CHECK SPELLING, RUN-ONS, FRAGMENTS, AGREEMENT, MODIFIERS.

Style

USE IMAGERY, PARALLEL CONSTRUCTION, ANTITHESIS, RHETORICAL QUESTIONS, ALLITERATION, ONOMATOPOEIA, COMPARISONS.

Visual Cues and Appearance

SIMPLIFY THE PRESENTATION WITH WHITE SPACE, HEADINGS AND SUBHEADS, BULLETS, BOLDFACE, UNDERLINING.

How Can I Spot and Correct Errors in My Sentences?

*Y*ou are revising a document and are satisfied with the content and organization. But you want to make sure that your sentences are correct and clear. What should you look for?

    While many things can go wrong with a sentence, making it either grammatically incorrect or simply awkward, this chapter highlights the more common problems business writers have with sentences. After reviewing a few of your documents for these problems, you will be able to zero in on your most troublesome areas and develop your own diagnostic checklist.

FRAGMENTS AND RUN-ONS: TOO LITTLE OR TOO MUCH

Fragments

By definition, a sentence has a subject and verb and at least one independent clause (aka complete thought). For example:

> subject   verb
> <u>Bond prices</u> <u>surged</u> on the good economic news.

This group of words conveys a complete thought and therefore is an independent clause—it can stand alone and be understood.

Length is *not* one of the criteria of a sentence. You can have a very short group of words that is a correct sentence and a very long group of words that is not. For example:

Sentence:	The market rallied.
Fragment:	As a result of the good news from Washington and the sharp upturn in consumer confidence, shown by a steady flurry of buying in retail stores.

Although the "sentence" has only three words, it matches the criteria for a sentence: subject, verb, complete thought. The fragment, on the other hand, does not render a complete thought. Readers are kept waiting for something to be said that completes the thought. They say: "As a result of these things, what happened?"

To make a fragment a sentence, insert the words necessary to complete the thought. For example:

Sentence:	As a result of the good news from Washington and the sharp upturn in consumer confidence, shown by a steady flurry of buying in retail stores, *stocks are soaring.*

Sometimes writers create fragments when they have an afterthought upon completing a sentence. They write that afterthought as a separate sentence. In tandem with the original sentence, the fragment makes sense, but independently it does not. To be a correct sentence, it must be able to stand alone. For example:

Sentence and Fragment:	While the project was tedious, it did serve as a good refresher by which a number of people could review some basic principles. *Brush up on some skills.*

You can correct a fragment by inserting what it needs to be independent, or you can rewrite it as part of the preceding sentence to which it is tied in thought. For example:

Revised, separate sentences:	While the project was tedious, it did serve as a good refresher by which a number of people could review some basic principles. *It helped them* brush up on some skills.

or

Revised, integrated:	While the project was tedious, it did serve as a good refresher by which a number of people could review some basic principles *and* brush up on some skills.

In some situations, fragments are acceptable in business documents. For example, transitions between one major aspect and another are often put in the form of fragments:

Acceptable Fragment:	So much for the plan. Now the actual performance.

Answers to rhetorical questions also may be written as fragments. For example:

Acceptable Fragment:	How can we accomplish these goals? With planning, perspective, and perseverance.

When you use fragments in these types of situations, be sure your readers will realize that you have written a fragment deliberately and that it is not just an error. When in doubt about that realization, do not use a fragment.

Run-ons

Another common problem with sentences is forcing too many thoughts into a sentence without the proper punctuation. Often this error is called a run-on. For example:

	— 1 —	— 2 —
Run-on:	We won the contract it takes effect in January.	

This run-on fuses two sentences (independent clauses) without any punctuation signaling the proper stop between them.

You can correct a run-on like this in two ways: by forming two complete sentences or joining the two in one with the proper punctuation—a comma and a coordinating conjunction. For example:

Two Sentences: We won the contract. It takes effect in January.

Comma and Conjunction: We won the contract, *and* it takes effect in January.

Only a handful of conjunctions are capable of joining two sentences with the help of just a comma. These coordinating conjunctions are *and, but, for, nor, or.*

Sentence: We could take this matter to litigation, *or* we could settle it amicably.

Sentence: The company had been in the industry for many years, *but* it somehow lost touch with its clients.

Sentence: Resumes are first screened by a secretary, *for* there are just too many for the director to review.

Other words that you might sometimes use in joining sentences require that a period or semicolon be placed before them. These are words such as *accordingly, also, consequently, furthermore, however, instead, likewise, moreover, nevertheless, then, therefore, thus.* Transitional phrases such as *for example, in fact, on the other hand, in conclusion, in the meantime* also need a period or semicolon in front of them when joining two independent clauses. For example:

Two Sentences:	First we interviewed the users. *Then* we developed requirements.
Two Sentences:	We have done quite well during the recession. *In fact,* business has even increased slightly.

One way to test for run-ons is to listen to the way you read the sentence. If you make a full stop, chances are you need a period and two separate sentences.

FAULTY AGREEMENT: THE START OF A MISUNDERSTANDING

In revising sentences, be concerned with two areas of agreement—between subject and verb and between each pronoun and its antecedent (that is, the noun it refers to). Let's look at each type of problem.

Subject and Verb

The subject and verb must agree in number. That is, a singular subject requires a singular verb; a plural subject requires a plural verb. For example:

Singular:	The <u>report</u> <u>is</u> ready.
Plural:	The <u>reports</u> <u>are</u> ready.

In such sentences agreement poses little problem. But agreement can be sticky when intervening words separate the verb from its subject. Writers will sometimes have the verb agree with the closest noun rather than with the subject. For example:

Incorrect:	The <u>date</u> printed on the day's tickets <u>do</u> not correspond to the date in the ledger.

The subject of this sentence is *date,* not *tickets.* Since *date* is singular, the verb should also be singular:

Correct:	The <u>date</u> printed on the day's tickets <u>does</u> not correspond to the date in the ledger.

Here's another example:

Incorrect:	The <u>director</u>, as well as all the staff members, <u>were</u> quite pleased with the result.

The subject of this sentence is *director,* not *members.* Since *director* is singular, the verb should also be singular:

Correct:	The <u>director</u>, as well as all the staff members, <u>was</u> quite pleased with the result.

Look for the subject and do not be distracted by other words that may appear before the verb,

Another troublesome area of subject-verb agreement surrounds indefinite pronouns. Words such as *everyone, anything, nobody, each, either, neither* always take a singular verb, even though the implication is plural. For example:

<u>Everybody</u> assigned to the project <u>works</u> 10-hour days.

<u>Each</u> of the clients <u>has</u> a particular set of requirements.

<u>Everything</u> in his files <u>was</u> taken.

<u>Neither</u> of the companies <u>is</u> doing too well.

The indefinite pronouns *all, any, most, more, some, none* may take either a singular or plural verb depending on the noun they refer to. For example:

Singular:	<u>Some</u> of the documentation <u>has</u> been destroyed. *Some* refers to the singular *documentation.*
Plural:	<u>Some</u> of the files <u>have</u> been lost. *Some* refers to the plural *files.*

Here's another example:

Singular:	<u>None</u> of the art work <u>has</u> been assigned. *None* refers to the singular *work.*
Plural:	<u>None</u> of the sketches <u>have</u> been approved. *None* refers to the plural *sketches.*

Subjects joined by *and* usually take a plural verb:

<u>Procurement *and* distribution</u> <u>are</u> major productivity targets.

Subjects joined by *or, nor, either...or, neither...nor* take a singular verb when the subjects are singular:

<u>Procurement *or* distribution</u> <u>is</u> the logical place to start.

With these conjunctions *(or, nor, either...or, neither...nor),* when one part of the subject is singular and one part is plural, the verb agrees with the closer subject:

Neither price *nor* market <u>conditions</u> alone <u>are</u> enough to base the decision on.
I'm not sure if the secretaries *or* the <u>manager</u> <u>is</u> running this office.

In sentences beginning with *there* and *where,* the verb that follows must agree with the subject, which enters after the verb:

There <u>is</u> no <u>indication</u> that the company is slipping.

The verb *is* agrees with the singular subject *indication.*

There <u>are</u> sixteen <u>vendors</u> capable of providing this service.

The verb *are* agrees with the plural subject *vendors.*

As in some of the examples above, don't get fooled by other words surrounding the subject. Find the actual subject and have the verb agree with that. For example:

Where <u>is</u> the costs and benefits <u>analysis</u>?

The verb *is* agrees with the singular subject *analysis,* not with the other words in between.

When the subject is a collective noun (*team, class, crew, management, committee, family*) the verb is singular if the noun is being considered as a group. If the context shows the noun referring to the individuals in the group, use a plural verb.

Singular: <u>Management</u> <u>has</u> certain goals that may conflict with those of labor.

Management here connotes a body acting as a single unit.

Plural: Our <u>management</u> <u>represent</u> many different viewpoints and backgrounds.

Management here connotes a group of individuals.

When the relative pronouns *who, which, that* are used as subjects, use a singular or plural verb depending on the noun the pronoun refers to. For example:

Singular: I have created the list <u>that</u> <u>is</u> to be duplicated.

Use the singular *is* because *that* refers to the singular *list*.

Plural: Here are the reports <u>that</u> <u>contain</u> all the information on the project.

Use the plural *contain* because *that* refers to the plural *reports*.

Singular: These are the slides accompanying the speech, <u>which</u> <u>is</u> to be delivered tomorrow.

Plural: These are the slides compiled from a number of presentations, <u>which</u> <u>have</u> been given throughout the year.

Here is another, slightly trickier example:

Plural: The VP of Finance agrees with those executive committee members <u>who</u> <u>approve</u> the expansion.

Use the plural *approve* because *who* refers to the plural *members*.

Singular: The VP of Finance is the only one of the executive committee members <u>who</u> <u>approves</u> the expansion.

Use the singular *approves* because *who* refers to the singular *VP of Finance*.

Pronoun

Use a singular pronoun to refer to a singular noun and a plural pronoun to refer to a plural noun. Do not let words between the two cause you to use the wrong pronoun. For example:

Incorrect:	The <u>telecommuter</u> can be more productive than traditional office workers because <u>they</u> eliminate transit time.
Correct:	The <u>telecommuter</u> can be more productive than traditional office workers because <u>he or she</u> eliminates transit time.
Incorrect:	Corporate <u>cultures</u> are nebulous but real, and <u>it</u> must be considered when planning strategic alliances.
Correct:	Corporate <u>cultures</u> are nebulous but real, and <u>they</u> must be considered when planning strategic alliances.

Use singular pronouns to refer to indefinite pronouns such as *person, one, any, each, neither, either, everyone, anybody.* For example:

Incorrect:	<u>Everyone</u> must take responsibility for <u>their</u> own career advancement.
Correct:	<u>Everyone</u> must take responsibility for <u>his or her</u> own career advancement.
Incorrect:	Looking at the two companies, we find that <u>neither</u> have increased <u>their</u> profits this year.
Correct:	Looking at the two companies, we find that <u>neither</u> has increased <u>its</u> profits this year.

PRONOUN REFERENCE: A SOURCE OF AMBIGUITY

Another common pronoun error is being unclear about the noun a pronoun refers to. For example:

Ambiguous:	Jordan talked to Winthrop about <u>his</u> sales figures.

The sentence is ambiguous because it is not clear if the figures are Jordan's or Winthrop's. Restructure this kind of sentence to avoid ambiguity:

Clear:	Jordan talked about his sales figures with Winthrop.
Ambiguous:	Jackson sent Oliver the unedited draft, because <u>she</u> was leaving town that afternoon.
Clear:	Because Jackson was leaving town that afternoon, <u>she</u> sent Oliver the unedited draft.
Ambiguous:	Rewrite the introduction to the report and add graphics to <u>it</u>.

Add graphics to the report or to the introduction?

Clear:	Rewrite the introduction and add some graphics to the report.
Clear:	Rewrite and add some graphics to the introduction to the report.

Keep pronouns close to the words they refer to, with few nouns between them. If other nouns separate the pronoun from its antecedent, readers may misread the sentence or passage. For example:

Ambiguous:	Personal computers have changed the way people in offices throughout the world do business and interact with each other. <u>They</u> are used in a range of activities, from record keeping to design.

Because *people* and *offices* are plural nouns close to the pronoun *they*, readers may at first assume the pronoun refers to one of those words. Avoid this kind of ambiguity by either restructuring the passage so the pronoun is closest to the noun it refers to or replacing the pronoun:

Clear:	Personal computers have changed the way people in offices throughout the world do business and interact with each other. <u>Computers</u> are used in a range of activities, from record keeping to design.

Clear:	The way people in offices throughout the world do business with each other has been changed by personal computers. <u>They</u> are used in a range of activities, from record keeping to design.

The pronoun *this* is another major source of confusion. *This* normally is used with another word—*this problem, this approach. This* may be used alone, but only if its antecedent is absolutely clear. For example, "The temperature in the computer room was 85 degrees. *This* was entirely too high."

Confusion reigns if the reader must ask *"this what?"*

Confusing:	It is imperative that communications with Finance be improved to ensure all potential liabilities are properly identified. *This* may involve further education of existing staff.
This what?	
Clear:	It is imperative that communications with Finance be improved to ensure all potential liabilities are properly identified. *This level of identification* may involve further education of existing staff.
Confusing:	The standard procedure calls for us to date each resume that comes in, review them all for the basic requirements, and forward to the hiring manager those that match the basic requirements. *This* is not happening.
Clear:	The standard procedure calls for us to date each resume that comes in, review them all for the basic requirements, and forward to the hiring manager those that match the basic requirements. *This procedure* is not being followed.

You can also avoid confusing your readers by not using one pronoun in two or more ways in the same sentence or group of sentences. For instance, we often use *it* as a definite pronoun—referring to a thing—and as an expletive, introducing a sentence, as in

It is impossible to determine the winner at this time.

Using the pronoun in both ways in close proximity can confuse the reader. For example:

Confusing:	Here is the schedule for next month. *It* is obvious that *it* requires a strong effort from all of us.
Clear:	Here is the schedule for next month. *It* will obviously require a strong effort from all of us.

INCONSISTENT SHIFTS: DISTRACTING, SOMETIMES CONFUSING

Avoid illogical shifts in your sentences. *Be consistent in using the same voice, tense, person, and style.* Making illogical shifts can distract the reader, and possibly even confuse.

Voice Shift:	When a *manager wants* to discipline an employee, *it should be done* in private.

The shift is from active to passive voice without need for it.

Consistent:	When a *manager wants* to discipline an employee, *she should do so* in private.

Both clauses are in active voice.

Tense Shift:	Assume you *are planning* for retirement and *wanted* to invest some money. There is an illogical shift from present tense to past tense.
Consistent:	Assume you *are planning* for retirement and *want* to invest some money.

Both verbs are in present tense.

Person Shift:	If a job *applicant* expects a response on every resume submitted, *you* are sadly mistaken.

This sentence contains an illogical shift from third person (*applicant*) to second person (*you*).

Consistent: If a job *applicant* expects a response on every resume submitted, *he or she* is sadly mistaken.

Both *applicant* and *he* or *she* are third person.

Style Shift: Our presentation displayed our expertise in the area and our industriousness in researching the question, resulting in our *blowing the competition out of the water.*

This sentence contains an illogical shift from a formal to a colloquial style.

Consistent: Our presentation displayed our expertise in the area and our industriousness in researching the question, resulting in our *totally eliminating the competition from consideration.*

The style throughout is formal.

MISPLACED PARTS MAY LOSE YOUR READER

In reviewing your sentences, look to see that modifying words, phrases, and clauses are near the words they modify and are in the proper position, before or after.

Words that have *a limiting effect usually go before* the words they modify. That is, place words such as *almost, even, hardly, only, nearly* immediately in front of the word they modify. For example:

Incorrect: We *only* make afternoon appointments.

As written, this sentence implies that the person's activities are limited to making appointments, which is not likely to be the intended meaning.

Correct: We make *only* afternoon appointments.

This sentence implies that all the appointments made are for the afternoon.

> *Incorrect:*   The indictment *almost* charges the entire department.

This sentence implies the indictment comes close to charging but does not quite make the charge. That meaning is probably not intended.

> *Correct:*   The indictment charges *almost* the entire department.

This sentence is probably closer to the intended meaning—that almost all members of the department are charged in the indictment.

Placing modifiers incorrectly may result in some confusing, even unintentionally amusing, sentences. For example:

> *Incorrect:*   I borrowed a computer from a friend with a faulty hard drive.

That friend is indeed in trouble.

> *Correct:*   I borrowed a computer with a faulty hard drive from a friend.

> *Incorrect:*   The dealer claims there was an injustice done to him in the first paragraph of his letter.

Is that where the injustice was done to him?

> *Correct:*   In the first paragraph of his letter, the dealer claims there was an injustice done to him.

Some misplaced modifiers are said to *dangle,* because the word they are intended to modify does not appear in the sentence. For example:

> *Incorrect:*   Reviewing the report, three glaring errors popped out at me.

Who or what was doing the reviewing? It certainly wasn't the errors. So *reviewing the report* has nothing to modify. Therefore it is dangling. Correct the dangling modifier by inserting into the sentence the word the phrase modifies:

> *Correct:*   Reviewing the report, *I saw* three glaring errors.

Here's another example:

Incorrect: Designed by consultants, we often have to spend days
cleaning up their system mistakes.

As written, this sentence says *we* were designed by the consultants. The
sentence probably should indicate that the systems were designed by consultants. You can make that message clear by inserting the word to be modified
close to the modifying phrase:

Correct: We often have to spend days cleaning up mistakes in
the systems designed by consultants.

OMISSIONS AND ILLOGICAL COMPARISONS

Writers sometimes inadvertently drop a word when they join two items. For
example:

Omission: The successful candidate will be proficient and have
familiarity with a wide range of software.

As written, the sentence says the candidate should be *proficient with.* That
is not the proper construction. It should be *proficient in.*

Complete: The successful candidate will be proficient *in* and have
familiarity *with* a wide range of software.

Include all words that are necessary in a joint construction.
Here's another example:

Omission: Our firm never has and never will practice discrimination.

As written, the sentence does not complete the expression starting with
never has. Complete the sentence by inserting the proper verb form to go with
never has:

Complete: Our firm never has *practiced* and never will *practice* discrimination.

Sometimes we write comparisons that are ambiguous or seem illogical because we omit words. For example:

Illogical: Our department's productivity exceeded any other department.

As written the sentence compares two different items—one department's *productivity* against other *departments*. Be sure to state what you mean in the comparison:

Logical: Our department's productivity exceeded the productivity of any other department.

Logical: Our department's productivity exceeded that of any other department.

Logical: Our department's productivity exceeded every other department's.

— Sentence Diagnostic Checklist —

Review your sentences for

FRAGMENTS

RUN-ONS

SUBJECT-VERB AGREEMENT, ESPECIALLY WHEN

   ❐ *Words comes between subject and verb.*

   ❐ *The subject is an indefinite pronoun (such as*
        everyone, anything, most, none).

❑ *Two subjects are joined by* and, or, nor, either...or, neither...nor.

❑ *The subject follows the verb.*

❑ *The subject is a title in plural form.*

❑ *The subject is a relative pronoun*—who, that, which.

PRONOUN AGREEMENT, ESPECIALLY WHEN

❑ *Words come between the pronoun and its antecedent.*

❑ *The pronoun refers to an indefinite pronoun, such as* person, one, everyone.

PRONOUN REFERENCE, ESPECIALLY WHEN

❑ *Two nouns could possibly be seen as the antecedent.*

❑ *The pronoun is* this *or* it.

ILLOGICAL SHIFTS IN VOICE, TENSE, PERSON, STYLE

MISPLACED PARTS:

❑ *Be sure modifiers are near to, immediately before or after the words they modify.*

❑ *Avoid dangling modifiers by always including the noun modified.*

OMISSIONS AND ILLOGICAL COMPARISONS:

❑ *Do not drop needed words when combining two items.*

❑ *Complete comparisons to avoid illogical or ambiguous statements.*

What's the Difference Between Affect and Effect, Imply and Infer, and Other "Look-Alike"/ "Seem-Alike" Words?

In revising a document, you are not sure if you have used certain words like <u>credible</u> and <u>credulous</u> or words like <u>flaunt</u> and <u>imminent</u> correctly.

Or you want to understand once and for all the difference between those words that either look alike, such as <u>cite</u> and <u>site</u>, or seem to be so similar in meaning, like <u>fewer</u> and <u>less</u>, that you use them interchangeably.

Or you feel you know the proper use of words like <u>notoriety</u> and <u>simplistic</u> but you find people using the words differently. Are these people wrong or are you?

Choosing incorrectly from among word groups like <u>assure</u>, <u>ensure</u>, and <u>insure</u>; <u>allusion</u> and <u>illusion</u>; <u>continual</u> and <u>continuous</u> may be more troublesome to your image than to your message. For, generally, most readers will know from the context what you mean if you use <u>disinterested</u> instead of <u>uninterested</u>, but they may realize that you don't know there is a difference.

To raise your writing to a higher level, let's take at look at some words that are misused frequently in business writing. And let's try to learn the distinctions between them.

Forty-four Sets of Troublesome Words and How to Use Them

affect, effect. *Affect* is the verb; *effect* is the noun.

> *The new system did not affect operations.*

> *But it did have an effect on attitude. Effect* can be used as a verb to mean to bring about, as in:

> *New managers seek to effect change.*

> But using *to bring about* in such sentences causes much less confusion.

affect, impact. *Impact* is a noun and should not be used as a verb, as in:

> *The procedure will affect (not impact) three departments.*

> But many business writers and speakers use *impact* as a verb and may some day make that use "legitimate."

agree to, agree with. *Agree to* means *to give consent,* as in:

> *I agree to your request.*

> *Agree with* means *to concur,* as in:

> *I agree with the majority opinion.*

a lot, alot. The correct form is always two words—*a lot.*

allusion, illusion. An *allusion* is a reference to something, as in:

> *The writer made frequent allusions to the company charter.*

> *Illusion* means *a false impression or erroneous understanding,* as in:

> *I have no illusions about our chances of winning this engagement.*

alright, all right. As with *à lot,* the correct form is two words—*all right.*

among, between. Use *between* for two and *among* for more than two, as in:

> *There was no animosity between the two executives. There was, however, disagreement among the four managers.*

When expressing a relationship of one thing to more than one other, you may use *between:*

> *We want to locate our new headquarters about evenly between the three divisions.*

amount, number. *Amount* refers to quantity or mass, as in:

> *Large amounts of food were eaten at the company picnic.*

Use *number* in referring to items that can be counted, as in:

> *We expect a large number of people to attend.*

bad, badly. Use *bad* as an adjective before a noun, as in:

> *bad cholesterol.*

Also use *bad* after a verb of being, such as *am, are,* or *feel,* as in:

> *I feel bad about the loss.*

Use *badly* as an adverb to modify an action verb, as in:

> *She reacted badly to the medication.*

being that, being as how. Neither is acceptable. Use *because* or *since.*

can, may. Use *can* to express ability, and *may* to express permission, as in:

> *As soon as you tell us we may begin, we can assign a project team.*

cite, site. *Cite* means *to quote or mention,* as in:

> *Can you cite your sources for those statistics?*

> *Site* means a particular place, as in:

> *They have selected a site for the new mall.*

complement, compliment. *Complement* means *to add to,* as in:

> *Jackson's analytical skills will complement Johnson's creative skills.* (Remember the *e* as in *complete.*)

> *Compliment* refers to praising or flattering, as in:

> *We received a compliment from one of our clients.*

continual, continuous. *Continual* means *repeated frequently*, as in:

continual renewal.

Continuous implies *without interruption*, as in:

continuous performances.

could have, could of. *Could of* is never a correct substitute for *could have* or the contraction *could've*.

credible, creditable, credulous. *Credible* means *believable*, as in:

This resume is impressive but is it credible?

Creditable implies *worthy of credit or praise*, as in:

They gave a creditable presentation.

Credulous refers to a person's level of believability, as in:

Having great trust in them, I listened credulously to their claims.

different from, different than. *Different from* is the correct form in writing and in formal speaking situations, though you may hear *different than* in informal conversation.

disinterested, uninterested. Use *disinterested* to suggest an impartial third party. Use *uninterested* when referring to someone who has no interest in the issue.

due to, because of. Do not use *due to* as a preposition meaning *because of*:

The project was postponed because of (not due to) budgetary problems.

Use *due to* immediately after *is* or *was* to mean *attributable to*, as in:

The failure was due to system overload.

elicit, illicit. *Elicit* is a verb meaning *to draw from*, as in *to elicit a response*. *Illicit* is an adjective meaning *illegal*, as in:

The broker was charged with engaging in illicit activities.

eminent, imminent. Use *eminent* when referring to someone of great distinction. Use *imminent* in speaking of an event that is about to happen soon.

ensure, insure, assure. Use *ensure* to imply *make sure,* as in:

> *To ensure punctual delivery, provide all details asked for on the shipping labels.*

> *Insure* means *to give or take insurance coverage on something,* as in:

> *The juggler insured his hands for $1 million.*

> *Assure* means *to provide a level of comfort,* as in:

> *We can assure you the check is in the mail.*

famous, notorious. Use *famous* when referring to someone's renown for doing something good or for having an admirable quality, as in:

> *She is famous for her insightful summations.*

Use *notorious* to describe someone renowned for negative qualities or accomplishments, as in:

> *He is notorious for leaving major projects until the last minute.*

You can usually substitute *infamous* for *notorious.*

farther, further. While some dictionaries see these words as interchangeable, some restrict *farther* to references to distance and *further* to mean *in addition.* If you think your audience is up on this sort of thing, use these words in this way, just to be safe.

fewer, less. Use *fewer* in referring to countable things, as in:

> *We had fewer applicants this year than last.*

Use *less* in referring to degree or value, as in:

> *But the candidates showed less ability than last year's.*

flout, flaunt. *Flout* means *to scoff at,* as in *flouts the law. Flaunt* means to display ostentatiously, as in:

> *The new director flaunted his recently attained status.*

good, well. Like *bad* and *badly, good* and *well* differ in use. Use *good* as an adjective before a noun, as in *the good manager,* and after verbs of being, such as *am, are,* and *feel,* as in:

She is good for the company, and I feel good about our chances.

Use *well* to mean healthy, as in:

You look well,

but *good* to mean *attractive,* as in:

You look good (properly dressed.)

Use *well* as an adverb to modify an action verb, as in:

The new procedure works well.

head, head up. Down with *up.* People *head* committees.

imply, infer. The speaker or writer *implies;* the listener or reader *infers.*

The letter implies we erred.

You can't infer that for the letter.

irregardless, regardless. Irregardless is always incorrect, *regardless* of how you feel about it.

it's, its. The apostrophe here *does not* signal possession.

it's = it is. It's an unrealistic approach.

its = possession. Its philosophy is weak.

lay, lie. Lay means *to place or put down,* as in:

Lay the cards on the table.

Lie means *to recline.*

me, myself. Use *myself* to intensify emphasis, as in:

I myself will do it.

Also use myself as a reflexive, as in:

I questioned myself about it repeatedly.

Use *me* in all other instances. For example:

Call my assistant or me (not myself) with your questions.

over, more than. *Over* refers to space, as in *over the city. More than* is used with numbers, as in *more than 15 violations were noted.*

precede, proceed. *Precede* is a verb meaning *to come before,* as in:

Who preceded Cynthia as President?

Proceed is a verb meaning *to move forward,* as in:

Let's proceed with caution.

preventive, preventative. *Preventive* is the correct form.

principle, principal. A rule or truth is a *principle,* as in:

The principle behind the policy is control.

Principal is usually an adjective meaning *main or primary,* as in:

The principal advantage of the policy is control.

Principal can also refer to a top school administrator or officer in some companies.

simple, simplistic. *Simple* means *plain or uncomplicated,* as in:

The solution was simple but effective.

Use *simplistic* to refer to an idea or plan that is overly simple and ignores real complexities, as in:

The recommendations were simplistic, showing little understanding of the real issues.

there, their, they're. Use *there* in referring to place, as in:

Put it there.

Or as an expletive at the beginning of a sentence, as in:

There is no call for that.

Use *their* as the possessive pronoun, as in:

Their RFP is unclear.

They're is the contraction for *they are.*

unique. The word means *one of a kind,* so a thing or event cannot be *somewhat unique* or *very unique.* It's just *unique.*

up, raise. *Up* is an adverb. Don't use it as a verb, as in *to up the percentages.* For this idea, use *raise.*

who's, whose. *Who's,* like *it's,* is not a possessive. *Who's* means *who is,* as in:

The manager is the one who's responsible for approving the changes.

Whose is the possessive, as in:

It is the manager whose approval is required.

who, whom. *Who* refers to the doer of the action; *whom* to the recipient:

The employee who offers the best suggestion wins the award. (who offers)

Wilson is one person in whom I had complete trust. (had trust in whom)

<u>Hint</u>: use *who* where you'd use he *(he offers)*
use *whom* where you'd use him *(in him)*

verbal, oral. *Verbal* refers to reducing ideas to words, either spoken or written, as in:

The testimonial gives verbal expression to our feelings.

Oral refers to spoken communication, as in:

An oral agreement was sufficient for both parties.

— Troublesome Word Checklist —

Use *Affect* as a Verb, *Effect* as a Noun.

Use *Between* for Two, *Among* for More than Two.

Use *Amount* and *Less* for Mass or Degree, *Number* and *Fewer* for Countable Things.

Write *I Feel Good or Bad,* When Referring to Sensibility; Write *I Feel Well* When Referring to Health.

Remember that *Complement* Has an *E,* as in *Complete.*

Continual Implies Pauses; *Continuous* Doesn't.

Disinterested, not *Uninterested,* is the Word for Impartial.

Use *Due to* Only After *Was* or *Is.*

Ensure Means to Make Certain; *Insure* Implies a Policy Coverage.

The Speaker or Writer *Implies;* the Listener or Reader *Infers.*

Notorious is Used When Referring to One Who Is Known for Negative Qualities.

It's Is Not a Possessive, But Means *It Is.*

Preventive Is the Correct Form, Not *Preventative.*

Simple Is Uncomplicated; *Simplistic* Is Naive.

Who's Is Not Possessive; It Means *Who Is.*

How Do I Avoid Using Sexist Language, Even Inadvertently?

You are answering a blind ad and do not know the sex of the person who will receive your letter. What greeting do you use in the salutation?

Or you've just come back from a management seminar where you learned that sexism in any form can seriously harm a manager's image and effectiveness, to say nothing of chances for advancement. How do you make sure your language isn't sexist?

Or, though you consciously try to avoid sexist language, words and phrases that may be considered sexist do creep into your writing without your realizing it. How can you cleanse your writing of inadvertent sexism?

Perhaps, because you are a woman, you feel sexist language is not an issue for you. But indeed it is, as many women perpetuate sexism by using much of the language that men are often criticized for using.

To eliminate sexist language from your writing, spend some portion of your revising time on this important issue. What exactly should you look for? Let's see.

HOW TO AVOID INADVERTENT SEXISM

English has been skewed toward male dominance for many years. As a result, many people—including women—use sexist language inadvertently. To see if you are using sexist language—and thereby offending a good portion of your audience—answer honestly the questions below.

A Sexist Language Checklist

NO   YES

___   ___   1. Do you describe the women you write about in greater physical detail than the men you write about?

___   ___   2. Do you refer to adult women as *girls* or *gals* and refer to adult males as *men*?

___   ___   3. Do you routinely provide information about the marital status of women you write about but then not about the men?

___   ___   4. Do you use *woman* as a modifier, as in *woman engineer*?

___   ___   5. When you do not know the name of the person you are writing a letter to, do you automatically address it *Dear Sir:* or *Gentlemen:*?

___   ___   6. Do you exclude women from many occupational categories by using terms ending in *-man*, such as *Congressman, businessman, repairman?*

___   ___   7. Do you believe sexist writing is a trivial concern?

If you answered YES to any of these questions, you are probably guilty of using sexist language at least occasionally. This use, of course, does not make you a sexist, but it does jeopardize your relationship with some of your readers and can undercut your effect on them. Included among those readers are men as well as women.

What kinds of expressions might seem sexist and offensive? The rest of this chapter outlines some of the most common ways people allow sexist language to enter their documents. Once you know what to look for, you can apply some of the suggestions for changing to nonoffensive phrasing.

HOW TO SUBSTITUTE THE GENERIC FOR THE SEXIST TERM

Most sexist language shows a male dominance. Try to avoid using words that reflect maleness. Use a generic form of the word instead. For example:

Sexist	Generic
mankind	people
manpower	work force, staff
average working man	average wage earner
mailman	mail carrier
salesman	sales representative or associate
man hours	cumulative hours
businessman	business executive
man in the street	average person
forefathers	ancestors
man-made	synthetic
policeman	police officer
fireman	fire fighter
chairman	chairperson
craftsman	artisan
stewardess	flight attendant
junior executive	executive trainee
anchorman	anchor
statesmanlike	diplomatic

As you can see, a generic alternative is usually available to replace the sexist term. You may have to think about the concept some, but eventually you should be able to come up with a suitable, nonsexist substitute.

HOW TO HANDLE THE PRONOUN PROBLEM

Substituting a generic alternative is fairly easy. But the sexism issue is more difficult to deal with when pronouns are involved.

For example, when we make a reference to an indefinite singular person, tradition has taught us to use the male pronoun, which is sexist:

Sexist: A good manager knows the strengths of *his* staff.

To avoid the sexist emphasis, use *his or her.*

Nonsexist: A good manager knows the strengths of *his or her* staff.

But using *he or she, his or her, him or her* repeatedly becomes awkward:

A good manager knows the strengths of *his or her* staff. *He or she* must also know the weaknesses of *his or her* people. *He or she* cannot expect to get blood from a stone or settle for mediocrity.

Avoid the awkwardness by using the plural:

Good *managers* know the strengths of *their* staffs. *They* must also know the weaknesses of *their* people. *They* cannot expect to get blood from a stone or settle for mediocrity.

Or, use the second person, *you,* instead of the third person, *he* or *she,* and address the reader as *you*:

To be a good manager, *you* must know the strengths of *your* staff.

SPECIFYING GENDER AND OTHER SUBTLE FORMS OF SEXISM
NOT FOR WOMEN ONLY

When women played a minor role in business, a woman at the executive level or with major responsibilities was an exception. Thus it was rather natural for people to highlight the fact that a particular executive or professional was a woman. Doing so today, however, can be an insult, as if to imply that a woman at the upper levels or in the professions is still an anomaly.

So don't call attention to the sex of the individual, unless you plan to do so for both men and women:

> *Sexist:*   The consultant, a *female* partner in the firm, recommended sweeping changes.

And don't use physical characteristics unless you do so for people of both sexes.

> *Sexist:*   The litigation team was headed by Valerie Reed, an *attractive* and brilliant attorney, and Jack Weinstein, an experienced litigator.

Woman, Not Girl

It is also offensive to use the word *girl* when referring to an adult female. Do not use *girl* when you mean *woman,* or when the corresponding term is *man.* For example:

> *Sexist:*   *Girls* outnumber men in our office by six to five.

Women at Home Work, Too

Do not denigrate women who work at home by using *working women* to refer only to those who have salaried jobs. Instead use *salaried women* or *women who work outside the home.*

WHAT TO DO WHEN THE RECIPIENT'S SEX IS UNKNOWN

When you are writing to someone whose sex is unknown to you, avoid the sexist salutations *Dear Sir* or *Gentlemen.* Instead, use:

> *Nonsexist:*   *Dear Sir or Madam:* or *Dear Madam or Sir:*

If you know the person's title, or category in which the person can be placed, you may use that for the salutation:

Nonsexist: *Dear Human Resource Director:*
                      Dear PC Owner:
                      Dear Resident of Hillsdale:

— Sexist Language Checklist —

BE CONCERNED ABOUT OFFENDING PORTIONS OF YOUR AUDIENCE WITH SEXIST LANGUAGE.

USE A GENERIC SUBSTITUTE RATHER THAN A SEXIST NOUN, VERB, OR ADJECTIVE.

WHEN REFERRING TO AN INDEFINITE NOUN, USE *HE OR SHE,* NOT *HE,* OR USE THE PLURAL FORM OF THE NOUN AND PRONOUN.

DON'T CALL ATTENTION TO ONE'S SEX OR PHYSICAL ATTRIBUTES JUST WHEN IDENTIFYING WOMEN.

USE THE TERM *WOMAN,* NOT *GIRL,* FOR A MATURE FEMALE.

DO NOT USE *DEAR SIR* OR *GENTLEMEN* AS A SALUTATION WHEN YOU DO NOT KNOW THE SEX OF THE RECIPIENT OF YOUR LETTER.

Pesky Punctuation: How Do I Master It?

*P*erhaps *you've been having trouble getting positive responses to your resume, even when you feel immensely qualified for the positions. In following up, you get one kind human resource manager to confide that he disqualified your resume because of punctuation errors in your cover letter. Because of those errors, the hiring manager never even looked at the resume itself.*

Or you have just felt the sting of rejection when a report you have written comes back to you bloodied with editorial markings. On looking closely, you note that your supervisor has not commented whatsoever on your content. But she has marked up just about every sentence, putting in or taking out commas, periods, dashes, colons, and semicolons.

Or you have just moved into the office from a field job that required little writing. Now that you write letters frequently, you are having problems. You know the content of your letters inside out, but this punctuation thing is driving you crazy. "Why are they making such a fuss about it?" you ask.

Frustration is warranted in all three instances, because punctuation is indeed much less important than content, organization, persuasiveness, and many other aspects of writing. But punctuation is not unimportant. This chapter shows you how to master these pesky little marks.

PUNCTUATION: THE SIGNPOSTS TO CLARITY

Some people react strongly to improper punctuation, and that kind of reaction can severely detract from, even shatter, the effect of an otherwise fine resume, report, memo, letter, or proposal. Punctuating poorly, like wearing the wrong clothes at an interview, can disqualify you in the eyes of the readers and create a negative impression that your substance may never be able to overcome. Readers then focus on the punctuation errors rather than on the ideas. Soon they start thinking, "If this guy doesn't even know how to punctuate, how can I trust anything he puts in writing?"

So, proper punctuation is important to keep from alienating readers. It is also important for another reason. *Punctuation helps clarity.* The only reason we have punctuation is to provide direction to the reader as to how a passage should be read. That is, punctuation adds to the written word what speakers add to the spoken word with their pauses, halts, stresses, and changes in inflection. For example:

That's mine.

That's mine!

That's mine?

In other words, punctuation enables readers to determine how the words should be read—where they should pause, stop, raise or lower the voice, give added emphasis.

Punctuation, therefore, is not just a collection of arbitrary symbols created as a diabolical torture for students and business writers. It is a set of directionals that help make your writing more comprehensible and easy to read.

Comma (,): The Most Misused Mark

The comma is the punctuation mark that is most frequently *misused*. The many uses of the comma are governed by a number of rules. Here, however, we will focus on just a few, to get you through the most likely areas of difficulty with this troublesome little mark.

Before getting to specific ways in which to use the comma, let us focus on one general thought, the guiding principle to use when you are debating whether to insert a comma, a period, or no punctuation at all:

Read the sentence aloud and listen to your voice. Where you pause, insert a comma. Where you stop, insert a period. If the words do not naturally call for a pause or stop, don't use a punctuation mark.

This technique should enable you to deal with 90 percent of your comma decisions.

USE COMMAS TO PREVENT MISREADING

Some word combinations can be confusing, forcing readers to go back and reread. In such sentences, the comma can often prevent misreading. For example:

Confusing: In deciding to expand the management team broke with tradition.

The confusion enters because readers might read, *to expand the management team.* They will realize that was not the writer's intent and go back to reread. But readers should be able to get the idea easily on the first read. Prevent the need for rereading by placing the comma properly:

Clear: In deciding to expand, the management team broke with tradition.

Here's another example:

Confusing: If all items match the purchase order system schedules payment.

On the first pass, one might read: *If all items match the purchase order.* To prevent the possibility of this interpretation—even momentarily—insert the comma:

Clear: If all items match, the purchase order system schedules payment.

Here's another type of sentence in which confusion can be cleared up simply by inserting a comma in the right place:

Confusing: The firm must work harder for new business with more marketing and special inducements.

Is the firm looking for business that has *more marketing or special induce-ments?* No, but the sentence might be read that way. To prevent that confusion, insert the comma:

Clear: The firm must work harder for new business, with more marketing and special inducements.

Here's another example of this type:

Confusing: The project affects all major operations functions in distribution centers including receiving, checking, marking, and picking.

In this sentence, is the writer referring to distribution centers that handle these functions, as opposed to distribution centers that handle other functions? Or does the word *including* introduce the major functions affected? More than likely the writer is intending the latter message. The sentence therefore should be punctuated in this way:

Clear: The project affects all major operations functions in distribution centers, including receiving, checking, marking, and picking.

To avoid such ambiguity and to prevent rereading, read your sentences carefully, following the punctuation, as your readers will. If you think there is any possibility for confusion, rephrase the sentence or insert the proper punctuation to make your intent clear.

USE COMMAS TO SEPARATE WORDS, PHRASES, AND CLAUSES IN A SERIES OF THREE OR MORE

Series of Words: We are seeking candidates who are *knowledgeable, experienced, and reliable.*

Series of Phrases: This resume shows *a weak academic background, a lack of practical experience, but an admirable array of accomplishments.*

Series of Clauses: Of the three candidates, *Jackson did not impress me at all, Johnson might be adequate, and Wilson is by far my first choice.*

In short series—usually of words rather than of phrases or clauses—you *may* omit the comma before the last item in the series. For example:

We are seeking candidates who are *knowledgeable, experienced, and reliable.*

But in longer series, use the comma even before the final item. To have one less rule to remember, use the comma to separate *all* items in series.

USE COMMAS TO SET OFF NONESSENTIAL MODIFIERS

This rule refers to the way commas sometimes separate modifiers from the words they modify. For example:

A. The program, *installed only last month,* saves hours of keystroking.

In other sentences with a modifier in the same basic structure, the comma is not used.

B. The person *who uses the program* calls it amazing.

In both sentences, we find a group of words in the middle of the sentence describing or modifying another word. Why do we set one modifier off with commas and not the other? The answer depends on whether or not the modifier *is essential to the meaning of the sentence.* In A, the modifier is not essential. It merely gives more information about the program. To signify that lack of necessity, the writer sets the modifier off with commas. In B, the modifier *is* essential. Without it, readers might not know what person is being spoken of. Because the modifier is essential to the thought of the sentence, it is not set off by commas.

Here are other examples:

Nonessential: The system, *in use for six months,* is still not complete.

Nonessential: The staff, experienced and adaptable can work with it
                      as it is.

The modifier in each is nonessential because the main idea of the sentence
would not change without it. The modifier merely gives added information. A
comma is placed *before and after* each nonessential modifier.
    With essential modifiers, use no commas.

Essential: Organizations *growing too fast* often lose control.
Essential: Managers *who straddle the fence* often find themselves in
                   uncomfortable positions.

Without the modifier, a change would result in the main idea in each sentence. Therefore, the modifier is essential in each sentence, and not set off by commas.

Business writers often use *short* nonessential modifiers (called *appositives*) to give added information about people, companies, places, and other elements. In these instances, commas set off the short modifiers. For example:

Mrs. Wallington, *the company president,* introduced the new product.

XYZ, *a Fortune 500 company,* has faced these setbacks before.

Our MIS Director, *J. K. Daters,* developed the system in-house.

In sentences with these short modifiers, as in all sentences with nonessential modifiers, be sure to place commas both *before and after* the modifier.

Dash (—): For a Touch of Drama

The dash is a dramatic punctuation mark and should be reserved for those situations calling for drama and excitement. Use it sparingly to highlight or call attention to information. Let's look at two of its most useful applications in business writing.

Use Dashes to Set off Nonessential Modifiers That Require Emphasis

Like the comma, the dash can be used to set off nonessential modifiers. But unlike commas, dashes give greater emphasis and force to these nonessential words. For example:

Commas, Less Emphasis:	Using old-fashioned methods, perseverance and determination, this group succeeded where others had failed.
Dashes, Greater Emphasis:	Using old-fashioned methods—perseverance and determination—this group succeeded where others had failed.

Set off by commas in the first example, *perseverance and determination* seem to be almost a casual inclusion. But in the second sentence, the dashes call attention to the words emphatically.

The dash is not found on most typewriter and word processor keyboards. If you do not find it on yours, use the conventional substitute, two hyphens (--). Do not skip a space between the hyphens or between the hyphens and the letters that precede and follow them. This deviation from conventional spacing further accentuates the information set off by the dashes. For example:

> Out of the group of applicants--more than one hundred in all--only six had credentials to get beyond the initial screening.

Use a Dash to Introduce a Word or Words You Wish to Emphasize

The dash sends a signal to the reader that something important is to follow.

> A retailer needs three things to succeed—location, location, location.

> Above all, we must dedicate ourselves to one goal—being the best we can be.

Use a Dash to Separate a Summarizing Clause from That Which Precedes It

> Instead of consolidating the company, he diversified it; instead of cutting back, he poured money into it—in short, he took a gamble and won.

> Commitment to research, money to fund it, and top-quality people to conduct it—that's all this company needs.

Because dashes are so dramatic, they should be used judiciously. If overused, or used improperly, they lose their effectiveness.

Parentheses ( ): To Diminish Importance

Parentheses ( ) enclose incidental matter within a sentence. In a way, parentheses serve the same function as commas and dashes in setting off nonessential modifiers. But parentheses generally signify that the matter enclosed is *only remotely significant* to the idea of the sentence. The parentheses, therefore, would be at the opposite extreme from the dash. While *the dash highlights* more than commas do, *parentheses deemphasize* more than commas do. For example:

> Our sales figures this year (see Table I) reflect our strong marketing effort last year.

> The company failed for three reasons: (1) lack of leadership, (2) inadequate controls, and (3) an inaccurate understanding of its customers.

Very often the material in the parentheses has no grammatical relationship to the sentence.

> The letter I refer to (dated June 23) states our position on this matter.

Sometimes an entire sentence will be placed in parentheses. Begin the sentence with a capital letter and end it with the proper end mark, placed inside the closing parentheses mark:

> According to a recent study, the average cost of making widgets has decreased by 24 percent over the last five years. (The study was conducted by the Widget Association of America.)

Note that parentheses come in pairs. Do not overlook the second one, particularly when the material it encloses is lengthy or comes at the end of the sentence. For example:

> Our weekly staff meetings have been losing effectiveness, particularly because of the way some members discuss issues. (You may recall how our last two meetings just dissolved rather than ended.) Some people seem to deal with personalities and personal agendas instead of the issues themselves.

Colon (:) Signals Something Special

The colon is a rather formal punctuation mark with limited functions. The most visible use of the colon is in separating minutes from hours and in the greeting of a business letter. Another major use of the colon is in signaling the reader that something special is to follow. Let's look more closely at these uses and at some related concerns.

USE THE COLON IN GREETINGS, TIME FIGURES, SUBTITLES, AND BIBLICAL CITATIONS

Dear Ms. Johnson: Dear Mr. Garth: Gentlemen:

Some writers use the first name only in the greeting of a business letter. This informality is acceptable in some circles. If you do use the first name only, you may follow it with a comma, as you would in a personal letter, or with a colon.:

Dear Cynthia,   Hello Marshall,   Dear Bill:

In writing *time figures,* use the colon to separate hours from minutes, and minutes from seconds:

11:32 P.M.   4:26:16 A.M.

Use the colon in *subtitles:*

Fulfillment: The Bread and Butter of Mail Order
Quality Improvement Program: A Blueprint for Success

Use the colon to separate chapter from verse in *biblical citations:*

Leviticus 2: 3   Matthew 3: 4–7

USE THE COLON TO INTRODUCE MATERIAL

Use the colon *to introduce a list or series* of items. Sometimes such lists will be preceded by the words *as follows* or *the following.* In many instances, such phrases are implied by the colon:

The purposes of the study are many: to assess need, to offer solutions, to analyze costs versus benefits, to propose an approach to implementation.

The primary duties of the department are as follows: maintain files on all clients, document expenditures, and report irregularities in office practices.

Use the colon to separate two clauses, *when the second in some way explains or completes the first.*

We devised a new approach to reduce turnover: it is called empowerment.

We have completed a study of systems in the distribution center: they are obsolete and terribly inadequate for the volume of traffic in the DC.

Use the colon *to introduce a formal quotation.* A formal quotation would be a passage from a book or other document or from a formal speech. For example:

One of the cardinal principles of good managing is communication:

> Good managers maintain open lines of communication with their staffs. They inform the staff of department goals as well as accomplishments. And good managers develop ways of getting input from their staff members, to get the benefit of their ideas as well as to learn about their problems.

You may have noticed colons used to introduce the examples on many pages in this book. The colon is a shorthand way of saying *like this* or *for example* or some such phrase:
Also use the colon after for example:

Very often the material in the parentheses has no grammatical relationship to the sentence. For example:

In using the colon to introduce material, do not place a colon between a verb and its object or between a preposition and its object.

Incorrect: Under the reorganization, Public Relations will oversee: marketing, community affairs, and media relations.
(The verb *oversee* is separated from its objects.)

Correct: Under the reorganization, Public Relations will oversee *a number of activities:* marketing, community affairs, and media relations. (Rephrase the sentence into an *"as follows"* format.)

Correct: Under the reorganization, Public Relations will oversee marketing, community affairs, and media relations.
(Use no colon or any other punctuation mark between the verb and its objects.)

Incorrect: They claim that this promotion accounted for: increased traffic in the stores, the largest sales day of the year, and a 10 percent increase in charge card applications.
(The preposition *for* is separated by the colon from its objects.)

Correct: They claim that this promotion accounted for *significant gains in key areas:* increased traffic in the stores, the largest sales day of the year, and a 10 percent increase in charge card applications.
(Rephrase the sentence into an *as follows* format.)

Correct: They claim that this promotion accounted for increased traffic in the stores, the largest sales day of the year, and a 10 percent increase in charge card applications.
(Use no colon or any other punctuation mark between the preposition and its object.)

These examples show the impact the colon can have. The colon calls attention to the *as follows* material. In the sentences without the colon, the information receives less "fanfare." Therefore, besides using the colon correctly, use it in the appropriate situations for effect.

Semicolon (;): A Mark with Limited Uses

The semicolon is another punctuation mark that is frequently misused. This misuse is surprising because the semicolon serves only a limited number of functions.

Its primary functions are two:

❐ To join two sentences (main clauses) that are so closely related in thought the writer chooses to combine them into one

❐ To separate series of items that have commas in them

Let's look at each of these uses.

USE A SEMICOLON TO JOIN TWO SENTENCES

When two sentences are closely related in thought, you may want to stress that relationship by putting the two in one sentence. Use a semicolon to join the two:

Separate:	This report does not provide the original price and the sale price. It merely provides the sale price.
Joined by semicolon:	This report does not provide the original price and the sale price; it merely provides the sale price.
Separate:	In recent months, the Personnel Department has emphasized attitude over skills in hiring entry-level staff. As a result, we are getting better people.
Joined by semicolon:	In recent months, the Personnel Department has emphasized attitude over skills in hiring entry-level staff; as a result, we are getting better people.

In each pair of examples, writing the ideas as two separate sentences is not wrong. But joining them with the semicolon is the writer's way of stressing the relatedness of the two ideas. Use your judgment in deciding whether to keep the sentences separate or join them.

USE A SEMICOLON TO SEPARATE ITEMS IN A SERIES IF THE ITEMS CONTAIN COMMAS

Too many commas:	On the dais were Dr. Fainsworth, the research scientist, Ms. Millard, the company president, Mr. Dennis Sacker, the individual who invented the capsule, and two members of Congress.

Semicolons: On the dais were Dr. Fainsworth, the research scientist; Ms. Millard, the company president; Mr. Dennis Sacker, the individual who invented the capsule; and two members of Congress.

Replacing commas with semicolons in these instances is arbitrary. This use is based on common sense and a desire to simplify matters for the reader. Here's another example:

Too Many commas: New management sought concessions, contributions, and cooperation from the unions, loyalty, trust, and ten-hour days from middle managers, and an increase in productivity, quality, and commitment from each department in the company.

The sentence contains a series of three items or clusters. Each cluster, however, is a series unto itself, with a number of commas separating its own items.

❐ "concessions, contributions, and cooperation from the unions,"

❐ "loyalty, trust, and ten-hour days from middle managers,"

❐ "and an increase in productivity, quality, and commitment from each department in the company"

Each cluster has commas within and at the end, separating it from the next cluster. To help readers determine clearly and easily where one cluster ends and the next begins, use a semicolon to separate them:

Semicolons: New management sought concessions, contributions, and cooperation from the unions; loyalty, trust, and ten-hour days from middle managers; and an increase in productivity, quality, and commitment from each department in the company.

QUOTATION MARKS (" "): SYMBOLS FOR WORD-FOR WORD BORROWING

Place quotation marks before and after words taken verbatim from another source. The board's directive was explicit: "Increase sales by 15 percent over the next fiscal year."

When the quotation is broken up, be sure to indicate where the quoted material begins and ends by enclosing those words in quotes:

> "It is not unreasonable," the boards' directive read, "for the company's shareholders to expect such an increase."

Long Quotations

Do not use quotation marks for quoted material that runs more than four lines long. For such quotes, use a "block" form. That is, begin the material on a new line and indent the entire quotation:

> Regarding productivity, I remind you of Chairman Jackson's view:

> ❐ Productivity is certainly a key indicator of any company's success. Increased productivity reflects an execution of the corporate mission that is smoother, leaner, swifter. It implies that managers and employees are working smarter, if not harder. But there's the troublesome element with increased productivity. Is the company paying too great a cost from a human resource standpoint for the gains in productivity? In continually striving to increase productivity does the company squeeze the creative life out of its people?

Punctuating Words Preceding the Quote

Usually, a comma separates the words preceding a quote from the quote itself:

> The on-site supervisor said repeatedly, "The conditions on the job site are safe."

If the quotation is long and rather formal, you may use a colon to introduce the quote:

According to the policy manual: "All employees are expected to be in full uniform at all times while on duty. Proper identification worn visibly on one's outer garment is considered part of the official uniform."

When the quotation is short and follows grammatically what precedes it, you may omit the comma and colon:

The auctioneer barked "Sold" and we had ourselves a Rembrandt.

Other Marks with Quotation Marks

When words explaining a quote break up the quote, be sure to put commas before and after the explanatory words:

"We could not in all honesty," the CEO said, "expect our employees to make more sacrifices."

Note the commas and periods in the preceding example are *inside* the quotation marks. *Commas and periods always go inside the quotation marks:*

Our goal for the year is "to survive."

It was not a question of their "wanting it more," but rather a feeling of our "needing it less."

Place question marks and exclamation points inside the quotation marks when the quote is a question or exclamation. Place these marks outside the quotation marks when they apply to the entire sentence, not to the quotation:

The chairman asked, "How can we deal with such competition?" [quote is a question]

Who said, "This is an impossible task"? [quote is not a question]

The crowd cried out, "Hurrah!" [quote is an exclamation]

A Quote Within a Quote

Using the apostrophe key, create a set of single quotation marks (' ') to indicate a quote within a quote:

The defense attorney repeated, "I remind you, ladies and gentlemen, of the need to be convinced 'beyond a reasonable doubt' before you can find my client guilty."

Added Words

In some situations, to make a quote clear, you may have to add words that do not appear in the words you are quoting but were part of the original context. Place those added words in brackets ([ ]). For example:

The manager said that, "In the face of this competition, [our company] cannot just retreat."

— Punctuation Checklist —

WHERE YOU PAUSE, PLACE A COMMA.

WHERE YOU STOP, PLACE A PERIOD.

USE COMMAS TO PREVENT MISREADING.

USE COMMAS TO SEPARATE WORDS, PHRASES, AND CLAUSES IN A SERIES OF THREE OR MORE.

USE COMMAS TO SET OFF NONESSENTIAL MODIFIERS.

USE DASHES TO SET OFF NONESSENTIAL MODIFIERS THAT YOU WANT TO EMPHASIZE.

USE A DASH TO INTRODUCE WORDS YOU WANT TO EMPHASIZE.

USE A DASH TO SEPARATE A SUMMARIZING CLAUSE FROM THAT WHICH PRECEDES IT.

USE A COLON IN GREETINGS, TIME FIGURES, SUBTITLES, AND BIBLICAL QUOTATIONS.

USE A COLON TO INTRODUCE MATERIAL.

USE A SEMICOLON TO JOIN TWO SENTENCES.

USE A SEMICOLON TO SEPARATE ITEMS IN A SERIES IF THE ITEMS CONTAIN COMMAS.

USE QUOTATION MARKS TO SIGNAL QUOTED MATERIAL.

FOR LONG QUOTES, INDENT THE MATERIAL AND DO NOT USE QUOTATION MARKS.

SEPARATE INTRODUCTORY MATERIAL FROM QUOTED MATERIAL WITH A COMMA OR COLON.

PLACE COMMAS AND PERIODS INSIDE QUOTATION MARKS.

PLACE QUESTION MARKS AND EXCLAMATION POINTS INSIDE QUOTATION MARKS WHEN THE QUOTE IS A QUESTION OR EXCLAMATION. PLACE THEM OUTSIDE WHEN THE QUOTE IS NOT A QUESTION OR EXCLAMATION.

USE A SET OF SINGLE QUOTATION MARKS FOR A QUOTE WITHIN A QUOTE.

Problem No. 28

HOW DO I DEAL
WITH SPELLING PROBLEMS
MY SPELL-CHECKER CAN'T CURE?

You are a person who has always had problems with spelling. How can you deal with the problem once and for all?

Or you have just gotten a draft back from your manager who said little about your content but circled a number of misspelled words. You are miffed.

Or, although your word processing program has a "spell-check" feature, there are times when your spelling is so far off the mark even the spell-checker is confused and can't offer the correct alternative.

In each of these instances you are faced with one of the most basic of writing problems—spelling. Let's see what can be done about it.

SPELLING: A SMALL THING THAT SAYS A LOT ABOUT YOU

Spelling is a big factor in creating a negative impression. No reader will praise you for spelling all words correctly, but many will chastise you—or at least think less of you—if you have even one word misspelled. (It's the same with baseball umpires.) Accuracy is expected and wins no kudos, but if the spelling is wrong, just listen to the boos. People assume the people they do business with can at least spell correctly, or will take the trouble to use the resources available to find the correct spelling.

LOOK IT UP: A HABIT WORTH DEVELOPING

There are so many words in the English language that don't fit a pattern. For example, you may recall the ditty from your school days about *i* before *e* except after *c*. That can serve you well for a number of words, such as *believe, relieve, conceive, deceive.* But there are a number of exceptions to the "rule," such as *neighbor, weight, either.* The exceptions almost make learning the "rule" a fruitless exercise.

The same is true of a number of other "rules" or guidelines that try to group words into recognizable patterns. So, since learning the rules can take you only so far anyhow, it might be more productive to develop the habit of looking up words whose spelling you question.

One source you can go to is your spell-checker, if you work on a word processor. The limitation of the spell-check systems, of course, is that they will not catch the wrong word spelled correctly, such as *affect* when you need *effect.* And sometimes, if your original spelling is far off the mark, the spell-check system might not offer the correct spelling for the word you want.

In those instances, or in cases when spell-check is not available to you, you can go to other reservoirs of correctly spelled words. The dictionary, of course, is the major source. In addition, bookstores sell books that are simply lists of words, which probably contain most of the words you might use.

And this chapter has a list of words that businesspeople use and sometimes have trouble with. If you are industrious, you might develop your own "short list" of words you frequently have trouble with. When you are writing, check these lists first. If the word isn't there, go to your dictionary. But in revising a document, identify each word that you suspect might be misspelled, and check one of these sources.

What to Look For

What got the words that follow onto the "Most Troublesome List" in this chapter? Some tricky element in their spelling. That is, they cause trouble in one of the following ways:

- ❏ Is it *i* before *e* or *e* before *i?*
- ❏ Should the final consonant be doubled before adding a suffix, as in *recurring?*
- ❏ Should an *e* be added before the s to form the plural of a noun ending in *o,* as in *tomatoes?*
- ❏ Should the final *e* be dropped before adding a suffix to a word such as *argue,* to make *argument?*
- ❏ Should *ly* or *ally* be added to make an adverb from an adjective like *unbelievable?*
- ❏ Does the word end in *ance* or *ence, ant* or *ent, ible* or *able?*
- ❏ Are you misspelling the word because of a silent letter in words like *indictment?*

These are the issues that make spelling troublesome, so these are the aspects of the words in this list you should look for. Each time you check a word you are doubtful on, try to note the troublesome part of it. Noting the problem often enough may help you memorize the correct form.

But then again that may not happen. I for one can never spell *facilitate* correctly no matter how many times I check it. Some of us are doomed to be creative spellers. The best we can do is, as Casey Stengel once said, "look it up."

HARD-TO-SPELL WORDS

abated

aberrant

abeyance

abrasive

abrogate

abutment

abysmal

accelerate

accent

access

accidentally

acclimate

accommodate

accompanying

accumulate

accurately

achievable

acknowledg-ment

acoustical

acquitting

acreage

acumen

acute

adaptation

addendum

adhere

adhoc

adjunct

admittedly

advantageous

aegis

affable

affidavit

affiliate

affluent

aforementioned

aggregate

aide

algae

alienate

alignment

allegedly

allegorical

alleviate

allied

allocated

allotted

allude

amenable

amid

amorphous

amortize

analogy

analyze

analytical

ancillary

anecdotal

anemic

annals

annihilate

annuity

annul

anomaly

antagonistic

anticlimactic

antidote

antiquity

antithetical

anxiety

apparel

appellate

appraise

apprise

appropriate

appurtenance

arbitrary

arduous

arguably

arraign

ascend

assent

ascertain

assertive

assuage

asymmetrical

atrophied

attest

attrition

attune

atypical

augment

augur

aural

austere

automaton

autonomy

auxiliary

bailiff

bailiwick

baited

ballast

banal

bated

bearable

befuddle

begrudge

behemoth

beleaguer	cancelled	collaborator	contentious
believable	capacity	collateral	contingent
beneficiary	capital	commemorate	controllable
benefited	capitol	commencing	correctable
biannually	capitulate	commensurate	council
bias	capricious	commingle	counsel
bifurcate	carte blanche	communicable	credibility
bigoted	cartel	communique	crescendos
bilateral	catastrophic	commutation	critically
bipartisan	categorizing	comparably	crux
blatant	censure	compatibility	cryptic
bondsman	changeable	compendium	cue
bookish	channelling	competence	culpable
bookkeeper	chaos	complacency	cursory
boundary	chargeable	complement	cyclical
boutique	charlatan	computable	cynically
brochure	chattel	conciliatory	dearth
bullish	chronic	concisely	debatable
bulwark	chronicle	conduit	debilitate
buoyant	circuitous	congruous	debtor
bureau	cite	conjecture	decadence
bureaucrat	coalesce	connote	deceivable
cabal	coalition	conscientious	deceptively
cache	codicil	consignment	deemphasize
cadence	codify	consistent	deferred
cadre	coercion	consortium	density
calculated	coexistence	constituent	depict
calendar	cognizant	consumable	depressant
calibrated	coherence	consummate	descend
camaraderie	coincidence	contemptible	detectable

detente	ecologically	facetious	fractious
deterrent	economically	facsimile	fraught
detestable	edifice	faint	frenetically
detrimental	egoist	fallacious	futility
devaluation	egotist	fallible	gadget
deviant	elicit	familiarity	gait
devotee	eligible	fanaticism	gauche
diagnostician	eloquence	farcical	gnarled
diametrically	embarrass	fatalistically	gnash
didactic	eminence	fathom	gnaw
differential	emission	feasibility	goad
diffuse	employer	feign	gouge
digress	enigma	feint	graduated
diligence	en masse	felicitous	graffiti
dimension	ensue	felon	gravelly
discreet	epoch	ferret	gravely
discrete	errant	fete	grievance
dispensable	erroneous	fictitious	grievous
distraught	euphemism	fiduciary	grovel
divergent	euphoric	fixate	guarantor
divisible	evoke	flexible	guileful
dormant	exceed	flippant	gullible
drivel	excelled	fluent	habilitate
drudgery	exemplary	foible	haphazard
dual	expectancy	forbearance	harangue
duplicity	expedient	foremost	hassle
duress	explicable	forensically	haughtily
dutifully	extinct	foreword	hearsay
dynamic	fabricated	forfeiture	heinous
dysfunction	facet	fortuitous	heirloom

heroes	insular	leisurely	mitigate
heterogeneity	insurgence	libel	mobilize
hierarchical	integral	libelous	module
horde	intercede	lien	mogul
hysterically	intricacy	likelihood	moral
illegible	intrigue	lineage	morale
illicit	intuitive	liquefy	multiple
illiterate	inveigle	litigant	mundane
illusory	invincibly	livelihood	mutable
imaginable	iridescent	loathe	naive
immensely	irrefutable	maladroit	niche
immigrate	irresponsible	malaise	ninety
imminence	itinerary	malcontent	nondescript
impanel	jaded	maneuverable	nonexistent
imperceptibly	jeopardize	marginally	noticeably
imperil	jocular	material	notoriety
impertinent	judiciary	materiel	obsolescence
inapplicable	judicious	mathematically	occasionally
incipient	juridical	measurable	occur
incumbent	juxtapose	mediate	occurred
indolent	kindred	medieval	omit
inertia	kiosk	meliorate	omitted
infuse	knowledgeable	menial	operable
ingenious	kudos	meretricious	pageant
ingenue	labyrinthine	metaphorical	palatable
ingenuity	lackluster	mete	panacea
ingenuous	laconic	mileage	panache
ingrate	ladle	minutiae	panoply
insatiable	largess	misspell	paradigm
insoluble	legendary	misstate	paradox

parallel	precede	rein	salvageable
paralleled	precedence	reiterate	sanguine
paraphernalia	precis	reliable	satellite
paraplegic	precise	remediable	satiable
pare	prejudicial	reminisce	scathe
pathos	prerequisite	remittance	scavenger
paucity	prerogative	renege	schematic
peacable	prevalent	renown	schism
pecuniary	preventive	repertoire	scintillate
pedantic	prodigy	repertory	scour
penchant	quadruple	replete	scowl
penurious	quandary	reprisal	scruple
perennial	queue	resin	scrupulous
perspicacious	quotable	restaurateur	scythe
phenomenal	raconteur	revocable	secede
pinnacle	rancor	rhythm	sect
pithy	rapport	ricochet	seethe
placate	rapprochement	riddance	senile
placid	ratable	rife	sequel
plagiarize	raze	riffle	serialize
plague	recede	rogue	serviceable
plaintiff	recommend	roguish	sewage
plaintive	reconcilable	rudimentary	sidle
plague	recurrence	ruinous	simulcast
plateau	refer	sabotage	sinewy
plausible	referring	saboteur	skewer
pliant	refuge	sacrosanct	skittish
pollutant	refutable	sagacity	sleight
pommel	regimen	salable	sleuth
portrait	reimburse	salient	solicit

sparsely	synchronization	tousle	vise
spasm	synergy	tractable	wager
species	synod	transcendent	waive
specious	systemic	transferable	wan
spherical	taciturn	transmitted	wane
spigot	talisman	traumatic	warrant
spontaneity	tangible	treatise	wary
stamina	tarpaulin	triad	waver
statistically	taut	trivet	whet
stellar	tawdry	typically	whim
stoicism	tenacious	undue	widget
straitlaced	tentative	ungainly	wile
strategically	tenuous	unique	wiry
stymie	thematic	unkempt	woeful
suave	theorem	unwieldy	wrack
subdue	thieves	urban	wreak
subpoena	thorough	urbane	writ
subtle	tier	usurer	wrought
succor	timber	usurp	wry
suffice	timbre	vacuous	yacht
supple	tinge	vacuum	yawl
surfeit	tirade	vague	yeoman
surname	tithe	variance	yoke
surveillance	tithing	vein	yolk
susceptible	titular	vengeance	zeal
sustenance	toggle	venue	zealous
svelte	torpedoes	verbiage	
sycophant	torte	vetoes	
symbiotic	totem	vice	

— Spelling Checklist —

Do Not Rely Solely on Your Word Processor's Spell-Checkers.

Look Up the Correct Spelling of Every Word You Have Any Doubt About.

Watch for the Following Areas of Slip-Ups:

- ❐ i *before* e *or* e *before* i, *as in* belief *and* receive

- ❐ *doubling the final consonant before adding a suffix or not doubling it, as in* exceeding

- ❐ *adding an* e *before the* s *to form the plural of a noun ending in* o, *as in* heroes

- ❐ *dropping or leaving the final* e *before adding a suffix to a word such as* imagine (imaginable)

- ❐ *whether the adverb form ends in* ly *or* ally, *as in* successively *or* dynamically

- ❐ *whether the word ends in* ance *or* ence, ant *or* ent, ible *or* able

- ❐ *syllables or sounds in the word that may sometimes be slurred over in speech, as in* typically, *often pronounced as* typiclly

WHAT ABOUT ABBREVIATIONS, NUMBERS, AND OTHER TRICKY RULES OF STYLE?

Is it proper to use abbreviations in business documents? Which ones? When?

Sometimes you see numbers spelled out and sometimes you see them written as figures. Which form is correct?

Should job titles always be capitalized?

And what about the titles of books and things? Do you use italics, underlining, or quotation marks?

Is there a rule to govern the use of hyphens in word combinations?

Questions such as these trouble people who want to write effectively and don't want to distract their readers with even the most inconsequential of errors. This chapter gives guidelines for dealing with these bothersome little issues of correct writing.

ABBREVIATIONS: HANDLE WITH CARE

Although you want to keep your documents as short as possible, don't rely on abbreviations to do it. Particularly in the text of documents, generally avoid using abbreviations that you might use when writing for yourself, such as when taking notes.

There are some instances, however, when business convention allows abbreviations. Let's look at these.

TITLES WITH NAMES

Abbreviate titles attached to an individual's name, whether the title comes before or after the name. For instance:

Dr. Micera	Sen. Bradford
Gregory Avedikian, D.M.D.	Joseph DeMiglio, Esq.

Without a surname, however, you would generally not use the abbreviation:

After six visits to the *doctor*, the patient sought a second opinion.

Common business titles generally are abbreviated, even in the text and without a surname:

Our company has hired some of the brightest *CPAs* and *MBAs* in the industry.

AGENCIES AND ORGANIZATIONS

Abbreviate through the use of their initials the names of well-known agencies and organizations, such as:

IRS, SEC, FBI, ERA, NOW, NAACP, IBM, AT&T, and DOT.

If your readers may not be able to recognize the name of an organization or agency, spell out the name the first time you use it and put its abbreviation in parentheses. Use the abbreviation in subsequent references:

Department of Youth and Family Services (DYFS)

PEOPLE, PLACES, AND DATES

Do not use abbreviations for personal names, or the names of countries and states, days, months, and holidays.

Incorrect: *Chas.* toured most of our stores throughout the *US*, starting in *Calif.* and working his way to *NY*. He began in *Aug.* and concluded in *Dec.*, just before *Xmas.*

Correct: *Charles* toured most of our stores throughout the *United States*, starting in *California* and working his way to *New York*. He began in *August* and concluded in *December*, just before *Christmas.*

Use abbreviations for the names of states in addresses, such as:

Mayor Rudolph Kolb
123 Main Street
Ridgefield, *NJ* 07662

Spell out the words *street, avenue, company* when used in addresses and in the text:

The Whimp *Company*
555 Central *Avenue*
Potomac, WA 00199

We will move our headquarters from First *Avenue* to 17th *Street*.

COMPANIES

In writing the names of companies, use the official form of the name. If an abbreviation appears on company letterhead, use the abbreviation in your reference to the name. Included are abbreviations such as *Co., Corp., Inc., Ltd.*

THE AMPERSAND (&)

Use the ampersand (&) only if that is part of the official company name. Do not use it otherwise.

Correct: We have made a proposal to *P&G* to install new software.

Incorrect: Notices *&* warnings have been sent on many occasions.

Correct: Notices *and* warnings have been sent on many occasions.

LATINISMS

Some people use Latinisms as a short form for certain phrases. The most common of these are:

i.e.	that is
e.g.	for example
etc.	and so forth

Generally, restrict your use of these Latinisms to informal writing. In formal writing, spell out the English form of the expressions.

The main problem with these Latinisms is that many writers do not know precisely when to use them, and many readers do not know precisely what they mean. Some writers will use *i.e.* when they mean *for example*, thereby confusing, or at least distracting, the reader who does know the precise meaning of the term.

Some writers use *etc.* rather than providing the details needed to fill out an explanation, relying on the reader to do their job. Use *etc.* only after you have given enough details to be sure the reader understands the concept:

Incorrect: The report will cover operating expenses, *etc.*

Correct: The report will cover operating expenses, cost of goods sold, revenues, salaries, leases, *etc.*

Though the use of *etc.* is correct here, it is not recommended. Either provide all the items covered or indicate that the items listed are representative of the items covered. For example:

Correct: The report will cover many financial aspects, *such as* operating expenses, cost of goods sold, revenues, salaries, leases.

NUMBERS: 10 IS THE TURNING POINT

In documents that use numbers extensively, as in a technical piece or a financial statement, use figures for all numbers.

In most other forms of business writing, spell out numbers under 10. Use figures for all others:

Correct: The department received *six* responses.
Correct: At last count, *77* districts had been heard from.
Correct: With *113* years behind it, the company is the oldest in the city.

One exception to this rule pertains to the use of a number to begin a sentence. When the first word of a sentence is a number, spell it out, regardless of what that number is. If you think such a long number is cumbersome, rephrase the sentence so the number does not begin the sentence. For example:

Incorrect: 266 days does not make a career.
Correct: Two-hundred-and sixty-six days does not make a career.
Correct: You cannot call 266 days a career.

Another exception to this rule pertains to situations in which the number does not stand alone. In those instances, regardless of the number, use figures. For example:

mixed numbers and fractions	62 1/8	3/4
percentages	39 percent	39%
decimals	5.4	12.6
volume, chapter, page	Volume 3, Chapter 9, page 20	
statistics	dropped from 9 to 5	
exact amounts of money	$8.93	
time	6:38 P.M.	

For *dates and addresses*, use figures:

January 7, 1942	28 Chris Avenue
1995–1996 season	P.O. Box 388

CAPITALIZATION: DON'T OVERINDULGE

As a general rule, capital letters designate a *specific* person, place, or thing. If you keep that rule in mind, you will limit your use of capital letters and the tendency of some writers to use capital letters excessively.

What to Capitalize

THE NAMES OF PEOPLE, PLACES, ORGANIZATIONS, HISTORICAL PERIODS AND EVENTS

Cara Marie Antico	Rotarians
San Antonio, Texas	Hall of Fame
American Medical Association	Environmental Protection Agency
The Middle Ages	The Great Depression

THE NAMES OF PEOPLES AND LANGUAGES

Serbs	Croat	Slavic	French

THE FIRST LETTER IN DIRECT QUOTATIONS

Who said, "The business of the country is business"?

DIRECT QUESTIONS WITHIN A SENTENCE

The main issue is: Do we in fact want to diversify that far afield?

WORDS IN TITLES, HEADINGS AND SUBHEADS, EXCEPT FOR INTERNAL ARTICLES, CONJUNCTIONS, AND PREPOSITIONS

Titles	Headings, Subheads
The Cost of Doing Business	Conditions for Filing a Claim
Inside Today's Conglomerate	In Search of Profits
The Wall Street Journal	

JOB TITLES WHEN THEY PRECEDE A PROPER NOUN

Special Agent Rogers	District Director Sharon McCarthy
Vice President Smith	Dean Winters

What Not to Capitalize

GENERIC JOB TITLES

Incorrect: The *Merchandise Manager* is responsible for those decisions.

Correct: The *merchandise manager* is responsible for those decisions.

GEOGRAPHICAL DIRECTIONS

Incorrect: Travel *South* for four miles until you reach the main highway.

Correct: Travel *south* for four miles until you reach the main highway.

But *do* use a capital to designate a specific section of the country:

Correct: The company began in the *Southwest* and then slowly moved *westward.*

NAMES OF SEASONS

Incorrect: History has shown that business picks up in *Summer.*

Correct: History has shown that business picks up in *summer.*

ITALICS, UNDERLINING, AND QUOTATION MARKS

Widespread use of word processors and laser printers has made italics an issue for writers. Given this interesting typeface, however, many writers use it indiscriminately, often to the point of weakening its impact. Here are correct uses of italics found most frequently in business writing.

When to Italicize

TITLES OF BOOKS, NEWSPAPERS, MAGAZINES

In other words, italicize the title of any *long* work, published or not:

In Search of Excellence	*Trouble-Shooter's Manual*
The Washington Post	*Fortune*

But enclose titles of short works in quotation marks. That is, titles of writing such as articles, chapters, and codes would not be italicized but be put in quotation marks. For example:

> According to an article in *Forbes* called "When Businesses Fail," the principal parties show much greater imagination in rebounding than they did in running the business.

> Chapter 2, "Focus on the Customer," in the company manual *What We're All About,* sets the tone for the entire work force.

Letters, Words, and Numbers Used as Letters, Words, and Numbers

> The contract is explicit in its use of *exchange* not *refund.*
> When writing to a client on behalf of the company, use *we,* not *I.*

> Because of the poor quality in the fax, I misread all of the *1s* as *7s.*

Foreign Words and Colloquial Expressions

> We are on solid ground *vis-à-vis* the impending investigation.

> At times like these companies just have to *bite the bullet* and move on.

To Stress a Word or Phrase

> Considering our past experiences with her company, we will not accept her request for our services *under any circumstances.*

Caveat: Do not rely on italics to give emphasis to words that are not emphatic. You will be better served by limiting your use of italics and working to find more powerful words.

Legal Citations

The names of the participants in the case are italicized, but all words surrounding and within the citation are not.

> *Smith* versus *Jogens*
> *New Hampshire* v. *Madigan*
> the *Calendar* case

Note: Use underlining instead of italics if you do not have access to italics. Follow the same guidelines. But do not use both italics and underlining in the same document for the same purpose.

HYPHENS: DO THEY REALLY MATTER?

Yes, they do. One service of the hyphen is to prevent misreading. For example, note how the following sentence can be misread without the hyphen:

> *Incorrect:* Each department must be concerned with cost control measures.

The problem in this sentence is that on the first read, readers might read *concerned with cost.* Readers would then see that is not the intent, but they should not have to go back and reread. A properly placed hyphen will prevent that:

> *Correct:*   Each department must be concerned with *cost-control* measures.

A more serious error can occur if the writer misplaces the hyphen in certain situations. For example:

> 10-foot lengths   10 foot-long lengths

So the hyphen is important for ease of reading and for clarity. Here are guidelines for using it correctly.

END-OF-LINE WORD DIVISION

Divide words between syllables:

> re-new   individ-ual   fore-most   manage-ment

In dividing words at the end of a line, do not isolate a single letter, even if it is a syllable:

> *Incorrect:* a-lone   a-typical   e-lement   fault-y
> *Correct:*   alone   atyp-ical   ele-ment   faulty

If you are not sure of the syllable breaks in a word, check your dictionary.

SEPARATING SOME PREFIXES AND ROOT COMBINATIONS

prefix and proper name	post-Johnson period
double vowel	pre-existing, co-opt
stressed prefix to avoid	
confusion with another word	re-creation, re-form

JOINING WORDS IN STANDARD COMPOUNDS

President-elect   attorney-at-law   sister-in-law

JOINING TWO OR MORE WORDS TO SERVE AS A SINGLE ADJECTIVE

a small-business owner
the best-selling author
a government-sponsored program
short-term goal
long-winded speaker

SPELLING OUT COMPOUND NUMBERS AND FRACTIONS

sixty-seven   thirty-four   two-thirds   five-eighths

When in doubt about whether to use a hyphen, consult your dictionary.

— Rules-of-Style Checklist —

USE ABBREVIATIONS SPARINGLY:

- ❏ *Abbreviate titles attached to individuals' names.*
- ❏ *Abbreviate names of recognizable organizations and agencies.*
- ❏ *Do not abbreviate names of people, countries, states (except in addresses), days, and months.*

❏ *Use abbreviations in company names only if an abbreviation is part of the official name.*

❏ *Use the ampersand (&) only when it is part of an official company name.*

❏ *Limit your use of Latinisms.*

WRITE NUMBERS AS FIGURES IN DOCUMENTS USING NUMBERS EXTENSIVELY.

SPELL OUT NUMBERS UNDER 10; WRITE OTHERS AS FIGURES.

USE FIGURES FOR MIXED NUMBERS, DATES, ADDRESSES.

DO NOT OVERINDULGE IN CAPITALIZATION:

❏ *Use capital letters for*
- names of people, places, organizations, historical periods and events
- direct quotations and questions
- names of peoples and languages
- words in titles, headings and subheads, except internal articles, conjunctions, prepositions
- job titles when they precede a proper noun

❏ *Do not capitalize*
- generic job titles
- geographical directions
- names of seasons

USE ITALICS FOR

❏ *Titles of long works*
❏ *Letters, words, and numbers used as letters, words, and numbers*

❏ *Foreign words and colloquial expressions*

❏ *Emphasis or stress*

❏ *Legal citations*

USE UNDERLINING AS YOU WOULD ITALICS WHEN ITALICS ARE NOT AVAILABLE.

USE THE HYPHEN

❏ *To divide a word at the line of a line.*

❏ *To separate some prefixes from root combinations.*

❏ *To join words in standard combinations.*

❏ *To join two or more words to serve as a single adjective.*

HOW DO I MAKE MY DOCUMENT LOOK INVITING?

Your proposal will be one of many. How can you make yours stand out?

Or, after working over a highly technical document, you feel you have simplified it and made it as user-friendly as possible. But it still comes across as a "heavy read," even to you. How can you "lighten" its look and make its detail more accessible?

Or, you've just drafted a letter your boss called "urgent" and rush it into her office. She looks at it and says, "Thanks. I'll read it as soon as I get a chance." Why doesn't she read it immediately?

In these situations you are concerned not with the writing itself but with the layout, the physical presentation of your words. Like it or not, the "packaging" does much to influence the reader's emotional response to the document, and even to affect the degree of comprehension. This chapter, therefore, gives you some techniques and guidelines for dressing your words in an inviting format.

HOW TO WRITE TO A VISUALLY-ORIENTED AUDIENCE

Ours is an age in which video is king. Even much of our music comes to us with pictures on television. One glance at popular magazines and newspapers shows the dominance of the visual image.

Since most readers of your business documents are products of this visual society, you have a better chance of reaching those readers if you cater to their appetites for the visual. I'm not suggesting that you become a graphic arts specialist, but rather that you be concerned about the look of your documents. Word processors and laser printers enable us to do many neat things just by changing typefaces and margins. But even if you use a typewriter, you can give your documents an airy and inviting look that will make readers want to pick them up and read.

Let's review some of the techniques and formats that you can use.

Break Up Solid Blocks of Type

There is nothing more daunting to a reader than facing a solid block of print. I speak of the page that seems to be a small rectangle of blacktop framed by a white paper border. Many memos, letters, and documents of all types seem to be just that. The writers cram so many words into such a small space. They single-space everything, and use a long line with very small margins on left and right. There are few paragraph breaks or subheads, leaving the reader no time to come up for air and think about what she has read.

Not only are such documents uninviting, but they also reduce the level of comprehension. That is, readers have a harder time with such concentrated text, particularly if the document runs a few pages or more.

And the reason for such concentration is not the concern with protecting the environment by saving paper. Writers often cram their message into a 2-by 7-inch block and leave the rest of the page blank.

To illustrate, let's look at two versions of the same memo. The first presents the information in a compressed format. The second version presents the same content in an airy format. Note the differences in the appeal and in the level of comprehension of each.

— COMPRESSED FORMAT —

To: All Department Managers   Date: 1/2/99
From: J. Peters
Subject: Certificates of Insurance

Marcia Pleasant of our Insurance Department has informed me of changes regarding Certificates of Insurance. Starting immediately, all vendors signing contracts for goods or services with our company will be required to provide us with a Certificate of Insurance, with our company indicated as the additional insured. These certificates will be required for all new contracts and renewals, but not for existing contracts. The certificate is good for only one year and must be renewed if the contract term is longer than that. This point should be noted in the contract. If you provide goods or services to outside vendors and they require a Certificate of Insurance from us, please call Marcia (ext. 1234) with the information. She will handle it from there. Please be sure all members in your area who negotiate contracts are informed of these insurance changes. I cannot stress too much the importance of this directive.

Note the difference in visual appeal, and in comprehension, in the following version of the same content. The wording is virtually the same:

— AIRY VERSION —

To: All Department Managers   Date: 1/2/99

From: J. Peters

Subject: Certificates of Insurance

Marcia Pleasant of our Insurance Department has informed me of <u>changes regarding Certificates of Insurance</u>.

<u>The changes are</u>:

1. Starting immediately, all vendors signing contracts for goods or services with our company will be required to provide us with a Certificate of Insurance.

2. Our company is to be indicated as the additional insured.

3. These certificates will be required for all new contracts and renewals, but not for existing contracts.

4. The certificate is <u>good for only one year</u> and must be renewed if the contract term is longer. This point should be noted in the contract.

<u>When You Provide the Goods or Services</u>

If you provide goods or services to outside vendors and they require a Certificate of Insurance from us, please call Marcia (ext. 1234) with the information. She will handle it from there.

<u>Important Note</u>

Please be sure all members in your area who negotiate contracts are informed of these changes. I cannot stress too much the importance of this directive.

What accounts for the difference in these two versions of this memo?

Compressed	Airy
1. Single-spaced	1. Double-spaced
2. Longer line, narrower margins	2. Shorter line, wider margins
3. All one paragraph	3. Four paragraphs
4. No highlighting	4. Underlining, boldface
5. No separation of detail	5. Detail in enumerated list, indented
6. No subheads	6. Two subheads

As you can see, the airy version uses no fancy software or graphics. But it makes use of the full page, double-spacing the text and using a shorter line, about 80 characters long compared to about 84. If your message is longer than this one and you want to keep it to one page, single-space the document, but widen the margins and increase the number of breaks in the page.

Another key difference is that the compressed version is written in one paragraph, which is bad purely from a writing standpoint. Because there are a number of different ideas presented here, the memo should have a number of paragraphs. Some writers forget what they know about good paragraphing when they write a memo, particularly a short memo. But as you can see, presenting each idea in its own paragraph does make the memo more inviting and easy to read.

Further, separating the key details from the rest of the text is a simple but powerful technique for highlighting those details and helping readers note all of them. The compressed version crams them, forcing the reader to ferret them out. Numbering them, on the otherhand, sets them off and helps readers distinguish one from another. Bullets or a lettering scheme could, of course, serve the same purpose as the numbers.

Finally, the subheads in the open version enable the reader to see at a glance the general areas of content in the memo. These sub-heads break the text, giving readers the breathing room they need between one idea and the next. With the last subhead (*Important Note*) the writer alerts the readers to an additional request, which might have been lost in the tight version.

By using these techniques, the writer creates a page with plenty of *white space*—the ultimate antidote to the solid block of print that turns readers off.

Select a Format That Suits the Information

In deciding on the format that will appeal to your reader, try to choose the format that best suits the material you are working with. Let's look at the most common formats.

The standard format for most business documents is an 8-1/2 × 11 page, with a single column of about 6 inches in width. Occasionally, however, you may be working with material that lends itself to a different format.

For example, readers can more easily grasp some material—such as terms and definitions—when it is presented in two columns side by side. Note the difference in comprehension in these two versions of the same content:

STANDARD SINGLE-COLUMN PRESENTATION

Our weekly group meetings seem to lose focus because of a number of bad habits people have in the way they discuss issues. These habits are not unique to our group but, in fact, are so common they have been cataloged and named. Please study these habits and consider whether or not you have them. If so, please try to break the habits at the next sales meeting.

The habits are these. Making an attack on the character of the person presenting the argument rather than on the argument itself. This habit is called Ad Hominem or Personal Attack. Another bad habit is appealing to what you think people want to hear rather than speaking what you think is right. This is called Popular Appeal. A third habit that derails our meetings is using Emotive Language, or highly charged words. A fourth bad habit is deliberately clouding the issue with unrelated facts or arguments. This is sometimes called Obfuscation or Pettifogging. And the last bad habit I see too often at our meetings is Assuming the Cause. That is, we assume that because one event precedes another it is the cause of the other.

DOUBLE-COLUMN PRESENTATION

Our weekly group meetings seem to lose focus because of a number of bad habits people have in the way they discuss issues. These habits are not unique to our group but, in fact, are so common they have been cataloged and named. Please study these habits and consider whether or not you have them. If so, please try to break the habits at the next sales meeting.

The habits are these.

Personal Attack or Ad Hominem	Making an attack on the character of the person presenting the argument rather than on the argument itself.
Popular Appeal	Appealing to what you think people want to hear rather than speaking what you think is right.
Emotive Language	Using highly charged words.
Obfuscation or Pettifogging	Deliberately clouding the issue with unrelated facts or arguments.
Assuming the Cause	Assuming that because one event precedes another, it is the cause of the other.

The two-column format for information like this just looks easier to deal with. And it is. By using the two columns, the writer makes the term-and-definition scheme clear from the start. Readers can easily distinguish terms from definitions and one set from the other.

Reading the terms and definitions when run together as in the first version is like remembering a telephone number given to you without the hyphens between area code and exchange and between exchange and the rest. With work you will get it, but the separation makes the number more easy to absorb.

PUT THE SUBHEAD TO THE LEFT IN LONG DOCUMENTS

Another format using columns places the subhead to the left of the material it introduces rather than above it. For example:

See Opportunity in Every Task

In any job, there will be tasks you like and others you don't. Some will seem significant and others quite mundane. On some projects top-level supervisors get directly involved, and you realize the high visibility you and the project are getting. At other times, however, you might think no one really cares.

But many careers have been made or shattered unwittingly. That is, the employee did a superlative job without realizing who was watching and how important the task was, and thereby became recognized by the company hierarchy. On the other hand, others have developed a bad reputation because of a lackadaisical attitude on what they thought was a rather insignificant chore.

The moral? Do as good a job as you can on every project. See every assignment as a potential opportunity for you to show your stuff. You never know who's watching or who might see this as a vital task.

Look Beyond the Scope of Your Job

To get ahead in a company you must, of course, learn all you can about your job and do it well. But you should also try to learn more about other jobs in your department, to see how your job fits in with the whole organization. With this knowledge you might be able to improve a process that you have only a part in. In a crunch, you may be able to step in and fill a breach, thereby calling attention to your readiness to move ahead.

This kind of format is good for manuals and other longer documents. This format forces you to put more white space on the page and create a more inviting look. The shorter column speeds the reading and raises comprehension.

SET OFF ITEMS IN A LIST ENTRY

When preparing detailed or annotated lists, set off one portion of the entry from the rest. You can do this simply by using two different typefaces or by highlighting one portion with underlining or boldface. Note the difference this simple change makes in the following entry from a list of completed projects:

Inventory tracking system. We installed a computerized tracking system for a major book publisher. This system enabled editors, marketing reps, and management executives with access to the system to call up at any time the current stock of every item in their inventory.

Inventory Tracking System. We installed a computerized tracking system for a major book publisher. This system enabled editors, marketing reps, and management executives with access to the system to call up at any time the current stock of every item in their inventory.

USE AN ANNOTATED FORMAT TO INSTRUCT

With some material you have the dual task of presenting the material and commenting on it, explaining it, or in some way calling special attention to certain portions of it. One way of making such material accessible is by annotating certain points in the margin next to the passage being explained. You have seen this technique used a number of times in this book. For example:

Dear SHEP Member,

benefit to the reader

As a frequent attendee at SHEP meetings, you know the impact the featured speaker has on the entire evening. Good speakers and timely topics generate a lot of discussion that often carries over long after dinner.

specific request

That's why, as this year's chairperson for dinner speakers, I'm polling the membership for ideas. Please take a minute to give me some TOPICS or SPEAKERS you think would invigorate our meetings.

directions

To simplify this process, call me at (222) 555-9999, or use the lower portion of this letter and return it to me as soon as you can. Thanks.

Sincerely,

Marsha Nichols

---

easy response form

TOPICS	SPEAKERS
_____	_____
_____	_____
_____	_____
_____	_____

Member: _____

The annotations in the margin explain to the reader the idea made at each point in the text. Although additional commentary may precede or follow the material, the annotations placed next to the text simplifies the reader's task. He does not have to go back and forth between commentary and text.

Highlight Subcategories

Sometimes you have a rather lengthy passage falling under a subhead. How do you break up material that does not call for another subhead? With such material you can highlight the initial word or phrase at various points in the passage.

For instance, assume that your subhead is *Steps Toward Improving Company Morale*. Because all the steps fall under this subhead, you would not separate them with another subhead. To break up a long flow of text, however, you might set off in some way the lead into your explanation of each step. For example:

STEPS TOWARD IMPROVING COMPANY MORALE

You can consider a number of activities to improve company morale. Here is a description of some of the more common steps that companies in our situation have used to affect morale.

1. **Come out of your office.** If you really want to know what's going on, you have to see for yourself. Make it a routine part of your day to spend time with various members of your staff—all of them at one time or another. Allow them to do the talking without your trying to respond to each issue at the moment. Showing people by your presence that you are interested in what they are interested in can do much to influence attitudes.

2. **Create a framework for involvement.** Besides the informal discussions you might have as you circulate the office, develop a framework by which you can get feedback regularly from the staff. The framework must encourage people to be frank without feeling they are jeopardizing their status.

3. **Review rewards system.** Take a serious look at the compensation process as staff members see it....

Another way of breaking up the text under a single subhead would be to print a key word or phrase in caps. For example:

ELEMENTS OF TIME MANAGEMENT

To make the most of the time you have, consider the following elements:

CONTROL. Realize that time can slip away if you are not in control of it and how you use it.

PLAN. Take a few minutes out of each day to plan the day's activities. These few minutes of planning are a good investment of your time, as they will generate many minutes or hours of more productive time.

SET PRIORITIES. Determine what has to be done first and why. People often lose time when they become involved in a minor activity, then find themselves rushing to complete a major task.

Make-It-Look-Inviting Checklist —

GIVE YOUR DOCUMENTS A LOOK THAT WILL APPEAL TO OUR VISUALLY ORIENTED SOCIETY.

BREAK UP THE SOLID BLOCK OF PRINT BY

- ❐ *Double-spacing*
- ❐ *Writing shorter lines and using wider margins*
- ❐ *Paragraphing*
- ❐ *Underlining and boldfacing*
- ❐ *Putting details in lists*
- ❐ *Using subheads*

PICK A FORMAT THAT SUITS THE MATERIAL:

- ❐ *Use a two-column format for material such as terms and definitions.*
- ❐ *Put subheads to the left of a smaller column in manuals and longer documents.*
- ❐ *Use an annotated format to instruct.*
- ❐ *Use a dual typeface or printing format for detailed or annotated lists.*

HIGHLIGHT MATERIAL WITH BOLDFACE, CAPS, OR ITALICS WHEN A SUBHEAD WOULD BE INAPPROPRIATE OR CONFUSING.

Index

A

Abbreviations, 303-5
  in address, 56
  in agencies/organization
    names, 303
  Latinisms, 305
  in names of companies, 304
  in names of states, 304
  in titles, 303
Abstract verbs, 195-96
Action verbs, 9, 194
Active voice, 113, 187-89
  examples of, 188-89
Address
  abbreviations in, 56
  envelope, 56
  numbers in, 56-57, 306
Adjectives, hyphens in, 311
Adjustment letters, 19-22
  compromise letter, 21-22
  conclusion, 22
  introduction of, 19, 20,
    21-22
  models of, 19, 20, 21
  presentation of information,
    19, 20, 22
Affect, effect, 261
Affect, impact, 261
Agencies, abbreviations of
  name, 303
Agree to, agree with, 261
Alliteration, 197-98
Allusion, illusion, 261
A lot, alot, 261
Alright, all right, 261
Among, between, 261-62
Amount, number, 262

Ampersand, 304
Antithesis, 200
Apology, in response to
  complaint, 32
Appendix, proposals, 103
Archaic language, 190-91
Attention line, business letters,
  57
Audit reports, 107-18
  audit summary, 108, 115,
    116
  change in format, 111
  content requirements,
    109-11
  example of, 115-17
  introduction, 107-8
  problems of expression/
    language in, 111-15

B

Bad, badly, 262
Being that, being as how, 262
Blind copies, business letters,
  58
Brackets, in quote, 290
Brainstorming, in preparation
  for writing, 162-63
BRS, 143
Business letters
  abbreviations, 56
  attention line, 57
  blind copies, 58
  complementary close, 49
  copy to, 51
  date, 47
  enclosure reminder, 50
  envelope, 55-56

full blocked format, 51, 52
greeting, 49
indented format, 51, 54
inside address, 47
letterhead for, 47
margins, 59
model letter, 48
modified blocked format,
  51, 53
multipage letters, 58
organization of, 55
page break, 58
postscript, 58-59
signature, 49-50
subject, 49
tone of, 67-68
typist's initials, 50

C

Can, may, 262
Capitalization, 307-8
  misuse of capitals, 308
  use of capitals, 307
Chronological organization,
  outlines, 151
Chronological resume, 120-28
  accomplishments, 127-28
  employment history, 124-26
  models of, 121
  responsibilities, 124-26
  summary, 120, 122-24
Cite, site, 262
Claim letters, 15-18
  model of, 16-17, 18
    presentation of informa-
      tion, 16, 17